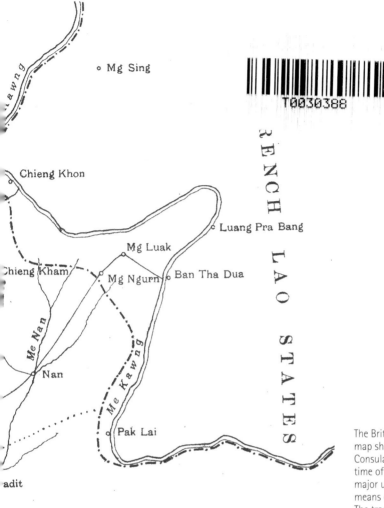

o Mg Sing

Chieng Khon

Luang Pra Bang

Mg Luak

Chieng Kham

Mg Ngurn   Ban Tha Dua

Me Nan

Me Kawng

Nan

Pak Lai

F R E N C H   L A O   S T A T E S

adit

ı

hitsanulok

ıpo

REFERENCE

Main Caravan Route............	════════
Trade Route...........................	────────
Railway.............................	────────
Chiengmai Consular District	....
Light Railways	+─+─+─+─+─+─+
New Cart Roads	─ ─ ─ ─ ─ ─
Mg (Muang) = Town	
Me = River	
International Boundary...........	▬·─·▬·─·▬

The British Foreign Office's map shows its Chiang Mai Consular District around the time of the Great War with major urban centres and means of communication. The traditional caravan routes from Yunnan through Chiang Mai and Lampang to the Burmese port at Moulmein can clearly be seen, as can the north's arterial rivers leading south. At this date, there were no roads in the north outside towns capable of taking motor traffic apart from the short road between Chiang Mai and Lamphun. The Northern Line of the State Railway has progressed to a point south of Phrae. It would be open through to Chiang Mai only in 1922.

Enchanted Land

Foreign Writings about Chiang Mai in the Early 20th Century

Enchanted Land

Foreign Writings about Chiang Mai
in the Early 20th Century

Edited by **Graham Jefcoate**

RIVER
BOOKS

First published and distributed in 2023 by
River Books Press Co., Ltd
396/1 Maharaj Road, Phraborommaharajawang,
Bangkok 10200 Thailand
Tel: (66) 2 224-6686, 2 225-0139, 2 622-1900
Fax: (66) 2 225-3861
Email: order@riverbooksbk.com
www.riverbooksbk.com

Editor: Narisa Chakrabongse
Production supervision: Suparat Sudcharoen
Design: Ruetairat Nanta

ISBN 978 616 451 064 7

Cover: On the Mae Ping at Chiang Mai in 1920, with the Nawarat Bridge
(built 1910) and the Presbyterian Church in the background and river boats
in the foreground. Photograph by Tanaka. Oliver Backhouse.

Printed and bound in Thailand by Parbpim Co., Ltd

Contents

Chiengmai Calling

What do you seek in this land of Thai,
Stranger from far away?
Scenes of beauty to charm your eye?
Hearts that are bright and gay?
Come up north and forget your ills,
Here we've no use for grief;
Rest your soul midst our brooks and hills,
Lovely beyond belief.
Our temples, wonderful as of yore
Glitter with every shade.
Hark! Our mighty elephants roar,
Toiling in forest glade!
Climb up high on our mountain fair,
Where rhododendrons grow,
Whispering pine trees scent the air
Rippling rivulets flow.
Chiengmai lads are steady and bold,
Whether in love or war;
Chiengmai maids are fair to behold,
Famous in lands afar.
Chiengmai folk, be they rich or poor;
Welcome you as a friend;
Northern memories shall endure,
Right to your journey's end.

Preface

The poem "Chiengmai Calling" was printed as an epigraph to Margaretta Wells' *Guide to Chiengmai*, which first appeared in 1962. Wells adds a note to explain that "Lotus", who signed the poem, was a pseudonym used by W. A. R. Wood, the former British Consul-General and a "distinguished and long-time resident" of Chiang Mai. Wood had written it especially for her book. Wood's memoir *Consul in Paradise* is one of the few examples of writing by members of the foreign community living in the north of Siam in the early twentieth century still to be found in bookshops today. It had first been published in 1935 under the title *Land of Smiles*.

Only a few hundred westerners (most of them from the British Isles and North America) lived in (or travelled to) the northern region before the Second World War. Though few in number, they left behind a considerable written legacy. Naturally, W. A. R. Wood features in this anthology of writings by Britons and Americans (and also a Siamese and a Dane) who lived in or visited Chiang Mai and the north of Siam (the modern Thailand) around a century ago. Few of the writings featured in this book apart from Wood's are currently in print or easily accessible and some remain unpublished and in manuscript. They include letters, memoirs, reports, articles in newspapers and magazines, poems, short stories and extracts from novels. Most of the writings are drawn from the period between 1910 when King Chulalongkorn (Rama V) died, and 1932 when a constitution was granted by King Prajadhipok (Rama VII).

The authors represented in this book are a diverse group of men and women who had come to the north as missionaries, "teak-wallahs", diplomats or travellers. Like Wood, some of them stayed in the north for most of their lives; others came only for a few weeks. Their writing is invariably personal and often vivid, describing, as it does, the hopes and aspirations of the writers, their personal relationships, the challenges they faced in their work and daily lives, and their recreational activities.

Needless to say, it reflects an early twentieth-century view of the world: views have changed as the world has changed in the century that has passed between them and us. Above all, the writing reflects the close bond many felt with the north of Siam, a remote, strange but beautiful land which some saw as a kind of Arcady or paradise but others felt was a "jungle prison".

The present anthology is a mosaic or a series of disparate impressions by very different individuals linked only by the impact the northern region had on their lives. It is a book to be read and not a scholarly edition to be

"The Ma Sa Ngoon, down which elephants had to drag logs before the chute was built." Note the markings on the cut logs. Oliver Backhouse.

studied. The texts are sometimes briefly introduced but have not been heavily edited nor extensively annotated. Obvious spelling errors have been silently corrected; otherwise, layout and punctuation are generally as found in the sources, and differences between British and American spelling have been respected. There was no standard way of transcribing Thai names or vocabulary with the Roman alphabet, and no attempt has been made to standardise it here. Some "facts and figures", a timeline/chronology, and a glossary of some unfamiliar terms can be found at the end, as well as information about the sources. Where dates are cited beneath texts in place of sources, these refer to dated letters.

Many of the illustrations found in the book are photographs drawn from the collection of Oliver Backhouse, to whom I am most grateful. Some of these were taken by Oliver's grandfather, Evelyn van Millingen, who was himself a "teak-wallah" with the Bombay Burmah Trading Corporation in the years 1923 to 1941. Other illustrations are from the editor's own collection or are reproduced by courtesy of the organisations credited.

I should like to thank Ajarn Pam Akrapisan, who has transcribed many of the texts and whose advice and assistance have been invaluable. I have used the collections of the Church of Christ in Thailand Archives at Payap University Library; the library of the École Française d'Extrême Orient at Chiang Mai; and the library of the Siam Society at Bangkok, and should therefore like to acknowledge the immense help of the staff at those institutions. I am also extremely grateful to the following for reading, correcting and commenting on the texts in draft: Paul Sullivan, Ronald Milne, Carol Biederstadt, Rebecca Weldon, David Lawitts and Janet Andrew. The index was provided by Janet Andrew. Any editorial or interpretative errors are of course purely the responsibility of the editor.

Finally, I should like to thank Narisa Chakrabongse and Chris Shelley at River Books for their advice and support for the project.

Chiang Mai, Nov 2022

Introduction

In 1867, the American Presbyterian missionaries Daniel McGilvary and Jonathan Wilson established a foothold in Chiang Mai (or "Chiengmai", as it was invariably spelt at the time), the capital of a remote region bordering on Burma and Laos. Divided into a number of semi-autonomous principalities under the suzerainty of Siam, this northern region is often referred to today under its ancient name "Lan Na". In the early twentieth century, however, it was known by westerners as "Laos" or "North Laos", its people and language being "Lao". In the decades following McGilvary's arrival, the "North Laos Mission" established stations not only in Chiang Mai but in most of the other major towns in the north of Siam, including Chiang Rai, Nan, Phrae and Lampang (which was known at the time as Lakon or Lakawn). Typically, each mission station comprised a hospital and schools as well as churches or chapels with small congregations of converts.

As the rival colonial powers Britain and France extended their territories towards Siam's northern borders, the region, despite its remoteness, took on an increasing strategic importance. Starting in the early 1860s, four British forestry companies (the Borneo Company Limited, the Bombay Burmah Trading Corporation, the Louis Thomas Leonowens Company Limited and the Siam Forest Company Limited) won concessions to exploit the pristine stands of commercially significant teak in the forests of the north. They established a presence in many of the same towns as the Mission, but were also present at Raheng (the present-day Tak). Enormous quantities of felled teak logs were floated down the tributary rivers of the north towards Paknampo (Nakhon Sawan) where they were assessed for taxation purposes, assembled into rafts, and floated down the Chao Phraya River to Bangkok for processing and export. Their journey from the north to Bangkok could take as long as five years.

The flag followed trade. In 1883, an Anglo-Siamese Treaty authorised

The Rev. Henry White and his family in
northern Siam.

the British to open a consulate at Chiang Mai. Britain's Siam Consular
Service went on to establish an intermittent presence in other significant
towns, the longest surviving being at Lampang, a major centre of trade
and commerce. As the Siamese government extended its control over the
northern principalities, government agencies also established themselves
in the north, many of them employing foreign (and especially British)
officials. Prime examples are the Ministry of the Interior, the Ministry of
Justice and the Royal Forest Department. International Courts at Chiang
Mai and Lampang adjudicated in cases involving British subjects, and
especially the many "British Asiatic subjects" who had migrated into the
north of Siam to find work or set up businesses. In 1913, W. A. R. Wood
estimated that there were some ten thousand British subjects in the north,
the great majority being Shan, Karen or Burmese. Only about seventy

of them, however, were "European British subjects". If we add to these American missionaries and others, we must probably conclude there were never more than a couple of hundred westerners in the north at any one time during the period.

Although their numbers were small, westerners clearly played an important role in the transformation of the north, economically, socially and culturally. The Mission introduced western education and medical practice. Westerners were closely involved in improvements in transportation and public health. The teak companies decisively changed the economy of the region. Although this process has been called "colonial", it was carefully aligned with central Siamese government policy which aimed to develop the region and to extend its own control.

The early twentieth century was therefore a period of fundamental change in the north of Siam, and no change was more significant than the reduction of its legendary remoteness. If in 1900 the river journey from Bangkok to Chiang Mai had taken several weeks, the opening of the Northern Line of the Royal State Railways in January 1922 (after fifteen years of construction), reduced the journey time to a little over twenty-six hours. Meanwhile, Chiang Mai itself was developing into something of a model town, with schools, hospitals, sanitation and public services that some considered superior to Bangkok's. "What Chiengmai does today", said W. A. R. Wood (with some exaggeration), "Bangkok thinks about tomorrow".

Mission elephants. From Freeman, *An Oriental Land of the Free* (front board).

The Back of Beyond

When a statue in honour of the late Queen Victoria was erected at the British Consulate in Chiang Mai in 1903, The Straits Times *in Singapore saw the event as the occasion for humour: "So far as the world at large and the British Empire in particular are concerned, Chiengmai is at the back of beyond". Nothing expressed the city's remoteness more vividly than accounts of the weeks it took to travel up from Bangkok before the Northern Line of the State Railways finally began to make its slow progress towards the North.*

At the Back of Beyond

Reginald Campbell (1894-1950) was a naval officer before joining the Siam Forestry Company as a forest assistant in 1919. After leaving Siam on grounds of ill health in 1924, he established himself as a professional (and prolific) writer, drawing on his experiences in the jungles of northern Siam in a series of novels and short stories. His memoir, Teak-Wallah, *which appeared in 1935, was his ninth book. His themes range from relations between teak-wallahs and northern women (in his early novels) to anxieties about physical dangers and even insurrection (in the later novels). Campbell chose the phrase "At the back of beyond" as the title of the first chapter of his novel* Uneasy Virtue. *Faith Tenterden has come a long way to visit her brother at what we assume is Paknampo. Patrick Tenterden is understandably concerned about her.*

In the smaller of two bungalows built in a clearing on the left bank of the river Me Lome at a point some two hundred miles due north of Bangkok, a man and a girl were seated.

Over their heads a punkah droned monotonously, sending whiffs of hot air through the suffocating room. Round a lamp suspended from the ceiling flying ants whirred ceaselessly, spilling their brown, wriggling bodies here, there, and everywhere over the hard teak boards of the floor. On the heat-blistered walls "chin-chock" and "tokay" lizards flitted, reaping a rich harvest of the insects of the night.

Queen Victoria's statue, erected at the British Consulate in 1903, but now in Chiang Mai Foreign Cemetery. The Editor.

Outside the clearing the stars sheened over the dry sand-bars of the river and the little native village of Sawankathai that trickled along the bank to the south-ward.

The tortured earth, free from the burning May sun for a brief twelve hours, stirred as if in travail.

Patrick Tenterden, rafting assistant of the Bangkok Wood Company, drew a worried hand through his curls.

"And why not, Faith?" he queried. "You're looking pale, and a little light chatter would do you good."

"I've got a wee bit of a headache," she replied.

"What a rotten thing it is to be a girl."

Faith Tenterden laughed. "Perhaps it is," she answered. "But never mind. I'll be myself tomorrow."

But the man was still anxious. "Look here, old girl," he said at last. "You oughtn't to stay on upcountry after the rains have broken, you know. There'll be malaria then, and I don't want you to crock up here miles away from any doctor."

"But I've only been here one month," she protested, "and I do so want to see the rafting when the river rises and the logs come down. Do you want to be rid of me so soon, Pat?"

Tenterden flushed. No, of course he didn't want to be rid of the dear, for he loved the little sister who was the only relation he had in the whole wide world. Still, when he had asked her to come out to Siam to see the lonely place in which he lived and worked, he hadn't quite meant her to settle down with him for several months.

"You know, Faith, that you're welcome to stay with me just as long as you like," he told her at last. "But if you got ill or anything . . ." He waved a vague hand through the drowsy atmosphere of the room.

Campbell, Uneasy Virtue, pp. 1-2

The Upriver Journey

Dr Edwin Charles Cort (who was known to his family as Charlie or Carl), married Mabel Gilson in Siam in 1909. They worked in Phrae and at Lampang before transferring to Chiang Mai in 1913. Dr Cort established a medical school at Chiang Mai (1916) and later a nursing school (1923). He succeeded Dr McKean as Superintendent of the McCormick Hospital, which was formally opened by H.R.H. Prince Mahidol of Songkhla in 1925. Dr Cort wrote various autobiographical sketches, but his full-length autobiography of 1946 (written with the aid of a ghost-writer) remained unpublished. Mabel Cort worked first as a teacher and later as a dietician at McCormick Hospital. Her letters from 1909 to 1932 (which are preserved in the Church of Christ Archives) are an important source for the life of the Mission and the Anglo-American community as a whole.

This upriver journey was the same one that Rev. and Mrs. Daniel McGilvary had made when they went to found the Mission in 1867. It was quite a trip. Loaded down with all the miscellaneous stores and supplies essential to the maintenance of remote Mission stations, it took us as long to travel the four hundred and fifty miles that lie between Bangkok and Chiengmai as it had taken for us to reach Bangkok from the Atlantic Seaboard.

Our route lay up the Menam Chao Praya River in Central Siam. It is the only great river system in the country, but, above Bangkok most of it is not navigable for draft vessels. So we were obliged to travel to our posts by sadaws, and if you have never travelled in a sadaw you have no conception of how slow and tortuous progress on the water can be.

The sadaw is a dugout some forty feet long. It has a slightly fan-shaped prow that rises to an angle of about thirty degrees. The stern is finished off with a fishtail six feet high. There are bamboo cabins for passengers and freight. Sections of the flooring open into holds for still more freight. And this long, heavily burdened, unwieldy boat functions by human motive power only. It is propelled against the current by four polemen equipped with fifteen-foot bamboo poles tipped with U shaped prongs. The trick was for the men to run to the top of the angled prow, engage their steel prongs in the river bottom or bank, bend their shoulders against the butts of these poles and walk down the inclined deck to the freight cabin – and so on and so on, foot by foot for the entire distance to Chiengmai. Yet, will you believe it, the men were surprised that we were surprised that they engaged in such a back-breaking, tedious business.

There were three such craft in our flotilla. [...] We resembled in a way one of those mixed parties of pioneers that sailed down the Ohio to colonize the Middle West. And the hardships confronting us were not too dissimilar, although for a time the voyage went well.

The first part of it carried us through the flat, alluvial plain of Central Siam. The river being in flood, we didn't see dry land for three weeks. It was dull and monotonous and the insects were maddening. The space inside a sadaw cabin isn't very large. And wasps are very quick. It was no good to sit still, for then the pests mistook you for a wall or piece of furniture and came down to rest on you. Being stung by one of them was like being burned with a red-hot poker and the pain lasted for hours. But when we reached the mountains the views and the weather more than made up for the dreariness and insects we had

"Om Loo". Slow progress through rapids on the Mae Ping during the dry season. Photograph by Philip Page, 15 March 1933. Oliver Backhouse.

endured. Now the scenes were wild and grand. Now the river rushed down a succession of canyons and ravines interspersed with foaming rapids that made navigation increasingly dangerous. Frequently we skirted the bottoms of precipitous cliffs, and how we managed to avoid being wrecked on the rocks only our steersmen could say. Picking our way through these rocks and rapids slowed our progress even more. There were now six boats in our little fleet and we understood why this was the minimum unit for upriver travel when we saw six crews hard at work hauling and poling a single boat through to clear water.

Cort, Yankee Thai, pp. 9-11

Sidling Slowly into Chiang Mai

Donald Eric Reid was born in Ceylon though of Scots parentage. In 1907, he joined Britain's Siam Consular Service, becoming Acting Vice-Consul at Chiang Mai in 1909-1910. He left the service in 1913 to become the editor of the Siam Observer. In the same year, he published his short-story collection Chequered Leaves from Siam. His 1920 novel Spears of Deliverance is the first full-length treatment of northern Siam in fiction. Here Reid (or the narrator of his story) recalls the days before the coming of the railway, when the trip to Chiang Mai (which Reid, following the example of Thomas Hardy, gives the fictitious name "Laowieng") took several weeks or months by boat.

So, after many days, the great barges slid slowly into Laowieng. ...

The current which, sometimes impetuously and in foaming fury, at others with dark and sullen underflow, but always relentless and steadily, had for so long opposed our progress, even now when almost conquered, abandoned its efforts only with the ill grace of a beaten child, and its last swirling shallow prolonged our final landing by a full half hour.

Painful progress indeed! Retrospective, the mind cannot but yield a meed of wonder at the thought of the long hours of grim, patient struggle upwards, ever upwards, that had at length prevailed against the doggedly-resisting stream. It is a broad and patent highway – this great river that traverses with all the devious directness of nature the plains and mountains lying between the capital and this far northern township. Its very obviousness has hitherto reconciled the mind of man to the excessive expenditures of time and energy demanded by the journey up-stream. Nevertheless, though it is a route which will ere long be abandoned for the shining track of steel that rips through the hills and plunges forward down the valleys, taking no count of current or flood, the great river will ever remain the artery of commerce in this land. Doubtless, in the years to come, when the aeroplane shall be a discarded invention, these same cumbersome *rua sadao* (barges) will still take their leisurely way up and down the broad bosom of the yellow Menam.

The journey up-stream is, in all ways, a type and example of primitive human endeavour that, with the minimum of machinery, and none of the labour-saving appliances which a more complex civilisation holds indispensable and even common-place, can be content to devote long hours to a difficult, toilsome and laborious method of locomotion without a regret for the inordinate expenditure of muscle and time involved. In this surely one sees again that truce with nature and her forces which man has always made, that submission to necessity which modern life in its haste grows daily more reluctant to yield. Yet there is satisfaction in these few hard-won stages, gained by the dint of an arduous and obsolete form of propulsion, which is unknown in all the facile triumphs of steel and electricity, for it is the reward of downright energy, the fruit of straightforward effort.

To one who comes from the more eager West this Iliad passage up-stream is a veritable revelation. But it is also a soothing experience, a lesson in long-drawn patience, and an insight into ideas Oriental and peculiar of the nature and value of time. Here a month is as a forgotten day, and a year a brief measure of a few breaths.

Not so long ago, the traveller who turned his face northward to the Lao country was condemned to traverse the entire distance by river. But nowadays one need not take to one's boats until, after a protracted and none too comfortable trip by rail, two hundred miles of the Menam have been left behind. – And the boats? Surely the quaintest of craft imaginable – these *rua sadao*, great squat barges of teak or rather monstrous punts, for all the world like those whimsical vessels that one sees on Egyptian inscriptions, wide of beam, shallow of draft, yet with holds of astonishing capacity, tapering forward into a steep and pointed prow, with behind a curving crest upreared like the triumphant tail of some huge scorpion, beyond which flops the unwieldy oar that serves as a rudder. Aft of all flutters the flag above the roomy cabin in which the wayfarer is to beguile the tedium of several weeks' transit upwards, ever upwards.

Four lusty hillmen, their glossy bodies and black tattooed thighs shining in the sunlight, are standing like copper statuettes by their bamboo poles. All aboard! The steersman, a skinny patriarch, deep versed in the knowledge of every pool and rapid in the river's course, grips with both hands his huge bludgeon of a helm. The first poleman runs up the narrow slanting prow: digs his bamboo firmly in the water, faces sharply round, and, having wedged the pole against his shoulder with a curious jerk, bends forward and stooping almost double, gives a long and steady thrust. As he descends another runs forward to take his place; the same action is repeated – then the third and the fourth, and the boat glides gently off with a pleasant swaying motion. When the first crew has finished its spell of twenty minutes, a relay of four fresh men take their places.

So we go on. Day follows day as leisurely as our boat pursues its calm way along the windings of the yellow stream upwards, always upwards. At first the course lies past parched paddy flats that glister in the haze of heat; then creeping along high wooded banks where the lips of the encroaching jungle seem greedily to lick the stream, over those yellow waters the perky king-fisher sits in wary watch; now by swamps from out whose grey slime the huge head of some wallowing buffalo is reared in stupid wonderment; here a village of brown thatched huts and a glimpse of naked children splashing at play in the stream; there the graceful slender pagoda of some sleepy riverside monastery seeming to nod with the palms in the breeze. So on from day to day upwards, ever upwards.

And now we are nearing the mountains. The character of the scenery rapidly alters. The water deepens. We hug the shore. Gorges open before us. The hills close round on every hand as if in frowning amaze at our daring to penetrate their ancient, unmolested fastnesses. Here the yellow river, otherwise a babbler, assumes a hue of meditative brown. Over the face of her deep waters are drawn the beetling brows of the eternal hills, shutting out the glooming eye of the rain-laden sky. The bed grows rocky and ever steeper.

Then one morning the roar of the first rapids reaches the ear. The polemen hitch their loin cloths up for the coming buffets. The steersman looks out his stoutest rope. From now onwards, progress is a slow succession of hard-won inches daily wrested from the maddening capricious flood. Half the time the men are in the water, hauling or pushing the boat, scrambling, shouting, panting, sliding on the slippery rocks. Always the sound of the mighty rushing yellow river fills the ears, but always we feel we are rising upwards, ever upwards, slowly, how slowly.

****

And so, after many days the great barges sidle slowly into Laowieng.

Reid, Chequered Leaves from Siam, pp. 201-205

The Coming of the Railway

In January 1914, The Bangkok Times reported that "very satisfactory progress" on the railway tunnel at Khun Tan had been made. "All Siam is deeply interested in the progress of this northern railway" as everyone was anxious to "do away" with the "long, tedious and expensive river journey". The project to build the Northern Line of Royal State Railways had begun in 1907 and the line had been gradually creeping towards Chiang Mai ever since, reducing travel times as it progressed. In fact, it took many years to complete the work, and the first through-train only reached Chiang Mai in January 1922. By the early 1930s, Chiang Mai could be reached by express within twenty hours from Bangkok and the city was becoming a tourist destination.

Explorers

Lucy Mercer Starling (1879-1968) was born in Hopkinsville, Kentucky, and studied there and at Western College, Oxford, Ohio. She sailed for Siam in 1909, becoming a teacher in Chiang Mai and Nan, and finally principal of the Girls' School at Lampang. During her early years in Siam she published widely in missionary periodicals. Her autobiography, Dawn over Temple Roofs, *appeared in 1960, but her most vivid writing is included in her letters to her parents which were published in the* Hopkinsville Kentuckian *newspaper, 1911-1914.*

The trip from Bangkok to Chiang Mai was always made by river and took from six weeks to three months, according to the state of the water. But the railroad was slowly creeping north, and our party would be the first to try the new route; so we had all the suspense and excitement of explorers. We were to travel two days by rail, and ten more by pony and chair.

The next morning my dreams were invaded by the "ding! ding!" of the alarm clock. It was early, and we dressed shaking with cold. The winter fog enshrouded every object and we moved through the mists like wraiths. Going to the station was an event and there was a crowd to see us off.

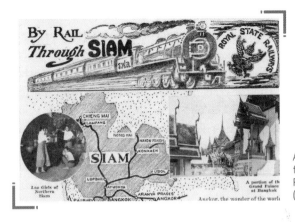

An advertisement for the Royal State Railways, about 1935 (detail). The Editor.

As we came in sight of the station there stood the tiny train, puffing as if eager to be off. There was only one train a day over the narrow-gauge railway. It would make four hundred kilometers that day to Phitsanulok, where we would sleep. The trains didn't run at night, for fear of being derailed by a roving elephant.

The coaches were European style and we got into a second-class compartment, upholstered in rattan. The British passengers traveled in a first-class compartment upholstered in imitation leather; otherwise the two were alike. Except for an occasional official, the Siamese traveled third class. With a warning "toot!" our train started and we waved goodbye to our friends. Almost at once we were out of the city and in the vast rice fields from which Siam's millions are fed. The plain, criss-crossed by canals, stretched to the horizon on every side.

Starling: Dawn over Temple Roofs, p. 13

Forces that Change

Robert E. Speer (1867-1947) led a Presbyterian "deputation" which visited missions in Asia in 1915. They spent about a week in Chiang Mai in May 1915.

The railroad which is being steadily finished from Bangkok to Chieng Mai has not yet reached Lakon. Regular trains are running only as far as Pa Kah. From there the German engineers who are building the road kindly sent us forward two long stages by construction train to

Meh Chang, whence we reached Lakon by ponies in a day and a half. I shall never forget the scene at the little improvised station at Pa Kah as our train came in just as the evening shadows were beginning to lengthen. All around was the great unbroken forest. Teak logs from old cuttings were lying where they had lain for years in a little mountain stream waiting to be driven out by flood and elephant, reaching Bangkok ten years perhaps after they had first been felled. The bamboo and thatch huts of the railroad laborers nestled together in a raw forest clearing. The neater houses of the German engineers stood among the trees on the hillside above. Back from the station were the encampments of the pack trains with the bullocks waiting to carry freight over the trails and the mountain passes into the open plains beyond. Wild-eyed people of half a dozen tribes, most of whom had never seen a railroad train before, looked on with wonder. The Chinese and Lao coolies who were building the road had finished their day's work. Nearby stood the Eurasian contractors or section superintendents. It was a strange mixture of race and speech, of old and new, of the forces that resist or only passively submit, and the forces that change and advance and create. Very much of what had been done was crude and imperfect and would have to be done again. The cost of maintenance and repair would far exceed the cost of first construction. In front stood the great and ancient forest, laced with lianas, dark and unmoved. Behind lay the fresh embankment and the new laid rails. "Here I rest," said the forest, "let no man disturb me." "Here I come," said life, the ever-onward, never-resting life of man, "make way for me." One could not have asked for a more vivid picture of the missionary enterprise or a clearer representation of its deepest problems than we saw that afternoon at Pa Kah as the long sunbeams lay athwart the tree trunks and the night gave the forest respite from man only until the day should break again.

Speer, Deputation Report, 1915, pp. 20-21

Express Trains

In his Bangkok guide, Erik Seidenfaden describes the service in the early 1930s …

The Northern Line of the Royal State Railways connects Bangkok with Chiengmai. the capital of the North. The main stretch between the two cities covers some 751 kms. At Ban Dara junction 458 kms. from Bangkok, a line branches off to Sawankaloke, 28 kms., the ancient capital of Siam, famous for its historical relics and ruins of centuries ago.

There are express trains with excellent day and night coaches, single and double berths compartments and restaurant cars running between Bangkok and Chiengmai. The journey occupies only 26 hours, and the time table is so arranged that daytime is spent in the most interesting part of the country.

The scenery along the Northern Line is incomparable in its grandeur. The Khun Tal Tunnel, at kms. 683, is 1,361 metres long, and is considered to be one of the most important engineering works of the system.

Rest-houses are maintained by the Royal State Railways at Lampang and Chiengmai. Good accommodation and excellent food can be obtained at both places. Many of the tourists visiting Chiengmai and Lampang find it convenient to make their headquarters there.

Seidenfaden, Guide, pp. 318-319

Travellers Need Good Heads

Rachel Wheatcroft (1869-1942) was an English artist who travelled to Siam independently in 1925. On a trip to the north, she visited Lampang (where she stayed with Lucy Starling) and Chiang Mai (where she stayed with missionaries and later David Macfie). Her illustrated travel book, Siam and Cambodia in Pen and Pastel, *appeared in 1928.*

On the railway line to Chiengmai there are several viaducts bridging whole valleys, fine specimens of pre-war German engineering. The rails run over open sleepers and the bridges are without any kind of parapet. The builder must have had a monkey's sense of balance, and only travellers with good heads can enjoy the wonderfully unimpeded view.

The Chiengmai Railway resthouse has a reputation for cleanliness and comfort; but I was fortunate in not having to put it to the test.

The picturesqueness expected of a royal town, the home of the Lao hereditary princes, still exists. Within the ramparts are fine temples, but the railway has had its inevitable levelling effect, and that approach to the town is nondescript and Westernised.

Wheatcroft, Siam and Cambodia, p. 251

The Trains are Crowded

Ruth Rickover (1903-1972), the wife of a well-known American admiral, visited Siam and Chiang Mai in 1938. Her interesting and entertaining travel book, Pepper, Rice, and Elephants, *appeared in 1975. Here she tells us about a journey upcountry on the Chiang Mai Express.*

The Chieng Mai Express leaves twice weekly at 6:00 p.m. and gets to its northern terminal at 2:30 in the afternoon of the next day. I went second-class which is all right, except that you sleep in full view of the whole coach unless you can induce the porter to give you a curtain. According to regulations you are supposed to bring one along, but the Siamese don't care for curtains since they enjoy being sociable on trips, even when asleep. So it is not easy to find one for, after all, this is a Siamese country, make no mistake – no special privileges for lordly whites!

The trains are crowded. People take along their babies, water-jars, silver drinking cups, kitchen utensils, bedding, and food in huge hampers. The corridors are so full of bundles that each trip to the washroom is something of a mountaineering excursion. The coaches are laid out like our pullmans, but have straw seats instead of upholstery. At night the porter brings a thin mattress, a sheet, and a pillow. I bullied him into giving me an extra sheet for a curtain, which he brought along grumbling audibly about unreasonable foreign nuisances. The good Rajdhani had given me a blanket and a sheet so I had all the bedding one normally needs on a train. I fixed one sheet as a curtain and made up my bed with hospital corners, admired by all the women passengers who thought these to be fantastically elaborate preparations for anything so simple as going to sleep. The temperature began falling and I was glad to have the blanket. When the Rajdhani boy brought it, it had seemed like a joke because it had been hot in Bangkok that day.

Rickover, Pepper, Rice, and Elephants, p. 182

First Impressions

Busy and Prosperous

The Irish cartographer James McCarthy (1853-1919) was head of the Royal Survey. Here, he gives his first impressions of Chiang Mai towards the end of the nineteenth century. The "full-sized billiard-table" he saw being transported upriver was presumably destined for Chiang Mai's billiard pavilion.

The town of Chieng Mai had a busy and prosperous appearance, and its modern improvements showed the influence of Western civilization. The river was spanned by a substantial teakwood bridge, erected by the late Dr. Cheek, who had also built a handsome teakwood church, with a tower, the centre of the Presbyterian mission. The steam saw-mill, which had been set up by the same enterprising American, was in active operation, with Kamu workmen, and substantial houses were rising all round. There was a residence for the English consul, houses and schools for missionaries, and a noteworthy structure, a fine billiard-pavilion. The pathways were excellent, and the water-supply was good. The main supply was brought a distance of 8 miles in open channels from Doi Sutep; but there were also numerous wells, and a spring of very pure water had been struck less than 40 feet below the surface. In the neighbourhood is a large swamp, which during the rains has the appearance of a lake, but which in the dry season affords an excellent clay for the making of bricks.

McCarthy, Surveying and Exploring in Siam, pp. 114-116, 123

A Picturesque Town

Eric Reid's protagonist Philip Harkness arrives in "Laowieng" at the landing-stage of the "Borneo Bornay Company".

It was nearly mid-day when their boats reached Laowieng. The picturesque town straggles along both banks of the river Meping, and over

Chiang Mai. The road to the railway station. Photograph by Tanaka. Oliver Backhouse.

it there hangs the shadow of Doi Saket, the mountain to which those of the European community who can possibly do so flee from the burning heat of sweltering Aprils. A pleasant town, Laowieng, where one has ever in one's ears the deep drone of the slow-moving, double rimmed bamboo water-wheels that line the bank and irrigate the paddy fields.

A long string of Lao women coming from market was filing past the Bombeo landing-stage at which Morland's boats had moored; and Philip's first impression of the place was that of a town full of women – for he could see no sign of men about. Residence confirmed this impression, the Lao woman here, as elsewhere, doing all the work, while their lords and masters approved their energy from the shade, recumbent and smoking a cheroot.

Philip was instantly struck by this train of quaint and dainty brown womenkind that went chattering and laughing past. It was his first sight of these women of the North with their swaying, double baskets full of rice, fruit, and the daily household marketing, their feet twinkling in and out beneath the vari-coloured *sin* (Lao girls' skirt) who cast occasional glances from capricious dark eyes upon the new arrival standing in their path regarding them thus curiously. They were so unlike the Siamese girls of Bangkok, invested somehow with the attraction of a femininity lacking in any Eve of the South, that, do what he would, Philip could hardly keep his eyes off them.

Reid, Spears of Deliverance, pp. 61-62

I Arrived at Harvest Time

Dr Cort describes the city as he first experienced it.

Strictly speaking, it consists of three cities. The core is the old city hemmed within the high, battlemented walls that did such yeomen service in the long ago when the people were waging eternal war with the Burmese or Siamese. Then, covering an area around the walled city some three hundred yards wide, there is an outer city, with dirt walls that are ringed by a creek which serves as a moat. This moat can be a wonderfully romantic place when the pink and white lotus are in blossom and the glow of the setting sun is reflected in the water. It used to be a natural breeding place for mosquitoes and malaria, but we managed to check that by introducing top minnows. They were almost as effective as oil for the purpose, and to the delight of every Romeo and Juliet about, they left the lotus plants to bloom unharmed.

Beyond the dirt wall lies the modern city, with its neat houses and well-laid streets spreading along the river bank. Across the river, where the Mission founded by Rev. McGilvary is located, is a suburb which very easily could be called a fourth city. It is connected with the eastern bank by a modern steel bridge that is impregnable to the floods which fill the channel from the beginning of August to the first of October. Numerous ruined pagodas suggest there must have been an earlier west bank suburb in medieval times, when Chiengmai attained the height of its importance as the capital of the North.

A water-wheel on a river near Chiang Rai, from Le May, *An Asian Arcady*.

I had arrived at harvest time. The rice had just been reaped and the bundles of grain were stacked in rustling walls around the threshing floors. The fields were yellow with stubble and everywhere were villages that looked like dark green islands shot through with tree and bush bordered creeks and irrigating ditches. In the distance purple shadowed mountains reached up to impressive heights. It was a magnificent panorama.

It wasn't long before the city claimed all of my attention and enthusiasm. I was particularly fascinated by the inner city, which was the first walled city I came to know intimately. Here stood the palaces of the Pra Chao, the hereditary chief of the state within the greater state. Here were scores of white temples with lofty roofs that were terraced down, usually, in three steps front and back. These temples had gables that were worth looking at time and time again. There was beautiful fretwork carving in teak. They were overlaid with gold leaf on a background of glass mosaic. Deep blues and reds and greens, and topping all this was a gracefully curved golden horn, the fingernail of Buddha pointing heavenward.

This quarter swarmed with priests and monks in their yellow robes, and for every priest and monk there seemed to be a dozen pilgrims. Chiengmai was the great place of pilgrimage of the North. The inner city, with its government buildings and official residences and its temples, was really the religious and administrative center of the province.

Then there was the bazaar. I have always had a weakness for them, and this one that lay between the outer dirt wall and the river was quite good. It was a conglomeration of fine brick buildings and wooden shacks. Here was held the open-air market. One of the sights of Chiengmai was the appearance at daylight of long lines of women and girls who came streaming in from the fertile plain to sell their wares and produce in this market. Each of them carried a pair of baskets slung on the end of a flat, limber bamboo pole which was balanced, effortlessly, on the shoulder. The younger women and girls wore flowers in their hair, a wreath of white blossoms around the top-knot, or a bunch of roses or orchids behind the ear. They made a charming picture in their brightly colored skirts, with their sleek black hair and lustrous dark eyes. The market made another interesting picture with its galaxy of colors and its assortment of wares. On low wooden tables that were supported by old bayonets and shaded by immense paper fans were all the foodstuffs of the region, along with earthenware pottery, handwoven cloth and an assortment of sauces, mostly with a fish, shrimp or crab base and amazingly odoriferous. When the sun reached its full heat I don't know which was more noticeable, the colors or the smells.

Throngs of good-natured people came and went, silent, dogs worked busily, buzzing, stinging flies came to sample what was being offered. And elephants swayed by, peacefully aloof. Trains of pack bullocks from the Shan States set the dust to flying. Yunnanese mule pack trains guided by slouching, sour-faced men from the hills moved slowly past. There were men and women carrying back-breaking loads, uniformed officials who were not. Everywhere were mobs of healthy, laughing, naked children. Everywhere were begging lepers, many of them horribly mutilated. To a newcomer it was all very exciting: a disturbing and interesting hodgepodge of beauty and squalor, bouncing health and loathsome disease.

Cort, Yankee Thai, pp. 18-20, 21-22

Reginald Le May Arrives in Chiang Mai, 1913

The present city lies on both banks of the river Mê Ping, but the ancient part of it is all on the west bank, the east bank being mainly given up to the houses of the European firms established in Chiengmai, the Mission compounds, with their school and church, and the beautiful park-like club. The old city, which is dominated by Doi Suthêp, a mountain rising behind it to a height of over 5000 feet, is, as Mr. Holt Hallett says, divided into two parts, the one embracing the other, on the south and east sides. The inner city faces the cardinal points, is walled and moated all round, and contains the palace of the Prince of Chiengmai. The outer city is more than half a mile broad, and is partly walled and partly palisaded on its outer sides. Both cities are entered by gates leading in and out of a fortified courtyard. A portion of the inner wall with the moat, with Doi Suthêp in the distance, is shown in the frontispiece to this work.

The chief buildings outside the ancient city on the western bank are the British Consulate, which lies some distance away to the south, and the Forest Department's house a little below that again. The house in which I lived was situated near the British Consulate, at right angles to the main road, and stood at the end of a wide extent of padi-land, which stretched away to the hills, almost as far as the eye could see. From my bedroom a clear, uninterrupted view of Doi Suthêp was to be had, and every morning, on waking, I could "look unto the hills."

Doi Suthêp is now used by the European community as a hill-station during the extremely hot weather of March and April, before the break of the rains, and many bungalows are dotted all over it, at heights ranging from 1200 feet right up to the top. At a height of 3000 feet there is the famous Temple of the Emerald Rice-Bowl, which is visited during the year by large numbers of pilgrims from far and near. I met there once myself a party of Shans, who had come all the way from Chieng Tung, at least 12 to 14 days' march distant, just on a pilgrimage, to pay their respects and then return the way they had come. It is possible, and even probable, that this is the temple referred to in a later chapter, as that on which the elephant rested, when he was carrying the relics of the Lord Buddha presented by Phra Sumana to the King of Chiengmai, as there are no known remains of a temple on the actual summit of the mountain.

Le May, An Asian Arcady pp. 79-80

The Bee Tree and Phya Nak

A giant Diptocarp, detached and magnificent in the Wat Luang grounds, was a subject not to be missed. Locally it was known as the Bee Tree, for the great honeycombs on its limbs. Wonderful trees in the exuberance and remoteness of their lives, their high branches a refuge for birds and monkeys where no shot can reach them. At the same temple the doorway and its approach were guarded by Phya Nak and his twin, wonderfully entwined. Crested and terrible he is, and in spite of his extravagant jewels, very impressive.

Wheatcroft, Siam and Cambodia, p. 253

PHYA NAK, WAT LUANG.

Out on the River Somebody was Playing a Flute

Ebbe Kornerup (1874-1957) was a Danish artist and writer. He travelled to Siam in 1926, entering the country from Burma and spending time at Chiang Mai. Unsurprisingly in view of the fact that his trip was more-or-less sponsored by the Siamese government, his book Siam *(1928) promoted the country as "the newest holiday land". It appeared in English as* Friendly Siam *in 1930 and in German as* Paradies Siam.

When the morning sun shone on the bridge and green bamboos and slender palms were mirrored in the quiet water, and the big bamboo wheels, thin as cobweb, churned water up out of the river, all was gay. People bathed or washed their clothes, beating them till they were almost ruined – this was their way of washing, for they seldom used soap. The sun played merrily on the yellow water, the roads were dusty, and strings of bullock-carts ground the dust about their wheels.

It was marvellous down by the river; the houses on stakes, the huts roofed with attap, the palms and the delicate bamboos, all the canoes, the well-made bathers, the life going on the roads beside the green river-banks – it all made Chieng Mai into an enchanting oasis under a turquoise sky.

And beside the river there were houses, big bungalows and villas with white walls and well-kept gardens. People went out early. The air was not exactly cold, but fresh. Far away behind the river were the wooded mountains. There was a caravanserai in a field; the unharnessed pack-oxen rested, chewing the cud, and the carts with their stowed-away goods stood in cool shadow under spreading rain-trees. These caravans, coming up from China, are a whole month on the way and bring porcelain, brassware, ponies, silks, brocades, and tea to Siam, and then go back the same way with rice, horn, stick-lac, wax, Japanese matches, and Japanese or European hardware.

At the hotel I shared a table with a young Siamese doctor who had qualified in Switzerland; we had met at his home in Bangkok; he was up here only to attend a princess who was ill. Every day the princess sent her servants with food for him on fine porcelain – Siamese curry, and many motley dishes – and he shared them in the friendly way, so we both had two kinds of food.

Women brought beautiful lacquer goods, silk cloths, shawls, old silverware, and spread them out on the veranda where they sat patiently all day long and watched for customers. Out on the roadway country people trudged past in single file; they came straight from the forests; wild and fearful, buoyant to their movements. When darkness suddenly descended they lit fires by the wayside and settled down for the night.

Twice a week only the express brought fresh arrivals; otherwise all was quiet and peaceful here.

Late one afternoon I borrowed the station-master's bicycle. Quite by chance. I happened to be strolling with my landlord, who stopped him as he rode by and introduced me. Without further ado I was given the bicycle. The Siamese are like that – always helpful.

I rode through the main streets, across the big bridge and turned northwards along the river. The sun was already behind the mountains, a rosy reflection fell on the old huts and lit up the opposite bank, where there was a beautiful garden of yellowish-green palms and delicate bamboos that leaned gracefully out over the yellow river. Boats and canoes glided downstream, children leaped and danced in the water. Men and women stood still, immersing themselves. It was the time of the evening bath. They rinsed their mouths and rubbed their teeth with their fingers. The banks were full of life. The big bamboo wheels churned on, fishermen cast their nets. People were sitting on the little bridges, fishing from lines. The smoke from the houses rose straight up into the air. It was perfectly still, and the air was pure after a brief shower. Often there was a smell of flowers – when there was not a stench from a sewer.

And then all those beautiful people, the lovely Lao women with flowers in their hair, dressed in red *palais* with a yellow cloth round their waists! The men, on the other hand, wore wide silk drawers of vivid crimson, blue, or green and with a silk scarf of a different colour tied tightly round their hips. They walked barefoot, swinging as they went. Their faces were broad and flat, with prominent cheek-bones and slanting eyes, rather reminiscent of the Japanese. Their figures were soft and rounded, they were plump, not very tall, and often exceptionally lovely. Entrancing women smiled friendly as they carried baskets on their light yokes. There were quantities of children, and people squatted on their heels quite absorbed in them, entirely forgetful of themselves.

The Viceroy lived on the road beside the river where the big houses and villas stood. I went there. A Lao boy in pale-blue Chinese drawers showed me up a high wooden staircase to the Residency. Inside, in a big half-open room, sparsely furnished. I met his secretary, who told me that H. E. Phaya Surabadindr would come at once ... would I sit down and wait? The Viceroy came. He was a man in the prime of life, a nobleman wearing Siamese dress, distinguished, clever, and with a bright, attractive smile and an aristocratic face. We sat down on a sofa; he welcomed me cordially and was very interested in my journey through Siam. What did I specially want to see? How long was I staying? I should have to spend a long time in Chieng Mai to see everything. He offered me his car; and all the time I was in this town it was at my disposal.

Then came tea. Pale tea in beautiful cups, and cigarettes with the tea. We talked for a long time. The sun had gone down. The lamps were lit. From the river below a cool breeze blew up on to the veranda and into the room. Somewhere or other out on the river somebody was playing a flute.

Kornerup, Friendly Siam, pp. 45-47

A Fairy-Tale Picture come True

Mary Lucretia ("Lou") O'Brien was the wife of Dr Henry O'Brien of McCormick Hospital. O'Brien had been born in Cincinnati and studied at Miami University, Oxford, Ohio. She edited Siam Outlook, *the Mission's quarterly magazine, in succession to Katharine Reichel. This is from a letter she wrote home soon after arriving in Chiang Mai.*

Before I begin to tell you about our house, an inexhaustible subject with me, of course, I want to tell you a little bit about the city, itself, so that you will be prepared for what you are to see when the carpet actually arrives and settles itself on the ground with a gentle little thud. In the very first place, and this explains much of the charm which Chiengmai had for me, there are mountains! Bangkok's one hill is one built of bricks, and I often found myself yearning for hills, gently rolling or steep, because

Chiang Mai: Wat Chai Si Phum, moat and wall. Photograph by Tanaka.
Oliver Backhouse.

my home city, Cincinnati, is built upon hills, and I love them. And so I
could hardly wait for my first glimpse of Chiengmai mountain. Then, too,
just across the road from the end of our compound is the lovely twisting
Me Ping River with its little island vegetable gardens and its interesting
river-craft. Add to this an old city wall, now crumbling all too rapidly, and
a moat filled with lotus blossoms, and the most colorfully dressed people
in the world, and you can begin to realize why Chiengmai people are just
as violent in their boosting as some residents of southern California, or
Florida. Really it is like a page from a fairy-tale picture book come true,
and I often have the feeling that I am dreaming. Old Buddhist temples
with gleaming tile roofs and queer figures at their entrances, Buddhist
priests in their yellow robes, Siamese and Laos, (this is Lao country in the
north) wearing trousers, blouses, *panungs* and *pasinns* of reds, purples,
green, orange, yellow, pink, blue, gold and every possible variation all
make a "splashy canvas" of the city.

There is a great long bridge over the Me Ping River, not far from us, and
all day long, from early until late, there is a steady procession of bullock
carts with their lovely, tinkly little bells, motor lorries, bicycles this is a
"bicycle town", pony traps, gharries, ricshas, and pedestrians going across.
It is fascinating to watch and to hear.

6 February 1927

My First Annual Meeting

Lucy Starling arrived in Siam in November 1909, in time to attend her first Annual Meeting of the Laos Mission which was held at Phrae (which she spells "Praa") in early December. William Reginald Dibb (1876-1918) of the Bombay Burmah Trading Corporation was to be one of the North's casualties in the Great War. Noting Dibb's "cordial welcome" to the delegates, The Bangkok Times *remarked: "In this north-land of few foreigners the gathering of so large a number means inspiration and pleasant social intercourse. Those newly out or returning from furlough brought enthusiasm fresh from the homeland.". (11 January 1910, p. 5). A "fruitcake tree" presumably had the shape of a Christmas tree.* Laos News *was a quarterly periodical published from 1904 by the Chiengmai Mission Press to promote the work of the Mission and to report on its activities to a wider audience in Siam and abroad. Its name was changed to* North Siam News *in 1916. It was relaunched as* Siam Outlook *in 1921 and, under the editorship of a series of women missionaries, began to publish more self-consciously literary essays and poems.*

The stranger in a strange land could have had no more beautiful introduction to that land than to have been brought into the atmosphere of the Annual Meeting at Praa. The trip overland from railhead to Praa was itself a preparation for the meeting. The slope of the verdure-clad mountains on either side, like steps unto heaven; the bewildering luxuriance of palms and ferns; the slender white trunk of the bee-tree rising high like marble pillars of a temple whose dome was the blue sky above; the garlands of vines that hung in festoons, or wreathed themselves around the white trunks, as if in honor of a conquering king; the stillness, broken only by nature's sweet music, the lullaby of the mountain stream and the whispering of the trees. The first night we raised our tent in the jungle and while the stars kept watch, slept peacefully and dreamed of home. How near God seemed, that first day in Laos, and with a deep sense of His abiding presence we came to Praa.

The meeting was good in many ways but the most memorable impressions made upon the writer were: the wonderful spiritual uplift and the delightful social intercourse.

The first day was devotional and on that day of prayer and thanksgiving the key-note was sounded that vibrated through the whole meeting. The first hour of each morning was devotional, the general subject being Prayer, and we drew very near to the business session which lasted until noon. A detailed account of the various business transacted will occur elsewhere, but I cannot refrain from saying that the spirit of devotion rested upon even this. Personal preference seemed to be laid aside, differences of opinion were adjusted without any friction, and the writer felt happy that she might be allowed to work in a mission that showed so much of the spirit of the Master.

Every afternoon came tea and tennis, Mr. Dibb of Bombay Burma Company, being the host throughout the week. Nor was this the only kindness shown us during our stay. The Praa Christians contributed a couple of beeves, rice, and fruit for our entertainment. And the Governor was most kind, expressing his desire that our mission at Praa be soon reopened, and promising to help in the establishing of a mission school. It was a pleasure of the writer to find that the members of the Laos Mission could maintain friendly relations with even the officials, and as Paul said "become all things to all men, if by any means I might save some".

But not the least pleasant feature of the meeting was the delightful social intercourse among ourselves. The two unoccupied mission houses were thrown open, and we crowded in twelve in each house, and the overflow in tents outside, with not a care for inconvenience. Through the kindness of Mr. Dibb two more families were accommodated in one of the Bombay Burma Company bungalows. It is quite proper to be frigidly polite to strangers where stiff collars and finger-bowls hold sway, but who would not thaw out and forget all laws of etiquette with dear Mrs. Taylor on the right, urging "Now, do have some more of this fruit cake. I don't want the trouble of putting it away," and Mr. Palmer on the left with "Here's a roast chicken Mrs. Shellman sent to you." If anyone had asked, "Have you seen our fruitcake tree yet?," the writer would have answered "No, but it must be a large one to bear such as enormous crop"; for the ladies who stayed at home had sent all sorts of dainties, to console us for their *absence*.

And then the evenings of music and games in the great rambling rooms! We worked well during the day, and the work only added to the zest of our pleasure; – clean, wholesome fun, with no bitter aftertaste.

It was a beautiful meeting. Would that every member of the Laos Mission might have enjoyed it with us! I thought often of the new injunction "Whether ye eat or drink, or whatsoever ye do, do it all to the Glory of God." With such a beginning may all our labor and all our pleasure in the year before us be to His Glory!

Laos News, February 1910, pp. 20-21

Much to Laugh at in Siam
By Charles Park, M.D.

I have now been in Chiengmai, Siam, for two weeks and am still quite verdant in regard to the customs and styles of the people.

I can say this for the climate that it is beautiful at present. Ideal, being like our Pennsylvanian September and October; as cold as 48 at night and reaching 80 at noon. This is the coldest weather ever seen here. The natives and Europeans alike suffer with the cold making business slow and hindering religious and school work.

The number and various species of animals are startling to say the least. We lack horses though and are compelled to use ponies which we find quite interesting. While contemplating the purchase of one lately, we asked the jockey to mount and allow us to see how the animal behaved. As soon as he had mounted the pony started for the tall timber running through some bushes and under a cocoanut tree throwing rider, tearing off the saddle, giving us a fine exhibition of Wild West sports – we did not buy.

Dogs are numerous. You see more here while travelling through the city than you would see at a dog show at home. Hundreds of dogs! Every household seems to have its share. They lie in the road and it is necessary to drive around them or run over them with the cart. The latter appeals strongly to me as it is my only chance at present to kill the poor brutes. They are outrageous looking animals in regard to their health, "Job's turkey" having no place in their class.* The natives do not get rid of them by killing

---

* "As poor as Job's turkey" is a nineteenth-century American expression.

them, because Buddhism does not allow them to kill anything, therefore the puppies are allowed to live starve and die as best they can.

There is much to laugh at in Siam and the foreigner is justified in indulging freely because the natives laugh at their own blunders. The boat sticks on a sand-bar in the river, and instead of using profanity as they would naturally do if they belonged to some of the other earthly tribes, the boatmen simply jump into the stream and while shouting and laughing at each other's efforts and mistakes they start the boat in motion again. Very much as boys would do in paddling a small boat about in a pond. The fact is they appear exactly as children in much of their work and customs.

One cannot avoid laughing at the native idea of styles in clothing, although at times there is nothing to laugh at.

It is a bit startling to the newcomer to see the way tobacco is used by the natives. Fancy the child of three, and I dare say less, smoking cigarettes, but it is the most natural thing in the world for him to do because his larger brother and sister, his father and mother, his uncle and aunt, his grandfather and grandmother all smoke. Why shouldn't he?

They are also very fond of chewing tobacco and the betel-nut which blackens their teeth. They are quite proud of their black teeth saying, that "shy dog can have white teeth."

We attended very interesting meetings this week (which is the Week of Prayer) and meeting have been held once or twice daily at some one of the houses, school buildings, or churches.

On this particular day of which I will write the meeting was held beside the chapel where there had been prepared a booth made of bamboo poles, palm branches and thatch, decorated by native flags, flowers and palm branches and portions of scriptures printed in the native language covered in bright colored paper covers. The Chapel was surrounded by bananas, orange and cocoanut trees and was a beautiful place to meet.

It is most encouraging to know that the native Christians are anxious to pass their Christianity on to their friends and fellow men, and they take every available opportunity for doing this, so during the special week of prayer they were busy distributing scriptures all around.

Although I could not understand the language and therefore did not appreciate the spiritual feast to its fullest, I came in stronger on the native feast of oranges, bananas, cocoanuts, rice, tea and sweets which were served later. I like the appearance of the native Christians and can see that they are greatly uplifted in all lines by becoming Christians. While they are becoming more and more enlightened there is yet much room for improvement in regard to the native customs, sanitation, agriculture and religion.

Laos News, January 1914, pp. 17-19

Wats and Worms
By Victor G. Heiser, M.D., and Wilbur A. Sawyer, M.D.

Dr Victor G. Heiser (1873-1972) was Far East Director of the Rockefeller Foundation's International Health Board. In January 1921, Dr Heiser and his colleague Dr Sawyer visited Dr Milford E. Barnes in Chiang Mai to observe the progress of the Board's hookworm eradication programme for which the city (and here the village of Sansai) was a pilot location. They also found time for some tourism..

From our seats near the speakers we could look into the eager faces of the attentive and respectful natives and could hear frequent murmurs of approbation. Although the meeting lasted nearly two hours, the interest of the audience was as great at the end as at the beginning. Dr. Barnes addressed the people first, speaking in Lao, the language of northern Siam. Their sounds and signs of approval showed how thoroughly they were convinced. They seemed to be ready to attempt the control of the parasite that was sapping their strength and holding back their prosperity. They were more than ready to follow the doctor's leadership in an attempt to secure for themselves, through better sanitation, another of the blessings of modern civilization. The next speaker was Major Boriracksha, one of the medical officers of the Siamese army detailed to assist Dr. Barnes. He waxed eloquent and used the chart and models freely. It was obvious from his gestures that he was enthusiastic. He gave the dramatic story of the hookworm's life from the egg to its adult stage – from the soil to the intestine. He explained the specifications for latrines so graphically that we could follow him in a general way without understanding a word. At the end of the talk the audience were shown the eggs and living larvae under the microscope. This was the final touch in bringing home the reality of the hookworm and in creating an intense eagerness to eject this unwelcome boarder and keep him out.

From Sansai we went to Chiengmai. Our stay there, though unavoidably brief, gave us an opportunity to see for ourselves that, despite the reputed conservatism of the Siamese, the hookworm work had been successful, and that the time was opportune for extending it to other parts of Siam and making the project truly national. But at Chiengmai we were not limited to the study of hookworm work, thanks to Dr. and Mrs. Barnes, who saw to it that we visited in our spare time all the principal beauty spots and points of interest.

An especially pleasant experience was our visit to the Chao Dara, widow of the late king of Siam and daughter of the last Lao king. The dowager queen received us cordially on a wide veranda, or outdoor parlor. She was a picturesque personage surrounded by her train of servants who entered and left her presence on their hands and knees. Of necessity we left to Dr. Barnes all conversation with our hostess, but we enjoyed the unique experience of being entertained by Siamese royalty. As a special favor we were allowed to see the garments which were being made under the direction of the Chao Dara for the fiancée of the king. The future queen had decided to use the Lao skirt, or *sin*, as court dress instead of the breeches-like *penung* worn by the Siamese women of the south. The looms had been set up in a spacious open-walled building. The expert women silk-weavers of Chiengmai had been gathered together and were hard at work making silk garments of most beautiful patterns devised by the Chao Dara. The colors were blues, pinks, greens, and reds, sometimes with added threads of gold and silver. In the middle of the floor sat a woman at work with a spinning wheel much like the ones exhibited in the hallways of Boston's first families.

There are several interesting industries in Chiengmai. In one section of the town we found silversmiths pounding metal into thin bowls on which they worked beautiful and characteristic patterns by beating against a

The hookworm lecture at Wat Sansai, January 1921. National Library of Medicine, Washington, DC.

background of hard wax. Hardly had we stopped to watch the work when women began to appear from several directions, bringing pieces of beaten silver which they soon arranged attractively before us. The men went right on with their work, leaving to the women the task of exchanging the beaten silver for our coined variety and its paper substitute.

We next visited the makers of lacquer work in a shop opposite one of the gates of the old city wall. From the shop one looked across the moat at the ruined brick wall and the overhanging palms and stately oil trees. Nearby a native, armed with a basket-like net hanging from the end of a long bamboo pole, was patiently fishing for the tiny fish that live under the lily pads. The round lacquer boxes, red, black, or black and gold, could be seen in every stage of manufacture. First the box was woven from bamboo fibre; next the interstices were filled with a thick material; and then a beautiful smooth surface of lacquer was applied, completely concealing the woven framework. With marvelous dexterity the fine patterns were then scratched on the surface and filled with pigment. Then we saw a pottery and watched the lump of clay on the potter's wheel rise, almost in the twinkling of an eye, into a tall jar, decorated and ready for burning. The market with its long lines of natives selling all sorts of fruits and small wares was not overlooked. It was there that we ran across palm sugar made by boiling down the sap of a palm. It had an excellent flavor and made a fair substitute for the much-missed maple sugar of the home country.

The greatest charm to the traveler in Chiengmai or Bangkok lies in the temples, or *wats*. Almost everywhere one turns there is a *wat*, glowing with blue and gold and red, or stately in its quiet ruins. The gateways are guarded by grotesque dog-like images that would frighten away the harvest of evil spirits, unless perchance they were protected by a sense of humor. The principal building, which is usually very beautiful, has at either end a series of overlapping gables, each of which is surmounted by a strange snake-like projection, suggesting to the I. H. B. mind a hookworm rampant. On the eaves are little bells to drive away evil spirits. They tinkle in the wind and add to the fascination of these charming buildings.

The Bulletin of The International Health Board (Rockefeller Foundation),
July 1921, pp. 21-25

Souvenirs

Chiengmai is a great centre for lacquer, very like the Burmese lacquer in type, and like the Pagan lacquer it was formerly all on a ground of red. Recently they too have branched out into red patterned with gold-leaf or gold-leaf on black, which, if not a return to an ancient fashion, must be an adaptation to small objects of the fine work often seen on the temple shutters and doors, and on the wonderful wat bookcases, of which a remarkable collection is in the National Library at Bangkok. The frame of box, begging bowl, betel set, tray or what not, is made of fine laths of bamboo plaited, and the lacquer applied in successive coats. Great skill is required to make the perfect shape on so uneven a surface and to retain the elasticity which is much valued. The designs are mostly traditional, but it is fascinating to watch the workman's unerring precision in spacing them – beautiful freehand work.

Small bronze weights, now superseded, in the shape of fantastic birds, dog-lions or, best of all, elephants, are delightful treasures still to be bought. Although the artists must constantly see elephants they have no copied air, but seem as much part of the artists' inner vision and as full of life as the gods and goddesses on the temple walls in astonishing contrast to their representations of mere human beings. The beasts of my own particular herd range in height from one and a quarter inches to six-eighths of an inch.

Much silk is woven at Chiengmai, a good deal of it like Korat, but less heavy and rich. Moreover it is made in short lengths of a little over one and three-quarter yards for *pasin*, the *panung* is not worn among the Lao. The range of colours is exquisite but fugitive like most Eastern vegetable dyes. Besides native cottons an immense amount of mercerised cotton is imported from Burma and is woven. It was to a Chinese merchant's shop that I was taken, but the weaving is probably Lao as much as Chinese.

Other souvenirs that may be bought are earthenware bottles for water, and beautiful baskets. Those that specially pleased me were made for marketing or carrying goods, strong and light and made of finely plaited bamboo. They are quite different in character, material and shape from the many Bangkok baskets.

Wheatcroft, Siam and Cambodia, pp. 258-259

Exceptionally Clean

Chieng Mai has grown far beyond the original site and is now a busy market town with rows of open-front stores selling every imaginable commodity. It is famous for an exceptionally clean market, owned by a public-spirited citizen who engaged an Englishman to put it into good condition and keep it so by putting every penny of profit into new cement floors, walls, fountains, and other improvements. This was my first encounter with such interested civic pride and service in this part of the world. I inquired about rental costs and found that a tiny cubbyhole costs two satang a day; a larger stand suitable for selling fruits and vegetables rents at five to six satang, depending on location; a small bakery shop in a good place costs ten satang. The Indian stores which sell yard goods, Bombay brass, and lacquerware pay thirty ticals a month.

Some lacquer and silverware is made in Chieng Mai. The silver-work is influenced by Burmese designs and features heavily embossed work, which I did not like as well as the shallower Siamese kind. Most householders have a few round silver bowls with stylized flower designs. The Chieng Mai lacquerwork is poor, but the weaving industry makes attractive sarongs. All these things are manufactured for the home market, not for tourists. Still, word had spread that I had arrived, and when we returned for lunch we found a number of ancient ladies squatting on the porch of the Collier house with silver items spread out before them. These were all articles they had used in their own homes and few of them appealed to me. Until I left, the porch was never empty. I did buy a silver bowl and told them what I wanted most was one of the small bronze weights in the shape of an animal that merchants used in the old days.

Rickover, Pepper, Rice, and Elephants, p. 191

Dorothy Le May's watercolour of Chiang Mai's walls, moat and mountain was published as a frontispiece to her husband's *An Asian Arcady*.

The Dreaming Walls:
Two Poems

The Moat, Chiengmai
By Mary Lou O'Brien

These crumbling walls did once behold
Grim warriors waging battle bold.
Antiquity breathes from them now;
The history of ancient Laos.
And lotus blossoms idly float
Upon the waters of the moat;
So still and sweet the way of peace
When war and all its discords cease.
O walls and moat which one time barred
The way of warriors battle scarred,
Rejoice to be a quiet spot
And for past glory sorrow not!
For we who gaze would rather see
Pink lotus buds nod lazily
And climbing vines embrace the walls
Than gallant men become war's thralls.

Siam Outlook, April 1930, p. 453

The Sunset Wall
By Kenneth E. Wells

This rugged breast that broke the hungry spears,
Hurled back the giant drum's defiant note,
That ran with blood unto the seething moat
Where locked in death were human hates and fears, –
How quiet now! - as one home from the wars
Sis, cane in hand, - dreaming in the sun,
Nor marks he mellow years that seem as one,
So swift they pass, so gently close the doors.
The tall new rice, the song at dusk, the slow
Blue smoke o'er golden thatch, the sunset flame
On Doi Sutep, - this too a dream? That same
Love song was sung a thousand springs ago
By one as fair, by beauty held in thrall.
A thousand summers hence young life will sing
Of love; and Beauty to this moat will bring
Fresh lotuses to grace the dreaming Wall.

Siam Outlook, April 1933, p. 128

Chiang Mai. The walls and moat. Photograph by Tanaka. Oliver Backhouse.

Language Study

The First Language Lesson

"Kah-kah, ki-kee, keu-keu, koo-koo", I intoned for the hundredth time, as I sat at a table with my language teacher. He had been abbot of a Buddhist monastery before his conversion and knew no English. His jaw was distended with a huge toll of betel, and his mouth was full of red saliva. This made it difficult for him to enunciate and impossible for the new student to understand what he said.

The ex-abbot read a syllable, and I repeated after him. Siamese is a tonal language, and while I was aware of the musical rising and falling of the voice, it was difficult to reproduce.

Starling, Dawn over Temple Roofs, pp. 29-31

This Annoying Tongue

Walter Leigh Williams (1889-1955) joined the BBTC after leaving Oxford in 1912, working at Lampang, Chiang Mai and at Paknampho. His memoir Green Prison *appeared in 1941, a revised, second edition renamed* Jungle prison, *following in 1954. Here he writes about the difficulty Englishmen have in mastering the language, even with the help of a "sleeping dictionary", in other words, a northern woman with whom a teak-wallah had made an arrangement.*

Our afternoons were reserved for shopping, sight-seeing, or studying the Siamese language. Siamese belongs to the Chinese family of languages, but its writing is borrowed from southern India. I had a nasty shock when I realised the difficulty of acquiring even a smattering of the language. It is mostly monosyllabic, with a comparatively small vocabulary, but the paucity of words is more than compensated for by there being five "tones." The same word can thus have five different meanings according to the way it is pronounced. There is also a complication of accents which still further increases the range. There is a word in the Lao dialect, spoken up-country, which has twenty-one different meanings! Unless pronunciation is meticulously accurate, one is unintelligible to all but the highly educated. Asking one's way of a jungle villager becomes a nightmare when it is realised that the words "far" and "near" are the same! Here is an example I came across later of the practical difficulties of this annoying tongue.

It has been said that Englishmen are bad at European but good at oriental languages. Siamese goes far to explode this theory, for it proved far too difficult for the average Englishman. Up-country the standard was deplorably low, and many a man who had been out twenty years was unable, in spite of a "sleeping dictionary," to give clear and precise orders or understand half what was said to him. Foreigners were, as a rule, better at the language than we were, but the number of Europeans in the country who could speak Siamese really well might be counted on the fingers of one hand. In addition to the vernacular, there is a polite or court language used in royal and highly educated society, whose intricate embroideries and niceties of nuance provide still further pitfalls for the unwary. A studious friend of mine mixed the two languages up when ordering his Kamu (coolie) cook to kill a chicken for dinner. His astonished staff gaped at something which might be roughly (very roughly!) translated thus: "It is our command that the feathered friend shall receive euthanasia in preparation for our banquet."

Jones and I waded into the Siamese grammar, and later found the long journey up-country an excellent opportunity for study and practice. I "swotted" up the language chiefly because I had nothing else left to read. It was not many months before I was interpreting for my seniors, and had gained a reputation for being good at the language, chiefly because I could write it with speed and tolerable accuracy. This does not mean that I was at all a Siamese scholar, but merely that I shone by comparison with the average "jungle-wallah," whose "howlers" were a perpetual delight to the local inhabitants. Yet the Siamese were marvellous at keeping a straight face whenever the white man had recourse to a useful and necessary word which can very easily be mispronounced to denote an equally useful and even more necessary natural function!

Williams, Green Prison, pp. 20-22

I Must Control my Tone

Mary Lou O'Brien chooses verse to express her horror of tones. This is in fact a part of a long, unpublished text in which O'Brien describes all of her early experiences in Siam in a kind of epic poem.

The language study, now my task, claims many hours of time.

And all the puzzles it presents I cannot tell in rhyme.

The way my voice slides up or down, or goes to heights unknown

Makes all the difference in the world. I must control my tone.

For if I say a word down deep it means another thing.

From that same word said sharp and high and with a nasal ring.

And often times I do forget and mix my tones up so

I may say the word for "stick" or "new" when all I meant was "no".

And "clothing", "mat", and "tiger" spelled the same, save this alone,

That each of these three meanings can be told from just the tone

Confuse me and upset me, and they make me yearn to quit.

Although I know that some sweet day I shall have mastered it.

21 August 1927

The Climate

The Most Trying Month of the Year

Reginald Stuart Le May (1886-1972) joined the Siam Consular Service in 1907 and was posted to the north of Siam as Vice-Consul at Lampang in 1913. He left the service in 1922 to become an adviser to the Ministry of Commerce under H.R.H. Prince Purachatra of Kamphaengphet. His account of the north of Siam, An Asian Arcady, *was published in 1926, and is widely regarded as one of the finest books about the region from the period. His* Siamese Tales *appeared in 1930. After leaving Siam on retirement in 1932, Le May became a celebrated scholar in the art and culture of South East Asia. He remained a tireless advocate for Siam/Thailand, even though he seems never to have returned.*

The climate of the North of Siam is one of greater extremes than the South or the Centre, and the rainfall is less. [...] In the winter months, from November as soon as the rains have ceased until the middle or end of February, the temperature of the North of Siam is delightful, ranging from 80° F. at mid-day to sometimes under 40° F. at night in a particularly cold season. It can occasionally be too cold to be pleasant, especially if one is travelling in the jungle, at the end of the year. I can remember one such New Year's Eve, when, putting up at a resthouse between Nan and Muang Pong, it was so cold that, although I went to bed enveloped in as many sweaters, overcoats and blankets as I could lay my hands on, I found it impossible to sleep, and eventually the wind proved so piercing that the whole camp rose and packed up at two in the morning, and we set out on our journey again with torches for our guide. It is of course the great range, at times of 45° F., between midday and midnight that makes the body so susceptible to the cold.

From the beginning of March until the break of the rains in May is a very trying period. The country is as dry as the proverbial bone, and the jungles present a sorry sight of carpets of charred leaves and stumpy trunks of trees, where forest fires have broken out. In April in Lampang one can see the fires - twinkling points of flame - all over the hills which encircle the city. Chieng Rai, which stands at the head of a wide, open plain with high hills behind on the Chieng Tung side, records, I believe, the highest temperature, going as high as 110° F. in April (as well as the lowest in the cold season); but Chiengmai, Phre and especially Lampang, are very hot for about three months of the year, when the nights are almost airless and the early mornings, too.

The rains, which last theoretically from May to November, are the same all over the tropics – receiving the warmest of welcomes when they arrive, but outstaying that welcome so long that, when they eventually do go, it is to a chorus of hearty cursing and relief at their departure.

June is a pleasant month, when everything in Nature is coming to life once more, and the air is full of a warm, soft breeze; but September is a difficult month, when the earth is sodden, and the air is dull and heavy with storms. Only the emerald-green fields of growing padi give promise of a better time to come. September is the most trying month of the year.

Le May, An Asian Arcady, pp. 83-84

Haze

The Anglo-Irish Dr Arthur [A. F. G.] Kerr (1877-1942) became the Medical Officer of Health for Monthon Payap based in Chiang Mai in 1903. Having established a reputation as a botanist, he joined the Ministry of Commerce as the government's first Chief Botanist in 1920. He retired and left Siam in 1932.

There is a good deal of haze during the hot season. It is most marked when there are long spells without rain. From the middle of March on to the break of the rains Doi Sutep is seldom visible from Chiengmai, though its foot is only three or four miles distant, while by 4 P. M. the sun is a dull red disc which can be gazed at without discomfort. Probably most of this haze is due to smoke from forest fires. All the deciduous forests, which predominate in the vicinity of Chiengmai, are burnt over at least once every hot season, these fires producing a great quantity of smoke which diffuses through the atmosphere.

Arthur Kerr, 'Meteorological Observations
made in Chiengmai, 1910-1914'

Suddenly a Sheet of Flame

One day was very much like another. I used to look forward to my unappetising tiffin if only as a respite from the eternal climbing. It was getting hotter and hotter every day. The trees were almost stripped of leaves, and the thick carpet of dead leaves was beginning to burn in places. Whether these jungle fires are started by the sun or by the natives is not known. They certainly sometimes blaze up in places remote from any human habitation. As the hot weather increased the long grass and the tall undergrowth withered and grew brittle as tinder. Suddenly a sheet of flame would roar up the hillside, and we would have to run for the shelter of a patch of evergreen. Often we would have to start a protective fire to give ourselves a margin of escape. The earth was baked, the air was full of dust and ashes, and sometimes the water-bottle was finished long before the end of the day's work.

Williams, Green Prison, pp. 114-115

We Sailed Through their Front Gates and Tied the Boat to their Steps

All northern towns were subject to periodic flooding. The floods of 1927 were said to be "unprecedented" and those in September 1929 were "the worst for thirty years". The railway line was washed away and roads throughout the region were under water. The Danish East Asiatic Company's offices at Phrae were "entirely submerged" and their "beautiful compound" wrecked. 200,000 ticals were made available for relief of flood victims. Here, Lucy Starling describes a flood at Nan in 1913.

We have had exciting times since I got my letter off to you last week. We had a hard rain Friday night, more rain Saturday. I went over to supper that evening, and as I went across the rice field, I could hear the backwater coming up, with a steady roar. The next morning when I awoke, I could hear the girls yelling, and suspected there was a flood on hand. When I got up all the back part of the school yard was flooded, from the back water. Our compound is high, so the river didn't get in at all from the front, but by night, both school houses were a foot deep in water, and it bad risen as far as the second step to the house. The man who went for my meals waded through water up to his neck. Of course there was no church that day for the road was covered in most places, and I couldn't even get the girls to settle down for a service in the morning, but late in the afternoon we had one. By Monday morning the water had gone down enough for Mrs. Taylor to get across by using a boat in one place, and being carried across in another, so we got a boat and went down to the south place. We sailed through their front gates and tied the boat to their steps. Their compounds are much lower than ours. There was no school that day, for the natives seem to think a flood is too interesting to allow of anything else being considered. So I went on home with the Taylors and spent the rest of the day with them. By evening seemed that the water had gone down enough for me to cross on horse back, so I started out. I held up my feet as high as I could, but in spite of all, I got wet to my knees, and the water filled my rubber boots. But by Tuesday morning I got across without a wetting, and ever since have been riding to my meals, like I did for so many weeks last year. But it is too late in the season for much rain now and the water is drying up fast. I think by another week, I shall be able to walk again. August is considered the month for floods but this time it was September 20th before we had any rain worth mentioning. The rain came just at the right time for the rice.

26 September 1913

Nuisances

Mosquitoes

The North of Siam compares very favourably with Bangkok as regards the number of mosquitoes to be faced, but, alas! the presence of one mosquito in Chiengmai often means malaria, while in Bangkok one may be bitten "to death" without any ill effects. The reason is that malaria is very prevalent among the Northern folk, while in Bangkok it was for many years almost unknown, though it is now said to be creeping in. I myself lived in Bangkok for over five years before I went North, and have now lived there for a number of years since my return without experiencing an attack of malaria, but I had not been four months in Chiengmai before I was laid up with a sharp bout. It may safely be said that practically every European living in the North has had malaria at some time or other.

Le May, An Asian Arcady, p. 84

That night we got a taste of the Raheng mosquitoes, as our nets on the top deck had been blown open by the night breeze while we were at dinner. The Chinese "boys," of course, had gone down town to the bazaar. We tucked our nets in before discovering they were full of hungry mosquitoes from the "jheel" which stretched behind Ellis's bungalow. There was nothing for it but to cover as much of ourselves as we could with the bed-clothes, and hope for the best. We spent a dreadful night, and in the morning our sheets and pillows were spotted with blood.

Williams, Green Prison, p. 54

Hornets

Walking down my drag-path another day, I suddenly heard a great rumpus among the elephants, roaring and trumpeting, and the shouts of the men, and a riderless female came dashing up the track towards me, followed by others. Next I met a thrown rider running after his charge, and he shouted as he passed me "Hornets, Master!" Soon I reached the scene of the stampede. High up in a tall resin-tree was a round object considerably bigger than a football – a hornets' nest. The tree grew just by the side of the drag-path, and it appeared that an elephant dragging a heavy log had bumped it into the base of this tree and so shaken it that the hornets were disturbed, and their scouts had swooped down on the elephants and stung them into bolting. From then on these dangerous insects – a dozen stings would send a man into a torpor – were so menacing that we had to cut a detour of our drag-path, which was an annoying waste of time. Finally, two of the camp Kamus offered, for a reward of five rupees each, to destroy the nest. They climbed the tree with huge resin torches in the middle of the night, and burnt the pests alive. It was a hazardous venture, and, I felt, cheap at the price.

Williams, Green Prison, pp. 178-179

Sand-Flies

Sand-flies were another joy. They flourished near elephant camps, and usually came to attack just as you were dropping off to sleep. Being very small, they easily passed through the holes in the mosquito-net and, settling in your hair, bit your scalp until you well-nigh screamed. One teak-wallah was so plagued with them that he thought if he were supplied with a very closely woven mosquito-net he would rest in peace, even if he were a trifle short of breath through lack of ventilation; so he wrote to a firm of outfitters in Bangkok asking then to send him a very "fine" net. And he got one. It had cupids on the top, pink and blue ribbons at the corners, cherubs – but why go on? He had been supplied with a bridal mosquito-net instead of the sort he wanted.

Campbell, Teak-Wallah, p. 38

Ants

I awoke one night with a pricking, tingling sensation all over my head, to find my hair a mass of tiny black ants whose pincer jaws were nearly a third the size of their bodies and could nip quite painfully. I turned on my torch, and yelled for the "boy," who arrived, gave one look, said nonchalantly "mot ngam," and went away again. I could see with my torch that a whole column of them had entered the tent, travelled across the groundsheet, climbed up the metal struts of my camp-bed, and were all over my pillow. The line of march was still intact when the "boy" arrived back from the servants' tent armed with a broom and half a dozen rags soaked in kerosene. First of all my bed had to be shaken out and remade, what time I combed the little pests out of my hair. Then they were all swept out of the tent, and the kerosene-soaked rags tied round the feet of the bed, an inch or so above the groundsheet, for, said the "boy," these "mots" (ants) will never cross kerosene. He was right: I was not disturbed again, and ever afterwards these precautions were taken nightly before the enemy's columns had advanced to the attack.

Williams, Green Prison, p. 173

Flit

Preparing the house before going on leave, Mabel Cort uses "Flit", an American insecticide, in her war on insect pests.

All the books have been dusted and sprayed with "Flit" – all the pictures have been taken out of frames, glasses washed, have been sprayed with Flit and put back in frames and packed in a trunk – most of the blankets have been washed and ready to pack. We are using tin lined boxes with "Flit" and moth balls and soldered to keep out insects which are moths, silver fish, white ants and cock-roaches, as well as rats if O'Briens won't keep our cats – which they are not inclined to do.

5 May 1927

Our electric lights are running very well but mosquitoes and biting insects are so bad these nights that you have to spray yourself with Flit four or five times an evening and keep Japanese incense burning round you.

29 July 1929

My First Acquaintance with the Elephant Leech

After walking on a bit, I felt an intolerable itching in the calf of my leg, and scratched at the place without looking. I felt something soft and slimy and bent down to see a horrible thing as big as a fat cigar. Its head was embedded in between a fold in my puttees, its tail in another fold. I wrenched it free (it stretched like elastic!) and flung it away with a curse. There was a sharp stinging sensation as it was torn loose, and when I took off my puttees on arrival at the bungalow they were soaked with blood. It took a lot of cold water to stop the flow, and then were revealed two pairs of small punctures in the skin, on which I smeared iodine. But this did not prevent a festering sore which lasted for days.

Williams, Green Prison, p. 57

His Snakeship

Lucy Starling confronts a snake on Doi Suthep …

Our cottage is built on the hillside, half way up to the ascent, and steps go down to the front porch instead of up. This morning I stepped out upon the front porch and was just starting up the steps when the girls called me to stop; and there, coiled up under one of the steps, was a brown snake. I called the girls to bring something to kill it, they brought a long bamboo pole, clumsy and too light to do any damage.

The girls (four of them) went around the side of the house, and came up behind me in the hall with the stick. After much debate the bravest of them gave the snake a punch, when he jumped clear across the porch into the entry, head up, mouth open and forked tongue darting here and there. We were all badly frightened, and the girls, after a wild hit or two, dropped the stick and ran. Two of the girls, before the fray began, had taken refuge in a little 4 x 6 foot room, and as soon as his snakeship got into the hall, he saw what he thought was an escape, and darted into that room. Well, for about ten seconds you would have thought every fiend in Laos was after those girls from their shrieks. But they finally managed to get out without being bitten. The room was dark, there being no window to it, and none of us relished going in for a further search. So two of the girls ran up some distance to get the only man around – our watchman having gone to the city for the day. He came down and took out all the mats and baskets, but there was no snake to be seen. But we found two holes in the mat walls through which he could have easily passed. You can imagine this knowledge did not make me any more comfortable. The man then went into my bath-room and searched, but declared there was no snake in there. The girls were just peeping around the corner, one of them stooping, so that her bare back was exposed. So in fun, I picked up a loose piece of chair bottom and had just drawn it across her back when the old man cried out, "poon! poon!" (there it is, there it is!) and there was another wild scattering.

On the floor of my bath room was a plank, on which was set the large earthen jar that holds the water for bathing. The snake had crawled under this plank and would have probably bitten me the next time I went to wash had it not been discovered. So he was killed, to my great relief. These rustic houses, with their mat walls, grass roofs and many rafters afford an ideal hiding place for snakes. This fellow was two feet long, with a red head and neck and dusty brown skin, with yellow flecks – very poisonous, the old man said. You may believe I said my prayers with a good deal of feeling that night.

30 November 1910

Tokay

Reginald Campbell's small terrier Sclave meets a tokay lizard …

In the evening I strolled round the compound if the drizzle wasn't too thick, idly looking at nothing in particular and followed by Sclave, who also seemed bored. Things livened up, however, when on one of these strolls he encountered a "tokay" lizard on the ground, a particularly fat, big specimen a good foot and a half long, resembling a miniature dragon. Every time Sclave made a feint at it, it swung round and presented a formidable array of needle-sharp, snapping teeth at him. But he kept on attacking (*he* was no coward), and at last managed to seize it across the back, whereupon he shook it exactly as a terrier shakes a rat; the force a dog can put into this action is astonishing, and the "tokay" didn't survive the treatment more than half a minute.

Campbell, Teak-Wallah, pp. 152

A Useful Pet?

If the tokay were only a little less shy it might be a most useful pet for the dinner-table, on those nights when plagues of various insects make it hard to keep them out of the food. They are frequent when the rains are due; one night it may be tiny beetles, another a kind of blue-bottle, ephemerae too, and cockroaches. The last-named, fortunately, are of a small variety about three-quarters of an inch long, but quite sufficiently objectionable. It is a matter for thankfulness that I only met the flying giant of sometimes nearly three inches singly. The big fellow with antennae nearly as long as himself is handsome, however much we may dislike his foolish face.

Revolting above all its kind is the red, flat, wingless cockroach, so hard to keep out of drawers and cupboards. I had some terrible encounters with him, but happily no losses. Choice clothes are the morsels in which he delights. He has the good sense to dislike napthaline, and in my warfare with him all sense of its fragrance was temporarily (and happily) lost to me. One piece of furniture in which he reappeared time after time must have been a breeding-place, and no napthaline could keep him away. It was finally freed of his presence by an internal scrubbing with the strongest hospital soft soap.

Wheatcroft, Siam and Cambodia, p. 183

Feathered Pests

Bert Deignan was a contract teacher at the Prince Royal's College during two periods between 1928 and 1937. A keen ornithologist from his youth, he later became a curator at the Smithsonian Institution and was author of the definitive Birds of Northern Thailand, *published in 1945.*

There are two birds which are responsible for many a bad temper in Siam. One of these is quite the most gaudy bird found in our gardens, but do not expect to see him unless you want to risk a stiff neck and a hot sun. He is most in evidence in the hottest months, on the hottest days, and during the hottest hours. Then, while everyone is trying to sleep, may be heard a "tunk-tunk-tunk-tunk-tunk", on and on and on, which unlike many monotones rasps the nerves instead of soothing. As it sounds like someone striking upon metal, he is called the Coppersmith Barbet. Being related to the Woodpeckers, he can not only climb the trunk of a tree, but can also bore himself a hole, and if you succeed in seeing him at all, it is likely to be just his head – but what a head! The throat is yellow and the breast and crown bright crimson, and the rest of his body is leaf-green. But since his voice is ventriloquial, his colors blending with the foliage, and his body quite small, most people will be satisfied to but hear him.

Our other feathered pest is the Tailor-bird, of whose nest, made of large leaves sewed together with cocoon silk, most everyone has heard, but which few have seen. It is very common in all the compounds, creeping like a small mouse in the hedges and bushes, and often visiting the verandah. The underneath parts are white, but its back is bright olive-green, and its cap is chestnut. It also sings most in the heat of the day when its sharp and monotonous "to-whit, to-whit, to-whit" rivals the song of the Coppersmith.

Siam Outlook, October 1929, pp. 374-375

Houses

Our House

Mary Lou O'Brien describes the missionary house she and her husband were allotted in 1927.

The house in which we are living is a great big house built some forty years ago, of teak, and it eats up furniture and calls for more: our worldly possessions are swallowed up in it, and we two fairly rattle around. But we are turning it into a home, and with our pictures up, our books in the teak book-case, our silver, china and glass in the teak china-closet, and best of all because it is a brand new possession and one of which I am still rather foolishly simple-minded, our piano in the living room, we feel established. Not for long however, for missionary homes seem to be not at all permanent, and when Dr. and Mrs. Cort, of McCormick leave on furlough in a few months, we are to move into their new home for their "furlough time", so that Dr. O'Brien will be just across the road from the hospital.

Nai Nung (Mr. One) is our *cone-yam*, watchman, and he sees that we are all safely locked up each night and unlocked each morning. He guards us all through the night. He has some sort of a home-made mandolin-effect instrument with two strings upon which he sometimes plays weird music as he makes his rounds, and it is remarkably reassuring. Nai Sam (Mister Three) is our "boy" who serves the meals, does most of the indoor cleaning, whitens our shoes and our topees, looks after the boiling of the drinking water (it all has to be boiled) and runs errands for us. Nai Nuan, a dear, faithful old man goes to market early each morning and then spends the rest of the day cooking what he has bought and a coolie waters the road in front of our place, cuts the grass, saws wood, takes care of the refuse, scrubs the porches etc. That is our household, and the entire cost of such a menage' amounts to very little, for their wants are simple

The Van Millingen family home in Chiang Mai, exterior and interior, late 1930s. Oliver Backhouse.

and their wages are low. Nuan can buy a chicken in the market for the equivalent of some twenty American cents, and he always remarks that it is very "*pang*" – expensive!

We sleep under mosquito nets, for these Chiengmai mosquitoes carry malaria with them, have dipper showers of water from great earthen ohms, read by kerosine lamps, for there is no electricity, eat butter from tins and drink canned milk; have our soiled linens and clothes washed every day by a tiny little Siamese "dhobie" who heats the water in Standard Oil tins over a charcoal fire underneath the house, and every noon we are visited by "silver women" who come to try to sell us Siamese silver, curios of all sorts and brass things. They are such interesting old women that we always visit with them whether we buy anything or not.

6 February 1927

Keeping House in the Tropics

Mabel Cort writes to her mother from Lampang in March 1911.

I am a very busy lady and the school only gets a part of my time. You would think that with a cook, a house-boy, a washwoman and a coolie I would be a lady of leisure. But I am not only keeping house. Sometimes I think housekeeping is the least important thing I do, and the conditions under which you keep house out here are quite different from home. We are in the tropics. It is hot all the time. We have no ice, so everything has to be fresh every morning or be recooked so many times no life is left in it. Milk must always be boiled twice, meat must be recooked at night and all vegetables thrown away. Everything must be bought of market women who try to get the highest price possible, and if I went to the market I would be cheated out of my eye teeth. In native eyes, we are all rich. Only the other day one of the missionaries sighed: "Oh, if I only seemed as poor as I am". Our cook has to search and bargain and it is often late when he gets back. Also, there are no delicatessens here, and all that you eat must be prepared in your own kitchen, and when you give a dinner or a tea you have to prepare everything at home. So being a cook is about all one person can really be. Then the houses are all dark oiled teak and all the doors and windows are open day and night.

This means that you are fighting dust or mould all the time, that everything has to be wiped up every day, floors and furniture. So the houseboy is busy getting breakfast, washing dishes, dusting and making beds, and the coolie wipes the floors, cleans the lamps, cleans the shoes, cuts the grass – some job in the rains –, trims the hedges, runs errands, cuts the wood for the kitchen stove, carries the water to the kitchen and the bathroom, and tends to the flowers if you have any.

And what do I do? Well, I plan my meals with the cook after he gets back from the market, for neither of us knows what he will be able to find. I go over his accounts and translate any recipe I want him to use that day. I give the houseboy instructions for the day. Since they are both excellent, intelligent Christian servants this part of the day is all right. But our coolie is quite different. He gets orders mixed woefully. One day I asked him to trim a very beautiful climbing rose. When I got back I found he had cut it back to the roots, so I shall have no yellow roses this year. Another time I came home unexpectedly from the hospital to find him washing my newly polished piano with the dirty water he had been using to wash up the floors.

But he isn't the only worry. The house isn't screened and we are at the mercy of white ants, silver fish, black ants, mud-daubers, scorpions, rats, mice and bats, *and* flying cockroaches. I have to look into every box, closet and trunk to be sure there are no insects in them. That has to be done once a week without fail. Silver-fish eat great holes through your books, cockroaches chew the covers and mud-daubers build nests on the pages. Your best wool dress or coat shows a great moth hole when you inspect it some morning, and all your leather boots and shoes have to be kept well-oiled if you don't want them to rot on you. Sometimes I think I am just a floorwalker. If you forget the servants you pay an awful price. Eternal vigilance is the price of keeping your possessions. But that is enough about the house.

25 March 1911. Printed in: Cort, Yankee Thai, pp. 54-55

… and from Chiang Mai in 1915 …

I thought to get your letters off before the eleventh hour, but as usual did not attain to my ideal, because someone fooled with the typewriter yesterday and it took Charlie a half an hour this morning to fix it, and it is nearly school time now. I am undertaking a good many things these days and I often don't get entirely through. This house has polished floors throughout and no large rugs and everything is open and used every day, so that keeping it presentable is quite a question. I now have no room woman, as I am trying to save, so I have to take care of our bedroom and our boy is only a school boy, and so can't be here long hours, so that I work as hard as I can go from breakfast time till nine and then I do not get back till twelve. In the afternoon I do my sewing and mending, teach Sawang algebra and Cornelia arithmetic, and my days are so full that letter writing is an extra. We get up a little after five, have prayers before breakfast and I usually get the washing ready or sort the ironed clothes for mending. I have not begun my real sewing yet. But my mending basket is full all the time, especially of stockings. I was somewhat dismayed the other day when Charlie invited all the Collins and Park families to tiffin, for I am not settled yet and the guest room had nothing done. We have only two table cloths here and six napkins both of which I had to have washed and ironed that morning, and as the boy and I did not get back till twelve it meant some hustling. I and Charlie go to market to get tinned milk and curry powder and the cook had to get the tiffin alone. I worked as hard as I could rush till a quarter past nine and did get things done and the tiffin was good but that was only because Noi Weng is a good cook. You see I have to plan the menus, see that the work in the yard is attended to and also look after the chickens and see that the eggs all come on in. We are getting about ten eggs a day and they might easily disappear if they did not know that I was on the job as to speak. The men are also working on the garden and I ought to attend to that.

10 July 1915

Our "Country House"

Rev. William Harris was born in Princeton, New Jersey, and educated at the university there. In 1899, he became principal of the Chiengmai Boy's School, which was renamed The Prince Royal's College (PRC) by Prince Vajarivudh, the Crown Prince, when he visited Chiang Mai in 1906. Harris was a leading member of the Anglo-American community, becoming active in the Gymkhana Club and the Chiengmai Library Association. From about 1917 to 1932 he also played a leading role in Chiang Mai's first municipal council. In 1950, he wrote an unpublished memoir in the form of notes he called 'Recollections'. Cornelia Harris had been born in Chiang Mai, the daughter of the Rev. Daniel McGilvary, the founder of the Mission, and of Sophia McGilvary. She shared the administration of the PRC with her husband. Here Dr Harris writes about the "manse" or "small native house" in which he and his wife stayed when visiting a country congregation.

In 1898 I was given the oversight of the Me Dawk Dang ("River of the Red Flower"). The chapel was at this village; but there were Christian groups living in villages from a mile to five distant from the chapel.

A small native house and lot, next to the chapel, was offered for sale; and this I bought for a small sum of rupees 240 ($80). The house consisted of a fairly large bedroom, in front of which were a covered porch and an open veranda; at the side was a small kitchen, separated by a narrow passageway. Like most native houses, it was raised on posts about five feet from the ground. Before we occupied the house, I took boiling water and applied it liberally to destroy any inhabitant there might be; and I built a small bathroom about four feet square at the rear end of the passageway.

Harris, Recollections, p. 29

Building a House

Almost every Laos man can plan and build his own house and fashion some, at least, of the ruder tools he needs on his farm and in his home. Some one in every village can boss the job of sawing any lumber he may need. With a piece of hoop iron, a file, and wood that is at hand, he will make the saw he needs. Better saws can now be had of German make, and many are sold, but much lumber is still sawed, and well sawed, with the rudest tools.

The frame of a Laos house is like the frame our grandfathers made, a few heavy timbers mortised together instead of many smaller ones. The walls are paneled like a door, and are completed ready to set in place before the "house-raising" begins. Posts, sills, plates and rafters, the entire frame is carefully fitted together, piece by piece, and carefully numbered, bamboo for the floors and thatch for the roofs are also ready, and a pig and other supplies for the feast as well. The lucky day is determined upon, and all the village is invited to the "raising." Work often begins before it is really light, for it would be ill luck if even a post hole were dug the day before;

material may all be ready, but the actual work of erecting the house must be completed in a day. Many hands make light work of the heaviest tasks, and a small house is often completed before noon.

Freeman, An Oriental Land of the Free, pp. 56-57

A Jungle Bungalow

Leigh Williams describes the jungle quarters of a teak-wallah.

On the eighth day I arrived at Ban Mai, the headquarters of Muang Wung forest. Set in the middle of a grass lawn, which is bounded on three sides by a hedge of hibiscus, on the fourth, sloping down to the river, stands a wooden bungalow of a type with which I was to become familiar. The roof is of thatch, the walls of plaited bamboo, and the floor of jungle-wood planks. The whole is built on stout wooden piles. A front verandah runs the breadth of the building. At each end is an enclosed bedroom, and the open space in the middle between the two bedrooms forms the dining-room. Opening out of each bedroom is a tiny bathroom containing a galvanised iron tub and a tall stone water-jar. The "usual offices" are at the bottom of the garden.

The ground floor or space underneath the bungalow was boarded up to form an office and a storeroom. Most forests had at least one of these "shacks," and after weeks in a tent, especially in the rains, it was a relief to have a roof over one's head for a few days while doing headquarters accounts or writing one's monthly report. The trouble about these jungle bungalows was that being infrequently lived in they are apt to become damp, and, unless one had a good caretaker, full of insects. The scorpion and mason-bee, in particular, infested them, and I have known their bedrooms contain a swarm of honey-bees or a flight of bats.

The caretaker of these jungle bungalows was usually dignified by the name of clerk. He was responsible for all the rice and paddy stored in the godowns for issue to the girdling or elephant camps by means of the Company's bullock caravans. He is also in charge of the stores – the dozens of pairs of elephant dragging-chains, tying-chains, hobbles, axes, spades, pickaxes, saws, and every form of tool used in the working of teak. His position as a buffer between the white man in charge of the forest and the local villagers is a delicate one. To refuse an occasional basket of rice to a friend would be churlish, yet if his defalcations are discovered he gets the sack. But if his loyalty to his employers becomes too irksome to his native friends, there is a genuine risk that his own sleeping quarters, if not the bungalow and godown, may be involved in a mysterious fire! But in spite of these disadvantages in his job, many a jungle headquarters clerk was able to satisfy both sides, and still collect a tidy "nest-egg" for himself!

Williams, Green Prison, pp. 82-83

Too Much Furniture

In Eric Reid's novel Spears of Deliverance, *Rarouey recalls Philip's taste in interior decoration …*

At this moment Philip who seemed to her now to have lost the dear familiarity of intimacy and to be merely her foreign lord, the white *nai* with the curly hair and the fierce eyes, Philip would be stretched on his long chair as she had so often seen him in the past, awaiting the advent of early tea, smoking a cigarette perhaps, and reading, yes certainly reading, for he seemed always to be reading.

She recalled the chairs and the tables of the verandah and the houserooms, a litter of books and cigarette tins, the deer horns and trophies, the rows of polished Buddhas on the shelves in strong contrast to the brightly coloured sporting and hunting prints decorating the walls, and all the furniture of the various rooms in the dwelling where the last few, brief years had been passed.

Farangs had always too much furniture in their rooms, she had long since concluded. Such an accumulation, in contradistinction to the bare simplicity of Siamese furnishing, she had regarded at first as odd and unnecessary, but accepted afterwards with a comic air of resigned co-proprietorship.

Reid, Spears of Deliverance, pp. 224-225

Food & Drink

Meals among the Northern People

Unlike the Southern Siamese, who take two meals daily at eight and at five, the Lao eat three times a day, at eight, at noon and at six. These meals are known as "Khao Ngai" (chao), "Khao Tawn" (tiang), and "Khao Leng" (kham).

The standard dish for all meals is curry and rice. Northern rice is, as I have said before, not like the rice grown in Central Siam, but is of a glutinous nature and, when cooked, is eaten in lumps rather like bread. The curries are made of fish, pork, beef, buffalo, vegetables, chickens, duck, and wild birds of all descriptions. Sometimes goat-flesh is also used, while bear and deer are considered a delicacy, especially among the jungle-folk.

After the curry and rice, betel nut is chewed, and this is followed sometimes by "*miang*," a species of wild tea, which is also chewed in small balls, like a quid of tobacco. Water is usually drunk after the meal, but not with it. Also fruit is usually eaten at odd times during the day, but not with a meal. The fruits to be found in the north of Siam are much the same as those grown in the South, but on the whole are perhaps not so good.

Le May, An Asian Arcady, p. 112

Foreign and Local Supplies

Remarkably, in the first decades of the century the foreign community imported basic foodstuffs once a year from England. If your house burned down, you could lose a whole year's supplies ...

The problem of stocking the larder was a real one until within quite recent years when stores and shops began to spring up like mushrooms. Now even those who live in the provinces need only to send to Bangkok for tinned goods of all sorts. But in the early days provisions of that kind, and clothing, notions [sic = rations?], equipment of all sorts had to be ordered from home, and they were ordered in big lots, a year's supply at a time. One of the missionary women added to an order which she was sending to a wholesale firm in England this item, two bottles each of currants and figs, as a special treat. At last, after a long wait, word came from the Mission godown at Bangkok that the shipment from England had come, and that it would be sent on to Chiengmai as soon as possible. Another long trip, this time by river, and then, what was the consternation of that missionary family, when among the other things they beheld two barrels each of currants and figs!

Siam Outlook, October 1928, p. 304

Early in the year we had sent in our orders to London for the annual food supplies. They would be almost a year reaching us. Some of the butter would have melted because of being packed too near the engine on the steamer. Other tins would have rusted from the water shipped into the river boats when going through the rapids. The flour would be sure to have weevil and would have to be sifted and sunned at once.

An order included a barrel each of flour and sugar, fifty pounds of butter, tinned milk, and whatever amount of tinned vegetables, meats, and cookies (biscuit to the British) that one wished. The newcomer usually ordered a large amount of foreign foods until accustomed to the local market, where the vegetables were few and lacked flavor.

Starling, Dawn over Temple Roofs, p. 68

As so frequently happens, Mabel's fever hung on until our two-week vacation was almost over. It wasn't a vacation or a honeymoon for her and the temptation was to try to grab a few extra weeks. But it was just a temptation. We returned to Bangkok to learn that the bungalow I had so painstakingly furnished had burned clear to the ground during my absence. It was a blow, for with it had been destroyed a year's supply of the staple groceries which had to be imported at considerable expense from London. Thailand produced no milk or wheat, and many other perishable foods were practicable only if they were purchased in tins. Prices for such foodstuffs were high in Bangkok and I had halved our budget by ordering commodities like milk, butter, flour, coffee, tea, sugar, and salt from London. What were we going to do about getting enough money to replace our loss? And what should we do for shelter? Mabel smiled all that aside. "We'll manage. Missionaries always manage. They have to. There's work to do, you know."

Cort, Yankee Thai, p. 45

During the Great War, supplies ran short in Chiang Mai and prices went up, as Mabel Cort reported. She asked her parents to send over glass jars for conserving fruits and vegetables.

There isn't a can of flour in the Mission that isn't full of weevils and a lot of our butter is uneatable. Potatoes are $5 per bushel and we did not think we could afford any when the man was around with them the other day and this afternoon we had a present of a large panful from Mr Atkins so we are just well off.

21 October 1915

In 1927, Mary Lou O'Brien was impressed by the fresh fruit and vegetables available locally. Such market produce had to be consumed fresh, or recooked or boiled, often more than once.

We have a remarkable variety of vegetables here including very fine tomatoes, of which I am inordinately fond, cabbages, to which I say ditto, turnips, beets, beans, peas (eaten pod and all), egg-plant, cucumbers, corn, lettuce, greens of many kinds, squash, potatoes etc. Haws from China come along with walnuts for sale, and we have many kinds of fruits.

6 February 1927

Mabel Cort describes her vegetable garden in 1919 …

Lettuce, parsley, turnips, tomatoes, beets all ready to use with corn and potatoes coming on and cucumbers coming on too.

19 February 1919

… and Lucy Starling in 1911 …

I am doing a little gardening this year – tomatoes, lettuce, and beans.

Food & Drink 73

Mrs. McGilvary has given me four rose bushes, and Dr. Kerr some cosmos, so I hope to have some flowers for the girls before long. I am also going to try a few raspberries, along the side fence. Mrs. McG. gets so much good from hers, and it is the only berry we have out here, so they taste pretty good. She stews them a little and then puts them on plates in the sun for several days to dry, when they become like "peach leather." It is very nice for touring. I wish you would send me some nasturtium and sweet pea seed. If you order from the florist, tell them to send them in tin, or wrapped in tin-foil, for the action of the salt air spoils them sometimes, Mrs. Kerr says, though Mrs. M. thinks not. I should like to try some aster seed again, too, for those you sent me did not come up. If there is anything new in the flower line, that is pretty or interesting, get some seed, and send to Mrs. M. for she is so interested in those things.

I think I'll start out on my wheel this afternoon, and make some visits. Hope this delightful weather will keep up.

8 February 1911

Englishmen Discover Coffee

Mabel Cort introduces some teak-wallahs at Lampang to freshly-ground coffee …

As I have told you before, we have the provincial headquarters of several teak companies here, for several of the leased teak forests are situated in this section. There are many nice young Englishmen about, either public school men or university graduates and the relations between them and the Mission are most cordial. Carl takes care of them when they are ill, and we belong to the same polo club. The Mission has tennis once a week and tea is served and everybody comes. One Tuesday evening I thought I would do something different. I asked Mr. Pegg if he would have coffee or tea. He looked at me, startled. "Coffee? Why, I believe I'll try a cup. I've heard it isn't bad at all." We get green coffee beans from Java and roast them ourselves. Crystal (Kao), our cook, roasts them to perfection, and since I had that new wedding-gift percolator to use, the coffee was delicious. Every one of those tea-drinking Englishmen took three cups. One exclaimed: "This is ripping. How do you make it?" The ground coffee was brought out and the percolator, and I explained everything. Another man asked:

"No chicory in that coffee?"

"Certainly not, we don't adulterate coffee in America." He shook his head. "It is certainly delicious." Before they left they asked me to order nine percolators from Montgomery Ward's and nine orders went out in the last mail. We have an interesting life, don't we?

10 April 1911. Printed in: Cort, Yankee Thai, pp. 59-60

Ice-Cream

William Harris impresses some of his British friends …

Yesterday I gave the Englishmen a treat of ice-cream. They are very fond of it – and none of their cooks know how to make it. They certainly did enjoy it and had two helpings all round. They were like a lot of boys. As it was over a hundred – one of the hottest days we have had – it was more of a treat than ever.

1 May 1920

Ice cream also featured at the Corts' wedding anniversary party, the ice coming from Joe D'Souza's ice factory (Cort calls him "de Sousa").

Mr. de Sousa made ice for us and Barnes' Chinese cook made the cream, two kinds, vanilla and chocolate. We had two three-quart freezers and a little one quart one which we froze for the Prarachaya and which she enjoyed exceedingly.

Evidently, the Princess placed a large order …

Mr. de Sousa, a Portuguese Eurasian, has an ice machine which makes 225 lbs at a time and he made it a week for the Prarachaya and then his lubricating oil has given out and we have not had any ice for four days. It is very expensive so that only a few can make it regularly, but her Highness is one that can. She has to take forty lbs. a day.

Cort, 2 and 9 October 1920

Betel-Chewing

Most of my readers know that betel-chewing is a common habit among Eastern races, but it is not all perhaps who know exactly how betel is chewed, at least in the north of Siam. The nut itself is not a "betel" nut, but is obtained from the areca palm.

This nut is ground with a kind of pestle and mortar, and is then mixed with white lime and dried tobacco in a little water. The red colour, associated with betel-chewing, is imparted by the addition of the bark of the *sisiat* tree (called cutch). The soft mass formed by all these ingredients is then rolled in the betel leaf, called *bai plu*, and a bite is taken through the mixture. As may be imagined, the taste is an acquired one. The ingredients are not, as a rule, mixed all together in the South, but are eaten separately; the cutch is, however, mixed with the lime, and then smeared on the leaf. Betel-nut sets are made in lacquer, silver, brass and gold, and an interesting collection may be made of the different kinds of lime-pots in use. Some of these are both original and charming in design and shape. The so-called "pestles and mortars" are also well worth attention from a collector's point of view.

Le May, An Asian Arcady, p. 113

Stewed Peanuts

Lucy Starling tries something new …

Today I tasted for the first time what is a favorite dish out here – stewed peanuts. I think they are first boiled in their skins – shells I mean, then they are shelled, and stewed with a cream dressing. Try it sometime. Another dish I like for dessert is rice and cocoanut milk. The rice is soaked several hours, and then steamed with cocoanut milk, which is prepared by grating the cocoanut and pouring water over it, then strain. If you want it rich, and I like it better, let it stand overnight, and skim off the cream. Sweeten a little if you like.

23 November 1910

Fruit

Strawberry. Though even now the cultivated strawberry can hardly be said to be well established in Siam, it is interesting to note that Holt Hallett records eating Mrs. McGilvary's strawberries, and, incidentally, drinking coffee made from her home-grown berries. Mrs. McGilvary's strawberries died out, but the plant has been re-introduced by Mr. A. L. Queripel.

Kerr, 'Notes on Introduced Plants in Siam', pp. 205-206

****

Lucy Starling tries bale fruit …

I am just forming a taste for very wholesome fruit, that I did not like last year – the "bale-fruit." It has a hard shell that must be broken with a hatchet, and the inside is a deep yellow, and tastes like a very dry peach, with a dressing of turpentine. Occasionally one may get a spoonful that is delicious. And the next mouthful has so much of the clear gum in it, it tastes exactly like the gum of the pine tree. It is about as embarrassing to eat in company as an orange; for it is full of seeds, that are coated with the gum, and it is almost impossible to get them out of your mouth, they are so sticky. I don't believe I would ever crave the fruit, but everyone says they have a great medicinal value, so I have been eating them this year, and they improve on acquaintance, at any rate one learns to endure them.

2 May 1911

… and durian

I ate a piece of durian the other day, – my first and last attempt. I had to hold my nose while I swallowed it. The meat is beautiful and creamy, and smells like a combination of glue factory, asafoetida, garlic and rotten eggs. I have never smelled anything like it in my life, and all the next day I tasted it on the spoon I had used, though I took a piece no larger than my little finger nail. It sells in Bangkok at from one to three dollars each, and is considered a great delicacy.

12 July 1911

Rachel Wheatcroft encountered the fruit on the overnight train to Chiang Mai ...

Too true it is that one man's meat is another man's poison. On this occasion my poison was durian: passing from the famous Bangkok orchards to the unhappy north where no durian grows. The possessor had it in his berth, two or three in front of mine, and it made the night hateful. The passage windows had to be kept tightly shut against its insidious smell, and as the outer windows must always be screened against mosquitoes, and more especially sparks, lest one wake in a fiery bed, as has happened to more than one traveller, the heat was hideous. The engines are run on wood, and tropical showers of sparks accompany the train. In such circumstances it was necessary to keep the most rickety fan imaginable going, which did not assist slumber.

Wheatcroft, Siam and Cambodia, p. 239

Prohibition

Towards the end of the fortnight's meeting, one of the senior missionaries' wives gave quite a big dinner-party, to which Brown and I were invited. Knowing that water would be the only beverage offered, several of the party of "jungle-wallahs" had "ginned up" at the club beforehand, and some had quite evidently overdone it. After dinner we played "parlour games" of the pencil-and-paper, educational variety. A "boy" brought a large stone water carafe with a tray of glasses, and put it on a table in the dimly lit verandah outside, for anyone to go out and help themselves when thirsty. By this time the primed-up ones had sobered down and felt dejected, while the others, in full alcoholic training after all these parties, were beginning to moisten their lips and look at their wrist-watches. Suddenly Brown asked our hostess if he could go out to the verandah for a drink, and returned after an appreciable interval looking more cheerful. He then suggested to one of the "hot" members of the party that he should try the water-jar. The other one blushed and gulped, but something in Brown's tone decided him. He went out and presently returned beaming. At intervals we all followed his example, and when my turn came I found the water-jar contained at least fifty per cent, whisky!

How thoughtful and tactful of our hostess, I thought. Debarred, if not by her own conscience, at least by the presence of other missionaries from providing alcohol openly, she had worked it this way. The evening ended better than it ever seemed likely to at first, and all went well until one of the male missionaries visited the verandah. He came back coughing and spluttering, with an expression on his face I shall never forget. Brown hastily gave a signal, and all we "jungle-wallahs" got up to go. On the way home I said to Brown how awfully decent it was of Mrs. X to provide liquor for us that way. Brown roared with laughter.

"I put a full flask in that jar myself."

Williams, Green Prison, pp. 97-98

Mrs and Mrs van Millingen and guests take tiffin on the verandah of their bungalow on Doi Suthep, 1930s. Oliver Backhouse.

Memorable Meals

Lucy Starling, Mabel Cort and Leigh Williams describe some memorable meals and also some forgettable ones …

A Perfect Breakfast

I walked along the river bank and paused under a huge banyan tree. The aerial shoots from the original trunk had taken root in the soil and developed new trunks over such a wide area that I thought I must be passing through a forest. This feeling was heightened as I looked up to the leafy canopy, so thick, that even at noon the passer-by was wrapped in deep shade. At this hour little fires dotted the gloom where market women were cooking breakfast. The titillating odor of frying bacon reminded me that my own breakfast was waiting, so I hurried on. Mrs. McGilvary was standing on the porch to greet me. "You are welcome," she said in her gentle voice. "Breakfast is ready. Dr. McGilvary got an early start to the country, so I am alone."

As we sat down, I saw on the plate before me a green fruit cut in sections. "The Siamese call this the "sweet, green orange," she said. "It is the typical orange of the North." I found it pleasant, but lacking flavor.

The next course was bacon and eggs. "We buy a slab of pork from the butcher," she said, "and soak it in a brine of saltpeter and brown sugar. We use rice chaff to smoke it in a little flue, and it will last for a week. You see we have no ice." No American bacon could equal this. The eggs she served were larger than those bought in the local market. "Some years ago we brought Plymouth Rocks from the United States," she explained. "The native stock is poor. In cooking we have to use a third more eggs than the recipe calls for."

She uncovered a plate on which there were some golden-brown muffins. "The seed corn came from South Carolina," she said. "We raise the corn in our garden and I grind it in our coffee mill." I never ate more delicious muffins.

"What is this?" I asked, as she passed me a porous dish of red sun-baked clay set in a bowl of water. It contained a white milky substance that had been whipped.

"That is buffalo butter," she replied. "It contains more fat than does cows' butter. Every morning I skim off the cream from the milk; then I stir it several times a day to keep bacteria from developing. This keeps it sweet; and when there is enough I make butter with a little hand churn." I found it sweet and palatable, but more like whipped cream than butter. If it were not stirred frequently it would become bitter. Most foreigners preferred to import butter from Europe in tins, even though upon arrival it was often rancid. When I exclaimed at the excellent cup of coffee, she pointed to the front lawn where a bush with shiny green leaves was growing, with tiny white flowers covering the branches. Soon there would be berries on the twigs. When the berries had changed to red, she would pick, dry, and grind them to brew the coffee such as I was now enjoying.

Toward the end of the meal the table boy brought in a plate of bamboo joints from which the green, tough outer coat had been removed. This was *khow lahm*, a favorite delicacy of the North. When I peeled it, a roll of glutinous rice was revealed. It had been mixed with coconut and roasted before the fire. It was food for a king.

The crowning touch to the meal was guava jelly. Through the window I could see the tree that bore the fruit. The guava lacks pectin, so tartaric acid had been added to make it jell.

Here was a perfect meal, all produced locally. How had Mrs. McGilvary managed to maintain such a high standard of living among a people who subsisted mainly on a diet of rice?

Starling, Dawn over Temple Roofs, pp. 21-23

Indigestible

This is Friday night, and I am just home from tea at Beaches'. We had a nice tea on the porch, – salad made of potatoes, cucumbers, a little onion, and mayonnaise dressing; chicken croquettes, bread and butter sandwiches, strawberry jam, pickles, tea, and for dessert, oranges and maraschine [Maraschino] cherries, with caramel cake. Enough to give one a nightmare, isn't it? Our Friday evening teas are very pleasant, but I think they usually manage to get together the greatest lot of indigestible stuff I ever saw.

Starling, 22 August 1913

Christmas Dinner, 1913

That night, Mrs. Taylor and I went down to Beaches' right after supper, and had an Xmas tree for the children; and they did have the best time over it. Then we went up to the church where Dr. Taylor had a magic lantern show for the people. Xmas day was a holiday of course, and that afternoon, we had games at the Taylors' and gave bags of candies and cakes to the children. Mrs. Beach gave the Xmas dinner, that evening. We five missionaries were there and the English consul. Everything was very nice. First course, tomato puree; second, venison, peas, mashed potatoes; third, duck, asparagus, cranberries, fruit punch; fourth, tomato gelatine, served as salad, light rolls; fifth, mince pie; sixth, candies, raisins, stuffed dates, coffee, olives, pickles, etc. Except that I felt stuffed, I suffered no ill effects from my late dinner; but Dr. and Mrs Taylor and Mrs. Beach are all sick.

Starling, 27 December 1913

Dinner at the Viceroy's

We had dinner at seven, and they had a regular English dinner, with course after course of meat. The first course was good hot soup; second, chicken and potatoes; third, some sort of stuffed meat, with too much onion to suit me, with mushrooms; 4th, salad offish, cucumbers, etc. with nice dressing, fifth, roast pork, peas, mushrooms, sixth, cake. With all this, we had bread, no butter, soda water, and wine served. There was another course, tucked in towards the last, of rice and curry. Nearly everything was stone cold, which spoiled it. The dinner was evidently gotten up with an eye to the foreigners, of whom there were three, and I was the only one of these who even made a stagger at eating; and I didn't see any of the natives who ate anything to speak of, except the rice and curry. And some of these passed that by, because it had grease in it. As every course was served, remarks were freely made, as to whether things were good or not; and usually, they were not good, according to their way of thinking. These people are a model of temperateness in eating, in comparison with us. I sometimes wonder if they don't think we are terrible gourmands, and I shouldn't blame them much, if they did think so.

Starling, 10 January 1914

An Elaborate Affair

Dr. Kerr left last Tuesday to enlist and so we had him to dinner. We also had a friend of his Mr. Morrison and Mrs. Harris and Mrs. Gillies. It was a much more elaborate affair. I had creamed soup, baked salmon, roast duck, sweet potatoes Southern style, peas, olives, tomato salad, charlotte russe. We are thinning out here fast. A new English bride however is on her way up river.

Cort, 5 August 1915

Christmas Dinner at the Barnes', 1918

Fruit cocktail, roast goose stuffed, mashed potatoes, peas, salad, mince pie, plum pudding, candies, coffee etc.

Cort, 19 February 1919

A Typical English Dinner

Mabel Cort found dinner at the Lingards was "typically English". After dinner, the party listened to Radio Manila but turned it off "as it was mostly jazz".

Appetizers of foie de gras on toast and roasted peanuts and for those that wanted it drinks – the soup, fish course, mutton from Bangkok with mint sauce, peas, potatoes, asparagus, olives, salted peanuts – then ice-cream with wafers – coffee – nuts and candies.

30 August 1930

Dinner at the Consulate

At the Consulate it was typically Danish, at least in 1930 …

Last night we went to the British Consulate for dinner and it was a Danish dinner as his wife is a Dane. [...] When we went to the table we had clear soup, frozen asparagus salad – celery and egg croquets [croquettes] – then steak done like a pot roast with boiled rice and olives – then little mince pies, coffee and candy. They served some wines but they all know we never take any.

Cort, 13 September 1930

A Chicken Dinner in the Jungle

I ordered dinner. This, as usual, consisted of chicken soup, followed by chicken rissoles, followed by boiled chicken. And what a chicken! Bought, in company with three others, for one rupee from the nearest village a couple of hours' march away, it had obviously never had a square meal in its life. Mosquitoes hummed around me as I ate, and horrible fat insects collided with the smelly kerosene lamp, and fell sprawling on the camp-table. It was an oppressive, depressing evening.

Williams, Green Prison, p. 165

A Dinner Spoiled

I now had an English-speaking Madrasi cook, who was very good indeed at every branch of his art. One evening my usually well-cooked dinner turned out to be a most unappetising mess, and the "boy's" explanation was that "cook is drunk". I rushed down the stairs and over to the cookhouse, where I found my "chef" sitting on the floor incapable for the moment of anything but a self-conscious giggle. I shook him roughly and asked him what he meant by it. He so far came to himself to swear this was the first occasion he had ever got drunk and added: "If Ramaswamy ever do this again, I beg Master beat it!" The "it" being his low opinion of himself if ever caught again!

Williams, Green Prison, p. 134

The Dinner was a Revelation

The dinner was a revelation, in spite of the fact that she'd only an ancient Kamoo to cook for her. We had tomato soup, I remember, tinned, of course, but delicious for all that, and served with tiny, square golden sippets; followed by snipe on toast, then barking deer, then tinned asparagus, then anchovied eggs, and then dessert and coffee. How the cook had produced such a meal at short notice was beyond my imagination, but undoubtedly his greatest triumph was the production of a menu-card – in English. Some English-speaking clerk of Scottie's must have written it for him, and after "kofi" it finished with the words:

"Thank you. Good nite, ladi and gentlemens."

Which we all thought rather pleasing.

As the meal progressed I found myself revelling in the peace and luxury of it all. Outside were the toil and the danger and the hardships of the jungle; in here, one seemed to bask in a sun-lit haven of peace. And soon that haven would be mine, mine, mine!

Campbell, Jungle Night, pp. 219-220

An Elegant Dinner Party

In the evening I was invited with the Colliers to an elegant dinner party at the Harrises – black tie for the men and trailing gowns for the women. Having never had any experience with missionaries, I thought of them as narrow-minded and dowdy. This party showed me that, as I ought to have known, missionaries are like other people. Most of those I met that evening were second-generation Chieng Maiers and looked like any other American physicians and educators. Dr. Harris himself was the very embodiment of the master of an exclusive private school, and his wife had the gracious ways of a great lady. Their beautiful home was filled with exquisite silver and brass objects given them by illustrious Siamese personalities. I was green with envy at the rows of bronze weights that ran along all the walls of the living room. Mrs. Harris had a complete set of all twelve animals!

There were a number of British teak industry people at the party, Chieng Mai's white colony being about equally divided between British teak and American mission people. My partner, one of the teak men, recognized in me a complete greenhorn and entertained me with the wildest stories about snakes and tigers and other dangers in the teak forests. He claimed that snakes run from humans and never attack unless cornered; that is, all but the king cobra which will attack man when it is nesting. It is the only cannibal snake, and the larger its size, the more deadly its bite.

Rickover, Pepper, Rice, and Elephants, pp. 199-200

Constitution Day, Chiang Mai, 1934, with the elephant that was to lead the procession and leading members of the foreign community in formal wear. Foreigners were expected to wear this on official occasions regardless of the time of day or temperature. Bangkok Times.

Clothes

More Comfortable Clothes?

Lucy Starling writes about the "Americanisation" of local clothes. …

You speak of the missionaries teaching these people to make more comfortable clothes. That is one thing the missionaries are trying not to do, – to change the customs of these people, except where their custom conflicts with health or morality. Some missionaries have tried to Americanize them, but have only succeeded in de-nationalizing them, putting them out of sympathy with their own country, and with no means of gratifying their new tastes. They are having some trouble with that in the Boys' School now. The boys have been taught to dress so fine, that some of them have taken to thieving and gambling to get money to gratify their tastes. And other poor boys say they cannot afford to attend school, because they haven't the money to dress, and are ashamed to be with other boys who dress better than they do. And then there is so much to teach these people, that is absolutely essential, that there is little time to bother with matters of dress. Our watchman's wife is unusually bright and quick, and yesterday I noticed that she made her youngster a pair of trousers with a drawstring around the top, – the first drawstring I have seen in this country. She had evidently seen one in our clothes. If you think the Siamese have too much cloth about their hips you should just see an Indian turban. I believe I could make a dress out of what they wrap around their heads. I don't see how they bear the heat.

12 July 1911

A White Suit

Our American friends were kindly and hospitable, and during my first fortnight in Chiengmai I found myself often wearing a white suit in the evening and sometimes (an unaccustomed horror after a year of open neck) the stiff collar which accompanies a dinner jacket. One of these occasions was when, in company with three other "teak wallahs," I was asked to dine with the Viceroy.

Williams, Green Prison, p. 148

Governor Hunt's Whites

In 1920, the American Minister made a trip to Chiang Mai from Bangkok. Mabel Cort describes him in a letter: "Mr. Hunt is a little fat man about sixty years old. He is not used to the ways in the East because he came up without a dress suit and here we follow European customs as all the princes have been trained there". At Chiang Mai, he was invited to dinner by Prince Bovoradej, the High Commissioner.

We were never able to convert the Prince, but that didn't prevent us from being friends. On one occasion he proved his friendship by effectively saving the face of the American community in Chiengmai. At that time the American Ministers to Thailand were usually political appointees, not career men. The incumbent at that time was a Mr. Hunt who had been seven times governor of Arizona before he finally was defeated for the first time in his political career. He decided to visit Chiengmai, and that was a fairly difficult trip still, for the railroad had miles to go before the capital of the North could be linked to Bangkok. He notified the Foreign Minister of his trip, which made it an official one. The Viceroy, of course, then had to give one of those big state dinners in his honor. At these state dinners full dress was obligatory. When we were coming in contact with royalty, for example, we all had to turn out in tails, top hat and what not even though we might be meeting the King at two in the afternoon. On the occasion of the state dinner for Mr Hunt, all the American community officials and the rest of the foreign communities were invited. At four o' clock in the afternoon Prince Bovoradej tore into the hospital on a bicycle. He was quite upset.

"I have just made an amazing discovery. That Minister of yours brought no dress clothes!"

That was a serious business. On official occasions you even had to be careful about keeping your coat buttoned. On one occasion a missionary going into the grand palace was stopped by a guard and had his coat buttoned for him before he was allowed to pass.

The Prince paced up and down, greatly agitated. "Do you suppose that I dare ask the British Consul General and the French Consul General and the other guests to discard formality and come in whites? I could send out a round robin telling them it is so hot that we have made it entirely informal and that everybody can wear white clothes."

I replied that I thought this would surely uphold the prestige of the Americans, and that we would be deeply grateful.

He beamed, greatly relieved. "I'll do it."

And off he went on his bicycle.

Cort, Yankee Thai, pp. 261-262

The Prettiest Hat from England

Lucy Starling has ordered a hat from England …
Last week, I got the prettiest hat from England. I don't know when I ever had one I like as well. Most of the women out here wear dressy straw hats, but it is not considered safe in the Orient, and the men all make fun of them for doing it; so I made up my mind that I would put my vanity in my pocket, so far as hats were concerned, and not wear anything but a cork hat. An ordinary hat is not considered enough protection from the tropical sun, and one may have sunstroke. So since I have been out here, I have worn plain cork hats, covered with drill, like the men's. I wasn't able to get a nice one, coming out, and there is no foreign market here. So I thought I would try ordering one from England, and it came by parcel-post last week. The shape is plain flat, and it is covered with pearl grey broadcloth, with a twisted sash of silk of the same color. It is lined with a pretty shade of green silk, and is very becoming. It was not expensive either, as hats go, and I feel that it is nice enough to wear anywhere in company with dress hats. It really hasn't been such a temptation to go without a dress hat here, as by the time they arrive from America, they are all floppy and banged up. I shouldn't like to be caught wearing some of the hats I have seen out here.

1 November 1911

Quite Coquettish

There were no English women up-country in those days, but several of the American missionaries were married, and their wives used to turn up in their best frocks to watch the inter-station and inter-interest polo matches. To a male eye their "kit" was smart and their hats quite coquettish, but this view might have been due to lack of standards of comparison. These Christmas meetings were almost the only occasions when one really saw anything of the missionaries, and they certainly took the social life of the station quite seriously.

Williams, Green Prison, pp. 101-102

A Mission Doctor's Day

A Mission Doctor's Day (and his Wife's), June 1911

Mr and Mrs Cort Senior had evidently asked their daughter-in-law Mabel what their son, Dr Cort, actually did on an average day. Patients on the day in question included a member of the local ruling house; a man who had fallen some forty feet and was badly injured; Dr Jonathan Wilson, one of the patriarchs of the Mission in North Siam; O. M. Peiniger of the Borneo Company Limited; and another Englishman with whom the Corts had become friends.

Lampang, Siam. June 10th, 1911.
You say you want to know just what we do every day, or, rather, that you would like a sample day. Well, here it is:

First of all, it is hot. 96 at midnight and I won't tell you what it is now, you would be too uncomfortable. We sleep on the verandah now, the one on the east side of the house. We have it fenced in with chicken wire so that sneak thieves can't run off with our furniture. It is better there than indoors, but it is still hot. This is Saturday morning. Breakfast and prayers are over.

Carl is over at the hospital, operating on a stone case. Suddenly there are footsteps on the porch. There is a voice asking: "Is the doctor in?" I meet Noi Wang coming to fetch me and outside I find an Englishman, Mr. Peiniger and a Lao Prince. Mr. Peiniger has a jumping tooth-ache. The Prince has not been feeling well for some time and wants an examination. While we are waiting for Carl to finish the operation in comes Mr. Vincent, the station treasurer, who asks for all of Carl's vouchers for the hospital. That done, a note comes from a sick Englishman across the river. He is feeling much worse. He has had appendicitis. He was getting much better and Carl hoped an operation wouldn't be necessary.

Now apparently it will have to be removed. It is like operating on your own brother when your patient is a man you have come to know so intimately. I send the coolie out to find the horse boy. Carl will need a pony. The Prince and Mr. Peiniger go over to the hospital and the cook comes in with two bad rupees he wants me to change for good ones. I have to get it from the safe. Then the Matron of the Girls' School needs market money and in comes the houseboy for his week's wages. But it is quiet now. The operation at the hospital is over, the tooth is filled, the Prince has been examined, and Carl has gone across the river on the appendicitis call.

Carl returned from his call in time for tiffin, but while we were eating it a call came in from the country. A man has fallen from a forty-foot platform in a village twelve miles down the river. He is very badly injured and they want Carl to examine him before they bring him in to the hospital. While Carl was getting his kit together I went over to the hospital to hunt up the crew of the hospital boat. An operation was necessary when they returned and I went over to help. We were through at 8:30 and what two tired mortals we were when we sat down to dinner. Carl makes his hospital rounds and then we go to bed.

At midnight the watchman arouses him for the nightly visit to Dr. Wilson. The poor man is at death's door, with a fast-growing throat cancer. By going over every night and putting fresh dressings on the cancer and giving the old pioneer a sedative Carl manages to give him a painless sleep that lasts until morning. So ends the day. During the week there is school. English and the Bible and organ lessons. And there are parents to see and children to mother and nurse and occasional trip to places that seem to be at the end of the world. And, usually, there are more operations than I have mentioned. So you see, we really work out here. And we love it.

Love, Mabel

Yankee Thai, pp. 60-62

A Professional Call under Difficulties
By E. C. Cort, M.D., Chiengmai.

For nearly twenty-four hours it had been raining steadily at a rate which if maintained for forty days in Noah's time, make the results easily understandable. But as "all things have an end" even this rain began to slacken and about 4 o'clock on a Friday afternoon Mr. Palmer and I started southward for a "week end" tour.

Two days before "Uncle" Ma, an old Christian from Ban Nong Tong, a village about thirty miles or more to the south, had come in for help as his wife was desperately ill, and was just about ready to worship the spirits and call in a spirit doctor. It was impossible to go just then, but he was given medicine and promised help as soon as possible. So the minister and the physician started out to wrestle with degrading superstition and disease.

As we crossed the river bridge we noticed that the river was bank-full but the real significance of this did not strike us until after passing through the "Chiengmai Gate" of the old walled city, a broad lake lay before us where once was rice plain.

Through this lake and covered by two feet or more of water lay our road. With the road that appeared ahead across the lake as a landmark we started in. Here and there swift cross currents showed the location of irrigation ditches. There had been bridges but as most of these consist of bamboo poles with earth thrown over them, their present existence was extremely doubtful. But like some other problems in life, the elucidation depended upon experimentation. The bridges were there. Then a bit of higher ground as we passed through a densely shaded village, then out to the plain again where lay another lake. The sun was setting and the lake was white and blue and burnished gold, while yonder was a patch of old, red Roman gold, and beyond where the plain was not yet flooded was the bright yellow green of the seed rice, then the village groves, a store of shades of deep green and beyond, again, the blue mountains, purple shadowed and capped with great cloud masses edged with orange and gold and pink.

Then again the road led through a village and out again upon another lake. Here the only landmark was the top of the raised bridge over a large creek. The bridge was probably intact, but under such circumstances the approaches are often missing. This would mean a swim in a very swift current if nothing worse. Again a trial and again a solid road beneath the ponies' feet. Then Ban Chang Kham where we were to spend the night. Here our progress was barred by a bridge like that which we had just crossed but with both approaches missing. We had to walk over a couple of elusive bamboo poles and the ponies swam through the creek.

One more stream, bank-full, kept us from the little chapel where we planned to spend the night, and they told us that it was not fordable. But we finally persuaded a man to wade in ahead of us and found we could just make it.

Then a change to dry clothing, supper and a little song service before the day's work was finished.

Early the next morning we started for Tong Tom with an elder as guide. Most of the way was over freshly plowed paddy land, now riding the ridges now plunging through the newly plowed earth which was covered by a foot or more of water, now through an irrigation ditch, sometimes deep but more often with perpendicular sides that made getting in and out difficult. After wading through a creek with sides too steep for riding we came into our village and stopped at a large, beautifully finished and spotlessly clean teak house where we intended to spend that night. After tiffin we set out again to Ban Nong Tong to see the sick women. As the river was still rising most of the way was under water. At one place we had to unsaddle and cross a narrow foot bridge while the elder swam through with the ponies. A little further on was a wide stream so deep that the smaller of the ponies had to swim. Here an amusing incident occurred. The landing place on the other side was a narrow point of land and my pony, frightened by the water came out with a rush that carried him over into deep water beyond and he plunged so in an unavailing effort to get up the steep bank that the elder became confused and started back to the other bank. The pony seeing the guide starting back thought it was his duty to follow, and did so, still plunging.

The poor elder thought his time had come and fled for his life, while it was with some difficulty that the pony was "reversed" and brought out on the proper side. During the rest of the trip nothing could persuade the elder to get near that pony!

Then we came to a deep current impossible to swim or ford, and bridged only by a slender log, half submerged. So we left the ponies in a nearby village and edging our way cautiously across the log proceeded to wade barefoot for another mile or two, and so reached a thatched bamboo house, the home of Loong Ma and his sick wife. Here to our great delight we found that the medicine already sent had routed both disease and "spirit doctor", and the sick woman though still far from entirely well, yet was able to sit up and the family very happy. After a little service of prayer and thanksgiving we had to hurry back to reach our stopping place, Tong Tom, before dark.

Then another song service for these people are very fond of singing. The next day, Sunday, we held a Communion service in the new house of an elder for they have the pleasant system among the Christians of dedicating a new house by a religious service.

Then we hurried back to Chang Kham where we held another Communion service in the little chapel.

The flood abated for a day and as a we returned home the next morning we saw great holes in the road with only narrow remains of bridges over them and we were very thankful that when all was under water, – we had found the bridges and missed the holes, and also thankful that we returned when we did, for had we delayed a day we would have been compelled to camp for ten days or more until the flood subsided.

Laos News, November 1909, pp. 105-108

Advice to New Missionaries

The Corts give advice to new missionaries in 1921 in the magazine Woman's Work for Woman. *Woman's Work was launched in New York in 1889 as "a union illustrated magazine published monthly by the Woman's Foreign Missionary Societies of the Presbyterian Church". Its aim was to promote the "missionary interest" abroad, and one way of doing this was to stimulate curiosity and an active engagement with the work of the foreign missionaries.*

Mrs. Cort, Siam: I have learned in seventeen years' service that I can teach all the mornings, visit in the afternoons, in a tropical country, yet be a good housekeeper too. I am a doctor's wife, I must keep his meals hot, no matter how late he comes in, I must train perfectly ignorant helpers to feel that when they cook the doctor a good dinner they are doing the Lord's work. Don't begin without a fireless cooker, aluminum utensils, no others last out there, thermos bottles that will not break even when carried on a bicycle or an elephant.

Dr. Cort, Siam: The missionary physician must be an oculist, an aurist, a specialist in nose, throat and intestinal troubles, a general practitioner, a surgeon, a dentist, a veterinarian, an elephant doctor, etc., etc. Most of all he must specialize in deficiency diseases, scurvy, rickets, hookworm, the world is suffering from them now. There is no help for them in heathen countries. If you are not taking with you the love of the Lord Jesus Christ in your heart you are taking nothing.

Woman's Work, August 1921, pp. 180-181

Truly a Gallant Man

Reginald Campbell is presumably describing an encounter with Dr Cort. "Inman" may well be based on A. R. Hanmer of the Bombay Burmah Trading Corporation who suffered psychotic episodes in 1923 and 1924 caused by cerebral malaria. On the second occasion, when he shot himself, Dr Cort and Arthur Queripel brought him back to Chiang Mai in terrible weather.

My transport I had sent in from the Mae Tang in the morning, and my boy had got everything ready against my arrival. Freshly-cleaned Lao silver bowls and ornaments winked in the light of the lamps just lit; on a round table was set a plate of salted almonds and a whisky decanter; a silver box of cigarettes was ready to hand. I sat down, lit a cigarette, poured myself out a tot of whisky, heard with satisfaction yet another furious gust of rain-laden wind roar round the bungalow.

My Siamese clerk eventuated out of the night, a tiny, inky chunk of the night itself:

"A good father has arrived. A good doctor father, and craves shelter," he announced in Lao.

A missionary doctor! I slipped on a pair of boots, flung a mackintosh across my shoulders, and, guided by a hurricane lantern, walked across the howling, rain-lashed compound. Standing by the office, in the comparative shelter of the porch, was a group of strange carrier coolies, exhausted and mud-begrimed; beside them was the taller figure of a white man, also a stranger to me.

"I'm Campbell," I said, and held out my hand to the tall figure.

"Shaw," was the answer.

I had heard of Dr. Shaw, and a finer man by all accounts did not exist. I gave directions for his coolies to be given food and shelter in our lines, then led the doctor into the light and luxury of Orwell's bungalow.

"Guess I can't come in here," he expostulated, with a rueful glance at his filthy clothing.

For answer I forced him into a chair and called for my boy.

"Take off the good father's boots," I told the Lao. "Then get a hot bath ready and put out some clean clothes. Also tell the cook there'll be one more master to dinner."

My own glass of whisky was still half-full. I took a second glass, poured out a tot, held it out to the doctor.

He shook his head, and I knew that he did so because of his calling. He had, I now saw, iron grey hair, a firm mouth, and wise, kindly eyes, at the moment clouded with fatigue.

"Where have you come from to-day?" I asked him.

"From Ta Nyong."

"No pony?"

"No."

Ta Nyong, twenty-five miles away down that awful Nakon road feet deep in mud. He'd marched that distance! I said:

"I'm the doctor now, and you the patient. This is the medicine I prescribe for over-fatigue," and again I pushed the glass upon him.

Still he was adamant, and I played my last card. "You've just done, for some reason, a forced march into Nakon, and now you're on your way back to your mission station – also by a forced march. Worried about your patients, I suppose. That right?"

"You've got it," he agreed.

"Not much good if you get back to your patients a crock, is it?"

This time he drank the whisky, and some colour stole into his cheeks. My boy then announced the bath ready, and in half an hour's time Dr. Shaw had rejoined me, looking a different being.

"Now," I said, pushing towards him some sardine sandwiches the boy had prepared for us to toy with before dinner, "who, or what, was the cause of that march?"

"Inman."

Young Inman, fresh from Cambridge and with the roses of English air and English beef still in his cheeks! I'd met him once or twice in Nakon – he was a teak-wallah of another firm – and a decent fellow I'd found him. What had happened to him?

I asked as much. The reply was:

"Malaria on the brain."

I thought I had heard of most complaints since I had been in Siam, and sampled a good many, but malaria on the brain was a new one to me, and it sounded grim.

"Inman ran away from his camp into the jungle," Shaw went on. "Simply didn't know what he was doing, and if it hadn't been for his coolies rushing after him, things would have been all up. As it was they found him, sitting on a log and dangling his feet in a *hwe*. So one sat down on each side of him, while the others went off post-haste to get hold of Berry."

Berry, I knew, was Inman's immediate forest boss, and a great "character." He was a magnificent polo-player. Had a little toothbrush moustache, and looked the perfect "My-God-Sir-What-the-Hell-d'You-Mean?" type of cavalryman, instead of a teak-wallah. He was also a bundle of nerves.

"Berry got Inman into a bungalow," the doctor continued, "and sent for me. When I arrived, Berry was almost in a worse state than Inman with the worry of having to look after him. Inman, apparently, had had a severe go of fever before rushing off as he did, and I could come to no other conclusion than that it had affected his brain. So I took him into

Nakon, and between you and me I'd have liked to have taken in Berry too. Man was in a terrible state of nerves, but he refused to come." The doctor paused. "Do you know," he added, "I'm more worried about Berry than Inman. Latter'll be all right if he leaves the country for good, but Berry …."

The doctor shrugged his shoulders significantly. And his words that night were strangely prophetic. Inman did leave the country and completely got over his trouble, but poor old "My-God-Sir" Berry died a few years later.

During dinner I mentioned my own trifling strawberry-face illness.

"What had you eaten that day or the day before?" was the prompt question.

"Curry, amongst other things," I answered vaguely.

"What odds and ends with it?"

I told the doctor. Coco-nut shredding, an odd nut or two, bamboo shoots possibly …

"Thought so," he interrupted. "Plain case of poisoning. Something you'd had out of that lot just wouldn't fit in with your system. Don't blame your cook, though; might happen to anyone."

So I had been poisoned, which was yet one more example of the remarkable facilities this country provided for dying in it.

Thereafter we talked of the weather, and the news, and cabbages and elephants and kings. We also, for some reason, had a long discussion about sheep and cattle-driving as depicted in the novels of Zane Grey. At ten o'clock I took him across through the fierce and relentless rain to our spare bungalow where he was to sleep. I shook him warmly by the hand, and that was the last I ever saw of him. Though I was up early the following morning, he had already gone, gone up that awful road to his hospital in which, for a mere pittance and thousands of miles away from his homeland, he did what he conceived to be his duty.

Truly a gallant man.

Campbell, Teak-Wallah, pp. 203-208

In Hospital

A Test of Skill and Nerve

The Presbyterian Board of Foreign Missions sent a "deputation" to report on the missions in Asia in 1915. During their week in Chiang Mai, they were witnesses to some dramatic events …

The hospital in Chieng Mai has a capacity of between fifty and sixty patients and is giving efficient service under Dr. Mason's care. The buildings and equipment have already rendered many years of service and are both in need of renewal. In the expectation that Chieng Mai is to become an important center for medical education in northern Siam plans have already been drawn for the re-building of the hospital, and it is to be hoped that the means may soon be found for carrying them into execution. In connection with the hospital we were pleased to find a clinical laboratory which was in active operation and rendering helpful service so far as its equipment permitted. In the work of the laboratory Dr. Mason finds very material help from several native assistants whom he himself has trained in the simpler laboratory procedure. Also in times of need in the operative work he calls to his aid Mrs. Mason who before entering the mission service had the advantage of ten years' training in the surgical clinic of Dr. Deaver of Philadelphia. What that aid means we had occasion to realize when on the last day of our stay in Chieng Mai it was found necessary to perform a most serious abdominal operation upon Mr. Gillies, one of our own mission staff. The operation was rendered necessary by the sudden perforation of a gastric ulcer from which Mr. Gillies had suffered for many years. The necessity of the operation was decided by a consultation of several physicians between six and seven o'clock in the evening. Under the prevailing conditions it seemed best that the patient should not be moved but that the operation should be performed in his own home. It was nine o'clock before the operating table, instruments,

The Mission Hospital at Chiang Mai, about 1910. From Freeman, *An Oriental Land of the Free.*

and other paraphernalia could be brought from the hospital and the operation actually undertaken. An abdominal section for such a purpose is a difficult and hazardous procedure under the best conditions. Under the circumstances prevailing in this case it constituted an unusual test of the skill and nerve of the operator. Dr. Mason, who performs the operation, had the assistance of both Drs. McKean and Dr. Cort, but it seemed to the anxious spectators that in this emergency he profited even more from the efficient aid of Mrs. Mason who, in this crisis, proved herself possessed not only of trained skill but of rare composure. The results of the operation we could not know at the time of our departure from Chieng Mai the next morning, but we all rejoiced really when, some weeks later in Manila, we learned that it had been entirely successful and that the patient was well on the way toward recovery. This experience brought home to all the members of the visiting party the heavy responsibility which the medical missionary must frequently assume in the care of his colleagues or the members of their families.

Deputation Report, pp. 173-174

The Opening of the McCormick Hospital, Chiengmai
Chinda Singanetra (A Medical Assistant)

Dr Chinda Singhanetra, one of Dr Cort's students at his short-lived medical school, was later a distinguished Chiang Mai physician in his own right.

The opening of the McCormick hospital which took place on Feb. 13th 1925 was considered a grand one. His Royal Highness the Prince of Sonkla who accepted the honour of opening had arrived from Bangkok the previous day and was here at 4:30 p.m. Every Government official and most of the merchants were invited. On the afternoon of the 13th, a tent was pitched in front of the operating building with chairs arranged in rows and a small stage in front for His Royal Highness himself. From 3 o'clock the guests began to come one by one until all the seats were occupied

The veranda of the new McCormick Hospital, 1925. The Editor.

and those who came after were obliged to stand outside the tent. At 4:30 His Royal Highness arrived with Madame Sonkla accompanied by The Viceroy, The Governor, Prarachaya, and his official guests. The moment His Royal Highness took his seat the opening performance was begun. Dr. J. W. McKean read a letter of congratulation from H.R.H. Prince of Nagara Svarga the vice president of the Siamese Red Cross Society introducing Major General Phya Vibul, Director of the Army Medical Department, and Miss Xavier, of the Public Health Nursing station in Chiengmai as the society's representatives. Rev. Banchong Bansidhi read verses from the Bible concerning the Lord's Commandment about care of the sick and Dr. Campbell offered the dedication prayer. Then Dr. E. C. Cort made a speech addressing His Royal Highness in Siamese concerning the rapid growth of civilization in both general and medical work, in Chiengmai compared with the past, and at the end of the speech, gave His Royal Highness the key inviting him to open the operating building. His Royal Highness' reply was a brilliant one, showing his interest in medical work and Christianity. He expressed a wish that this Hospital will save not only the body but also to save souls and restore them to everlasting life. He then handed the key to Prarachaya begging her to accept the honour of opening. The door of the operating building was opened and the guests were led to see the inside. We employees were kept busy explaining to them the two operating rooms, anesthetizing room, dressing room, x-ray room, laboratory, and doctor's office. From this building they were led to the hospital building, the wards and here we were also busy answering their questions concerning several things in the hospital such as sanitary toilets, shower bath, etc. Everybody seemed satisfied and felt as if there is nothing more needed. In reality these are only half done for the diet kitchen is still un-complete, and there are three more buildings promised. One Administration building promised by the Governor and two more wards promised by the leading merchants in Chiengmai.

This ward which was completed was in so nice order that it made my eyes dazzle to see it. I can really say that this is the best hospital I have ever seen during my whole life. Some doctors said this is the most up-to-date hospital ever built in Upper Siam. Most of the guests must have felt the same way for I heard one of them say this hospital looks exactly like heaven (he must have seen heaven in his dream or somewhere I cannot say, exactly.)

The operating room was so brilliant that there was almost nothing to say of it. The case for keeping surgical instruments was so clear that you did not see the glass at all. One of the guests told me that it was only a frame with no glass on, and I found out later that the glass walls were all broken during transportation. Luckily most of them did not notice it. After looking through every building the guests returned to their seats in the tent and we served them with afternoon tea. His Royal Highness left at 5:30 p.m.

This hospital was in the process of building for 5 years. Together there are 4 buildings. The operating building already stated; the ward can receive at least 64 patients; and another building called European ward, the funds for which were raised by the English teak companies in Chiengmai to accept only European patients. The last is the diet kitchen which is the best and most sanitary in Chiengmai. The funds for this kitchen were raised by Christian people in Chiengmai.

This hospital is situated on Doi Saket road two kilometres from the city, in a paddy field, a quiet cool place, the exact place for sick people. We citizens of Chiengmai will always be proud of this hospital. We cannot help thanking the good, generous heart of Mrs. McCormick who was so kind to us. If there is any way that we can express our gratitude towards her we would gladly do it without delay. And those who can think can imagine how heavy a burden it has made on Dr. Cort in this whole affair and to think of how splendidly he carried on the task. All we can do now to show them gratitude is THANKS.

Siam Outlook, April 1925, pp. 144-146

The Patient with Little or No Money

This is a "self-supporting" mission hospital. That means that aside from the salaries of the American staff and some supplies sent by guild societies, the running expenses of the hospital are met by its receipts in Siam, from the fees of patients and the sale of drugs. There is no subsidy, whether from America or Siam, and no endowment.

At the same time that the hospital charges fees appropriate to the means of the patient, its constant effort is to see that no one who needs medical care fails to get it because of lack of money on his part. This past year 120 sick people were treated without any charge at all, for a total of 3,155 days in the hospital. Still others could pay for only a part of the treatment they needed, the hospital assuming the rest. The money they paid is credited at a minimum rate of Tcs. 1.50 (or 67 cents) per day, for operations, food, injections, other medicines, etc. The remaining days of treatment they received were given them free of charge. In this way 169 additional patients received 2,714 days of treatment.

Thus a total of 289 out of 747 patients treated during the year received entire or partial free treatment. Out of 14,668 days of treatment given by the hospital 6,869, or 40 per cent, were not paid for at all by the patient.

Nevertheless, by careful watching of corners the year was closed out of debt.

McCormick Hospital report, 1927-1928, p. 4

Physical Plant

This year we have added two buildings completed and one under construction. The Maternity ward, the gift of Luang Anusan Soonthorn and his wife, is a beautiful ferro concrete building. It contains a six-bed ward floored with colored Italian tiles; a normal delivery room, an operative delivery room, and a scrub up room with floors and walls of white tile; a screened nursery with separate feeding and dressing room so arranged as to permit of isolation of babies from visitors; a service room, a two-bed private room, bath and toilet rooms.

The power building, a well-constructed edifice with cement floor and galvanized iron roof and walls, houses the Diesel engine, dynamo and batteries of the electric light plant, the pump for our water system and the four units of the laundry plant: washer, centrifugal extractor, drying tumbler, and ironer.

The administration building which will combine administration offices, examining rooms, rooms for X-ray and electric treatment and examination, which is the gift of the descendants of the old Royal Family of Chiengmai led by H. H. Princess Chao Dara Ratsami, Phrarachaya, and the Chao Luang, the Prince of Chiengmai, is under construction.

The hospital dairy of Anglo-Nubian goats and the hospital gardens and chicken farm have been increasingly useful in helping to provide an adequate diet for the patients.

McCormick Hospital report, 1928-1929, p. 5

H.R.H. Prince Mahidol of Songkla in Memoriam
E. C. Cort

Word has just come of the sudden death of the Prince Royal of Siam, H.R.H. Prince Mahidol of Songkla, after an illness of several months.

Siam has lost a great and able prince, a great and generous man. All who love their fellow men will mourn the loss of a man who gave himself and his possessions without stint in the service of his country and humanity.

Graduating from the German Naval Academy with very high honors, as a young man he returned to Siam and decided that the navy was not an outstanding need in this land. After looking over the field he decided that in public health was Siam's greatest need, and so with the permission of His Majesty, the King, he undertook the study of medicine. Prince Songkla graduated in 1928 from Harvard with high honors, where in a group of men famous for industry he was outstanding in his devotion to his work. On returning to Siam he desired to get a first-hand knowledge of Siamese medical conditions and so joined the staff of McCormick Hospital, where he served less than a month before the onset of his final sickness.

In opening the new McCormick Hospital in 1925, in furnishing the support of Dr. O'Brien since his arrival in Siam and other financial aid to the hospital, in addition to his joining the staff, he had shown himself a warm friend of the work. He was a supporter of the Boon Itt Memorial and of the Bangkok Christian College. Prince Songkla was the outstanding supporter of the Royal Medical School, and personally

From McCormick Hospital Report,
1929-1930.

provided scholarships for large numbers of men and women for study abroad. He gave himself and his means without limit in any cause that he believed would build up Siam physically, mentally and spiritually, and because he believed that the mission was doing these things he gave it his whole-hearted support.

Modest and very democratic, he was also a man of unusual charm, of great mental ability and of the finest spiritual qualities, and in his passing Siam, and we of the mission, have lost a great and helpful friend.

Prince Songkla died September 24, at the age of thirty-seven. His wife is a former student of Wattana Wittaya Academy, and there are three children.

Dr. E. C. Cort

Siam Outlook, October 1929, p. 365

At School

Mission schools were established at Chiang Mai in 1879 (for girls) and 1888 (for boys). The former was later known as the Prarachaya School and then as the Dara Wittaya Academy, the latter as The Prince Royal's College (from 1906). The government introduced compulsory primary education only in 1921.

Education Old and New

Up to the age of ten a boy remains at home, playing in the streets and generally running wild. At ten he is sent to the nearest temple school, where he is taught his letters and his prayers by the priests. His early years do not need much detail, for children are much the same all over the world, whether white or brown or yellow. All are apt to play truant from school whenever the opportunity occurs, and the punishment, when they are caught, is usually the same – a good spanking. The older form of education has, of course, now been modified by the new Compulsory Education Act.

When the boy reaches the age of fourteen or fifteen, according to his mental capacity, he will either leave the school or become a novice or acolyte; often, at this time, if he stays at school, he will change the name originally given him at birth. He will remain an acolyte at the temple for a year or two, and then will come the parting of the ways.

Le May, An Asian Arcady, p. 106

Compulsory primary education was introduced into Siam by the Education Act of October 1st, 1921, though it has not yet been put into force throughout the entire Kingdom. The Act decrees that every child, boy and girl, must attend classes given in the Siamese language for three years, between the ages of 7 and 14, the commencing age varying with each District; and, in addition, if the child does not intend to proceed to the higher secondary course, it must undergo a further two years' course of vocational training. This vocational course depends as to form largely upon the special activities of the District in which the school is situated, but it will in practically all cases be connected with some form of agriculture. Boys, on finishing their five years' course, may take up a higher technical course, but this is optional, and the great majority of boys leave school at the end of five years' training. Girls may take the higher technical course after three years at the primary school, thus receiving a well-merited recognition of their superior intelligence compared with boys. It is, indeed, not too much to say that, in the ordinary everyday practical affairs of life among the peasants, the average man is no match for the woman.

Le May, An Asian Arcady, p. 89

One Day at Prince Royal's College
By M. B. Palmer, Chiengmai.

Rev. Marion B. Palmer was a teacher at the school from 1906 to 1909.

The day begins early for some of the boarders as they tighten up their loose-fitting trousers and begin pounding rice long before the others are awake. A little later the boys that help prepare the rice and curry for the day get up and pound pepper or steam the rice that has been soaked in water all night or else prepare the curry for the day. At seven-thirty the food is usually ready and the boys squat in groups around little round tables about ten inches high while with fingers for knives and forks they satisfy themselves from the baskets of glutinous rice and bowls of peppery curry. At eight-thirty the boarders and day-scholars assemble in their respective classrooms while the teachers call the rolls and note the absentees, then in order and by classes the boys file from their rooms and march to their regular seats in the large auditorium for morning chapel which the teachers and Vice principal take turns in leading. Immediately after chapel comes the music period when hymns and anthems with the four parts are drilled until the boys sing quite well for Laos love music and have good ears for harmony.

From nine until twelve classes are held and various branches are taught from the alphabets of the three languages, (Laos, Siamese, and English) through preparatory, intermediate up to semi-advanced work in the three tongues, though the most advanced work is done in Siamese and English. Our most advanced boys are studying Geometry, General History, English Composition and correspondingly high work in Siamese including a course in Pali, the classic language of the country. After the noon hour the boys reassemble and study until three o'clock when the day-scholars who are not arrested for unfinished or poorly executed tasks go home and the boarders who are too poor to pay full board which is the case with nearly all of them go to their respective assignments of work on the campus. Some pull weeds out of the paths, some make new roads, while others water the plants and young cocoanut trees, or put in their time in hauling earth or sand for leveling or building up the roads. Everybody is busy and the routine goes along with very little friction. In the evening a study hour is held and prayers conducted by the teacher in charge, and lights are out at nine o'clock.

Laos News, May 1912, pp. 75-76

School Lunch

When it is time for lunch, out come little baskets of woven bamboo, filled with glutinous rice. The child squeezes the rice into a firm ball, dips it into a curry hot with chilies, and adds a bit of dried fish. The meal over, he runs his fingers through his oiled hair to remove the rice, wipes them on a post, and is ready for the writing lesson. After school he dawdles home, content with the day's work. On the way home he stops by the river for a bath and water sports.

Starling, Dawn over Temple Roofs, p. 99

Play, among the Lao

We have 110 girls in school this term, over half of them boarders, and they are so gentle and tractable it is a pleasure to work with them. It is pitiful to see how little they know about playing. Their greatest pleasure is watching us play tennis. A few evenings ago I heard an unusual noise under my window, and, looking out, saw a towel tied across the walk between the hedges. On either side of this stood a girl with a flat stick in her hand, and they were knocking across the towel a bundle of rags which they had tied up in some semblance of a ball. Later we took them out, and let each one have a few minute's real play with real racquet and balls, and, when I put the racquet in a girl's hand, she would gasp, as if to say, "Can this be really true, or am I dreaming?"

Starling, in: Foreign Post, May 1910

Corporal Punishment

Lucy Starling clearly believed in the principle "spare the rod, spoil the child" …

The other day one of the little girls got cranky, and wouldn't go to her class, mad at the teacher, I suppose. I told her twice to go, and each time she would start, and when she thought I wasn't looking, would stop. The second time, I got up, took her by the arm and led her to her class, giving her a spank at the last, to knock out her bad temper. When I came back to my own class, and took my seat, one of the little princesses said, in a most disappointed way, "When you whip, it doesn't hurt." I pretended not to have heard the remark, but I had a hard time keeping my face straight. The girls are often disappointed, because I don't furnish them enough entertainment in the punishment line.

22 August 1913

School Days
By Julia A. Hatch

Julia Hatch (1870-1934) was principal of the Prarachaya School (Dara Academy) from 1917 to 1926 when she left on her marriage to Dr Hugh Taylor of Nan.

The "Maids of Siam" appearing upon the cover of last year's November issue of *Women and Missions* are little pupils of Dara Wittaya Academy. This little group of four was playing under a big flowering tree in front of the old school house where one hundred of their play-mates were making merry. The dilatory Japanese photographer was too slow for the recording of the smiles which were called forth by the thought of having pictures taken.

From *Woman's Work.*

These girls of Siam are lovable and attractive. I wished that the change wrought in them by a few months in school might be depicted. At the beginning of the term, Mrs. Campbell brought two little nine-year-old girls in from a village across the plain. They were shy little tots but of determined minds. After a few days in these very changed surroundings where they were expected to sit up at a table and use a spoon in lifting the rice from the individual plate, instead of sitting on the floor and sopping bits of rice into a common bowl of curry, here at night they have to climb up on a white cot and sleep between two clean sheets instead of curling down upon a dirty mat on the floor, with the big buffaloes and cattle directly under the house, they took French leave for their home. Usually the mother gives up to the desire of the child. But in this instance, one mother had been a school girl for a short time years ago, so the runaways were promptly returned to school. They soon slipped into the new way of living and became happy and in two months time were so changed that they were hardly recognizable as they marched into church with a becoming "bob" and in their neat uniform.

A year ago a most woebegone appearing girl was brought into school by an uncle. Her grandfather had bequeathed her a small rice field, imposing the condition that she be placed in a mission school, that she might be taught "the Jesus Way". Both charge and guardian were trembling with fright and it required all my power of persuasion to keep the girl from breaking away and following the uncle as he left. Long standing ulcers disfigured the child and one could hardly imagine a more pitiful sight than she was that day, as the girls gathered about her to befriend her and as she stood for Miss Adams to take a snapshot of them. How I wish that Miss Adams could see her now, clean, healthy, attractive and intelligent. She has given her heart to the Savior. She loves to sing and has many songs by rote. When she visited her village a few weeks ago the uncle said that people came from all about to marvel at the change in the girl and to hear her sing.

Among our new teachers this year is the daughter of the Siamese Governor of Chiengmai. She was a pupil through our sixth Matayome grade. Later, upon her graduation from a High School in Bangkok, she was much sought after as a teacher in the government school here. In the securing of teachers for this, her father has the chief responsibility, and her mother is a patroness of their school. But the young lady, and a most lovely one she is, – said that as she was Miss Hatch's pupil she chose to be associated with her in teaching.

Custom allows the teacher to take considerable ease during the long, hot days of this tropic climate; but the young woman falls right into line with our Christian corps, devoting her time and strength without stint to the discharge of her duties as teacher of her class numbering more than thirty, and as Principal of the day school of more than one hundred at our old school building. To contrast this conduct with that of former times, and still quite generally proper for the daughters of titled Orientals, would require more space than is allowable here.

The future of the Kingdom lies in the hands of these "new women" of Siam who are to rock the cradles and swing the hammocks of the coming generation.

Siam Outlook, October 1925, pp. 8-9

Teak-Wallahs at Work

The Day's Work

Rise, in *your* imagination, above Piccadilly Circus. Wing, again in your imagination, east-south-east for seven thousand miles. Pass over Europe, Turkey, Persia, Afghanistan, the long Ganges basin, and you will come to the great belt of primeval forest that stretches across Burma, Siam and French Indo-China. This area of rolling, tree-clad hills, though dotted here and there with the tiniest of human settlements, remains as it was and ever will be – as vast and unfathomable as the darkest depths of the sea.

Hover over the Northern Siam portion. Watch, with that all-powerful imaginary eye of yours, the day's work of five lonely men, any one of whom might easily have been you if you hadn't taken that other job or been born a girl, of course. See these men's actions; read their thoughts. They are ordinary men, as we have seen, gifted with no great gifts and cursed with no great faults, yet shortly they are to adopt, of their own free wills, a course of action from which Horatius himself would have recoiled in the utmost alarm. But that is just the sort of thing we ordinary men are apt to do; we're so foolish that we can't realize what we're letting ourselves in for . . .

Vernon, back to work after his day's rest in the Ban Luang compound, toiled through his particular patch of rocky, heat-shimmering jungle. His patch was virgin forest, his job to discover, measure and girdle every suitable teak-tree in a one-hundred square-mile area due north of the Nakon road. In his boyhood days the word "jungle" had conjured up wonderful visions of exotic flowers, exotic birds, exotic perfumes, exotic skies; he had long ago discovered that the real thing, especially in the hot weather, was rather different. The predominant colour, for instance, was a harsh, indescribable yellow. The leafless trees, save for those that had been charred by some passing fire, were yellow; the parched ground was yellow; the brassy sky, the very air seemed yellow; he himself, for the first part of the morning at least, was yellow too – topee, hair, face, neck, shirt, belt, shorts, knees, puttees, boots, all burnt a dusty yellow by weeks of glare, though later in the day he would gradually turn completely black.

He had left his tent at seven in the morning. The first two hours of toiling through the wilderness had drawn a blank: not one single teak tree amidst those thousands of trees, but the next hour yielded fifty, all first-class pieces of timber. At each tree the same procedure was adopted: at a height of four feet six from the base the circumference of the tree was measured with a tape-line; if over six feet, the tree was then blazed as a sign to the following coolies for them to girdle, or ring it with their axes. Some trees, however, Vernon passed by: solitary ones and those growing on ridges were left to conserve the forest with their seed for those who came after.

At noon he sat down on a rotting log to consume a cold, unappetizing tiffin. By now he was black from head to foot through continual contact with the charred stems of bamboo and other vegetation that had been caught in the track of jungle fires. With blackened hands he devoured the chicken rissoles his cook had prepared for him at dawn, after which he drank from a porous earthenware jar, then lit a cigarette.

A tiny yellow scorpion ran out from the log on which he was seated and, seizing his stick, he pinned the creature to the earth with the metal tip. Tail twisted over back, the scorpion quickly stung itself to death in its

Chiang Mai. Elephant at work. Photograph by Tanaka. Oliver Backhouse.

Photograph by W. A. Elder. From Campbell, *Teak-Wallah.*

frantic endeavours to get free. Vernon flicked the body away, then called to his coolies to resume the day's work. Though the men were squatting but a few yards away, he had to raise his voice to a shout in order to make himself heard through the high, ceaseless din of the cicadas stuck in millions on the neighbouring trees.

At four o'clock he ordered a return to camp. The coolies, guided by jungle-sense, unerringly made a bee-line for it. On the way they passed the hide of a deer – a sambhur. The coolies, soft-eyed Kamoos from the wild hills beyond the French frontier to the north-east, conversed together in guttural monosyllables. From the tracks on the ground the story was clear: wild dogs had run down and slain the sambhur, whereupon my lord the Tiger had appeared, driven off the dogs and devoured the kill himself. And did not Ai Sow consider that the price of blue jungle cloth was prohibitive this year? So might one man in London Town say to another: "That refuge over there; pretty useful smash to bring the standard down! 'Bus, probably. Now about these shares . . ."

Back in his tent Vernon bathed, changed into black silk Chinese trousers and spotless white singlet – he was always careful of his appearance – and sat down to tea outside his tent. His camp was pitched in a small clearing on the one side of which towered a huge wall of rock. As the sun sank lower, the din of the cicadas ceased and other sounds became apparent. Long-armed, tailless apes, the silvery white gibbons, "whooed" to one another from the topmost branches of the forest; on the wall of rock the vulgar brown monkeys chattered and scolded in hundreds; an occasional barking-deer belled, sending great waves of hoarse clamour shocking through the trees; the sound was more terrifying than the coughing roar of a tiger, yet it came from one of the most beautiful and harmless creatures on this earth.

Tea over, and his diary written up, Vernon sank deep into his thoughts.

Campbell, Fear in the Forest, pp. 42-45

On the March

Alec Waugh (1898-1981), the brother of the much more celebrated writer Evelyn Waugh, travelled to Siam in 1926, taking an opportunity he was offered to visit the jungles of the north. He also visited Chiang Mai. Waugh drew on his experiences for two substantial short stories and the travel book, The Coloured Countries *(1930), which appeared in the United States under the title* Hot Countries.

The weeks we spent there were very like a picnic. But I could picture what the life of the assistant must be during ordinary periods. For months on end, through the sequence of rain-drenched weeks, he might never see a white man. There would be no cheery companionship at the end of a long day's marching; no antidote to the maladies of jungle life, the discomfort; the itch of prickly heat, the leeches, the mosquitoes and the mud-sores; the sandflies that no netting can keep out; the red ants that night after night make sleep impossible; the long depression of the September rains, when bedding and kit are soaked and for days it is impossible to wear dry clothing; the fever that takes its toll, slowly, spasm by spasm, of your vitality and courage. Fever comes suddenly upon you, and in a few hours you are incapable of movement. I remember returning to a compound where three hours earlier we had said "Good-bye" to a strong and vigorous assistant, to find waiting for us a pale, lined, white-faced figure laid out on a long chair, shivering with a rug over him. I could not believe that it was the same man.

Waugh, The Coloured Countries, pp. 149-150

"Boys"

Next morning I was called at six, and all my kit was piled on the elephants, who had been tied up and hand-fed the night before. Breakable stuff like crockery and bottles were packed into two large baskets connected by a bamboo carrying-pole and carried by the four coolies. My Chinese "boy" from Bangkok was now made cook, and I was given a Lao "boy" who could not speak a word of English, so for the first few weeks the cook's role was doubled with that of interpreter, not that his English was very good! A "sais" or pony-boy engaged for me by Smith completed my menage. He was to look after the regulation two ponies, one provided free by the Company on condition one bought another. For their upkeep we received an allowance of twenty-five rupees a month. Smith had got me a small bay as second pony. The other he sold me being the grey he had sent to meet me, an old polo pony called Rajah.

Williams, Green Prison, p. 76

Waiting for the Rise

In all I waited four weeks for that rise to happen, and how I got through them I don't know. I'd get up as late as was decently possible, linger over breakfast and a post-breakfast cigarette, drift down to the office, which was directly beneath the bungalow, find with an effort perhaps half an hour's work by paying some raftsmen who wanted advances, or by rationing them out some cane, and then, since walking was out of the question, up the steps I'd go again to the bungalow. It probably wanted at least another two hours before tiffin, and I'd start playing the gramophone I had and which invariably accompanied me wherever I went. I hadn't too many records, but these were used over and over again, particularly one called "The Gipsy Warned Me." How often Violet Loraine must have sung that song out over the depressing, drizzle-enshrouded river I cannot imagine; but her lovely voice brought back visions of when I had sat, entranced, and listened to her singing "Some Girl has got to Darn his Socks," in "Round the Map." Though she had worn glasses and was dressed in a black shawl, she had held that crowded audience of khaki and blue so that one could have heard the proverbial pin drop, and, sitting in that bungalow and listening to "The Gipsy Warned Me," I could see and hear her again as plainly as in those hectic War days.

After an hour or two of the gramophone I'd eat a heavy tiffin, then fall into a heavy sleep. Oh, the joy of waking up about four o'clock in the sticky heat of the bedroom, one's skin all oily, one's mouth like a chemical factory, and with the knowledge that one couldn't have a cup of tea! I just longed for tea then, and found coffee a poor, almost nauseating substitute at that time of the day.

After dinner I'd read the advertisements in the last batch of newspapers out from England (the news I had probably read long ago), then after a period of general mooning around, and a last vain glance at the Mae Yome for signs of a rise, I'd turn in. I was so bored I hadn't even the heart to summon my phantom naval friends, for they'd have been bored too. And I was too bored to take to solitary drinking. Hobbies? I tried to think of some, but couldn't.

The only changes from the general monotony were several slight goes of low fever I experienced. Malaria has many ways of coming out in a man; usually it brings a high temperature and ague, and can then be very dangerous. It was the fate of most teak-wallahs to have at least one bad bout which they were lucky to survive, but I myself never went in for anything worse than low fever as opposed to high. I generally felt it coming on in the evening; all day I'd be feeling tired and out of sorts, and about five o'clock the calves of the legs would begin to ache, the eyelids to sting, the head and nose to feel stuffy, and curious little, trickling shivers would come creeping over the skin, like cat's-paws of wind over sea. The skin also would be hot and dry, and I'd know for sure what I was in for.

Here is a typical Low Fever Evening in Sawankaloke:

"Boy!" I shout, "*ow heep yah mah.*"

In comes the boy, carrying my medicine-chest, a little tin box partitioned off for the various bottles of Burroughs and Wellcome tabloids. I take out fifteen grains of quinine and ten of aspirin, and swallow them with the aid of some lukewarm, filtered water.

"I'm going to bed," I say to the boy. "Light the lamp in the bedroom and bring blankets."

"Yes, master."

I walk from the living-room to the stuffy bedroom. Those shivers are trickling more and more over my skin, and though my brain is strangely active, I feel very tired physically. "I must bring on a sweat," I say to myself. "Then this confounded fever will go."

I slip off my day kit, which consists of khaki shorts and a white cotton shirt, and then, instead of putting on the usual night rig – black Chinese trousers and singlet – I don the thickest pair of pyjama trousers I can find, a flannel tennis shirt, a pair of thick socks, and a sweater. Clad now like a boxing instructor, but feeling very much unlike one, I get into bed, and on top of this already warm kit heap the blankets the boy brings me. The bed is a big square affair, part of the bungalow furniture, and I lie in the middle of it, with the blankets wrapped round me so that not even an elbow or finger is visible. I now have to await the coming of the sweat.

The two oil-lamps, one set on a table and one hanging from the ceiling, light the dark, wooden-walled room but dimly. Staring straight ahead of me, I see lizards crawling along the walls; most of them are little "chin-chocks," but one is a huge "tokay," and I watch him stalking a moth that has settled near him. Inch by inch he approaches it, first one scaly leg going out in front of him and then the other, and at last, when my nerves are almost at breaking point with suspense, there is a sudden jump, a snapping of teeth, and the moth is no more. Even into this room the law of the jungle has penetrated.

The noises of the night come faintly in through the open window: the hoot of an owl, the squeak of an otter, the faint breathing of the river. Then all minor sounds are drowned by the howling of a dog from the village nearby. The howl is taken up by another dog, and another, and another. Soon every pariah in the hamlet is voicing his lament to the weeping skies. Now high, now low, now long-drawn-out and now in sobbing ululation, and I muse on the Lao saying: "When the dogs howl, a spirit is passing."

Campbell, Teak-Wallah, pp. 151-155

The Loneliest Station Manager

Ellis was tall and athletic-looking, with blue eyes that occasionally seemed to gaze beyond one into vacancy. In the few days we stayed with him we both learned to love a charming personality, with an impish sense of humour and an amazing absent-mindedness. Fear was a complete stranger to him. He had been terribly mauled by a tiger, made an almost miraculous recovery, and still went on bagging them, generally on foot. His total at that date was over twenty tiger, easily a record for Thailand. Big-game hunting and a little farm in Sussex he had bought against his retirement and of which he showed us numerous photos, were his hobbies, but he was exceedingly well informed and could talk on almost any subject.

Yet this was the man who led the loneliest existence of any station manager in the country. Determined to save money rather than spend his salary in senseless and extravagant entertaining, he had consistently refused charge of the bigger stations, and ran the huge Raheng district with only one assistant, on leave at the time of our visit. [...] For at least nine months of the year Ellis lived entirely alone.

A glance round the room soon revealed one of his antidotes to solitude. He had a good library, ranging from the Victorian classics to the latest novels and autobiographies. One shelf was filled with books on Asiatic big game. He offered to lend us some of his books for the remainder of our journey, but, like fools, we declined, afraid of the delay and difficulty

Illustration by John Campbell to Reginald Campbell's story *The Temple of Ghosts*, 1930.

in returning them. What would either of us have given, a few weeks later, for something to read!

Williams, Green Prison, pp. 52-53

Nothing to Do but Read

There was nothing to do but read, read and read, and in a week I had finished every book and paper I possessed. Then I started reading the advertisements. At first they seemed clever and amusing, and full of a sincere belief in the virtues of the products they extolled. But when I had read them all through a dozen times, they revealed themselves as cheap and banal balderdash, obviously misrepresenting values, utterly without any claim to trust or interest. Finally I flung all the papers away, and started reading through the books again. Luckily, before I was quite sick of these, we broke out of the elephant grass into open and inhabited country.

Williams, Green Prison, pp. 64-65

An Inner Shrine of the Mind

Trying to maintain his interest in the subjects which had formerly attracted his curiosity and widened his culture, Philip read voraciously. His mind often protested, naturally. The brain can never apply itself when the body, pleasantly fatigued by a day in open altitudes, makes great demands upon the blood's best play.

But Philip stuck to it. He ordered shipment after shipment of pocket editions, finding them handy for stowing away among his jungle kit. Every day he read, and every day he thought of what he had read: he built himself an inner shrine of the mind: and every night he wrote a little of his thoughts and captured as many of his fugitive impressions as he found possible.

Eric Reid, Spears of Deliverance, p. 91

A Life Sentence

Twenty years in the jungles of Thailand sounds very much like a life sentence. And when most of that time was to be spent in one's own company, it might be said to amount to solitary confinement. Yes, there were occasions during the height of the monsoon, particularly at dusk, when, as I sat in my tent pitched in a small forest clearing, the dripping boles of the trees seemed to close in on me like the bars of a prison. I was a hundred miles – a week's march in that country – from the nearest native town. I was alone, except for half a dozen fever-stricken Kamus. You imagine my hand stealing towards the whisky bottle. And you are right!

Williams, Green Prison, p. 1

Dust jacket of Leigh Williams' *Jungle Prison* (detail). The Editor.

The Private Lives of Teak-Wallahs

The Problem of Sex

It was at a smaller dinner-party that I caught my first glimpse of the private lives of the "teak-wallahs." I had been invited to the junior mess of another firm who were housed in a barrack-like building which had several bed-rooms opening on to a long verandah. I had arrived too early, and my hosts were still changing. In front of three of the bedrooms sat a Lao girl, with powdered face and dressed in the most expensive lace bodice and silk *sin* (skirt). They were glaring at each other without speaking a word, but as I appeared at the top of the stairs each broke into a self-conscious simper. At that moment a door opened and a man came out of his bedroom.

"Hey, get out of this!" he shouted, and the three girls disappeared giggling down the passage to the servants' quarters.

"Sorry, Williams," he said. "These polls do love to show themselves off. I expect you'll be taking one on soon, eh? Keep 'em in their place, that's my motto."

The same man, much later in the evening, took me aside just as I was rising to go.

"I say, W., if at any time you want to take on a girl, let me know. My girl has a sister, a pretty little thing of sixteen, and a pukka virgin. As such, she would cost you one hundred rupees down, and twenty-five rupees a month wages. You're bound to come to it sooner or later – everyone does, you know."

"I bet you a fiver I never do!" I retorted hotly.

"My dear boy, I wouldn't take your money," he laughed.

"Good night!"

In course of time I discovered that he was right. Practically every man had his "girl" or more vulgarly "poll," and some of the "burra-sahibs," whom I should never have suspected of relations with native women, had quite large black-and-tan families. There was some justification for their mode of life, including the firms' ban on marriage, subsequently relaxed. A casual affair was quite rightly considered highly dangerous, as well as being beneath the dignity of a white man. To keep one's own mistress was the only solution of this problem of sex.

The cynical Brown was sitting up by himself having a last whisky when I got back to our mess. He had been to another party which was evidently quite a good one. When I told him what I had seen at the other mess, and of my bet, he laughed and said:

"You be wise, my boy, and try and stick to your resolution. These girls sound cheap enough on paper, a hundred "dibs" down, and twenty-five a month (less than you pay your cook), but believe me, you will have spent as much in the end as if you had hired a white "tart" to come out from home. These girls are damned good at wheedling. After a bit the wages aren't enough (to do the girls justice, I believe their parents pinch most of it): then she must keep a servant – at your expense, of course. Then she'll want expensive clothes to keep up the high social position of being your poll! Next, she'll want jewellery because Blank's poll has got it. You wouldn't believe what some of these fellows spend on the wenches. They get all sentimental and chivalrous-like about them, instead of regarding them as a bloody but necessary nuisance!

"I assure you that quite a few chaps are absolutely under their girl's thumb. They give in to their every whim, lend their people money, build them teak houses, buy them paddy-fields and then, when they go home for good (if they can afford to!) leave them a parting present of five or ten thousand rupees. And all this quite apart from the question of children. These girls, though they know more about prevention than most people, always try to have a kid as soon as possible, as they think it gives them a hold on you. Then the kids must be clothed and fed and educated. Why, some of these chaps even send them to school in Europe. So you watch it, my boy, or you'll find yourself a not-so-proud father in no time!"

I thanked Brown for his good advice, and turned in. I concluded that he was one of the few who had kept himself "pure," and that was a possible cause of his cynicism and irritability.

Williams, Green Prison, pp. 99-101

A Native Girl

In Reginald Campbell's novel Uneasy Virtue, *Leyburn makes a resolution …*

That afternoon, having finished his solitary tiffin, Leyburn sat in a long chair and stared moodily before him. The drink had half faded from his brain, and the uncomfortable conviction was beginning to dawn on him that he had made a fool of himself before Tenterden, which wouldn't do at all. He must keep firm hold on his nerves, he reflected savagely, otherwise he might fall sick and the be-all and end-all for which he was now living would never be accomplished.

Then memory of his visitor's parting words came back to him. "Take on a native girl." Why not? He'd finished with white women, except so far as his revenge was concerned, and he might as well do the same as many of the other jungle-wallahs did and take a brown woman to his bosom.

And it would help him, too, he reflected, help him to keep fit so that he would be cool and have all his wits about him when his time came.

And the native girl? Well, she would be all right, since he had no intention of leaving the locality for years yet, nor of asking for the transfer that had been suggested to suit the convenience of Raymond Saunders.

Having come to this decision, he called for his boy.

"Bid your wife come to me," he ordered when the man appeared.

Five minutes later she was standing before him.

"Lord, you sent for me?" she quavered nervously.

"Yes, I wish for a *meliang*. In the village of Muang Toom there are maidens?"

The Lao woman's lined face brightened. So the Lord Leyburn was taking a wife to himself at last, which was both meet and right and entirely as it should be.

"There are maidens," she repeated quickly.

"Good maidens?"

"Yes, lord, but they are of poor birth; they are of the jungle."

"It matters not. I wish for one."

"As your real wife? Not for one moon?"

"As my real wife."

Her eyes glinted. "You will give me commission, lord?" she asked anxiously.

"Yes"

"How much?"

"Ten per cent of the price of the buying."

A sigh of satisfaction escaped her, and she glanced out at the lowering sky before replying.

"Listen, lord," she said at last. "I will go, but the hour is late and the village is two miles distant. I will seek out a maiden this very evening, but she must be a good maiden, fit for a white lord, therefore must I choose carefully. I will sleep in the rest-house of the village to-night, and bring her and her parents back to your bungalow to-morrow morning. It is good?"

"It is good," replied Leyburn.

She slipped away on her errand, accompanied by two pleasantly intrigued members of the white man's household staff, and was lost to sight amidst the glooming of the trees.

Campbell, Uneasy Virtue, pp. 72-73

A Pair of Slippers

On arriving in "Laowieng", Philip Harkness, Eric Reid's protagonist in the novel Spears of Deliverance, *is introduced to his colleague's wife.*

"You'll see my girl presently. She has learnt to speak English, and I have taught her how to behave at table. And now, I assure you, she prefers European fashions of life to those of her own people. Wouldn't change for anything. Here! Bua Phang!"

Van Homrigh turned and called out through the door of the adjacent room, "We're waiting for you!"

A girl came forward. Pretty enough, and dainty in the usual Lao girl's way, she was dressed, with the taste that characterises her sisters, in a muslin and lace blouse and a skirt with the usual green and black stripes running horizontally across the upper part. Her face, however, was spoiled by an expression of permanent discontent, and she wore too much jewellery.

She came up to Harkness and held her hand out with supreme assurance.

"How are you?" she drawled with comical affectation in the best Van Homrigh manner. "Did you have a good trip up-river?"

Her lord and mentor was beaming in the background beaming with pleasure at seeing his pet go through the paces he had taught.

For a moment Philip was quite flabbergasted. He had seen Bangkok *mias* of many sorts, but none like this girl. The bare idea that she should appear so openly, and even sit at meals with Europeans was certainly in direct contrast to the surreptitious manner in which every Bangkok man of his acquaintance had conducted such household arrangements.

Then Van Homrigh broke out with some angry remark in Lao. The other white man thought he caught the word "shoes." He glanced down at the girl's feet.

She was wearing a pair of silver-embroidered Lao slippers, in entire keeping with the rest of her costume, and though her bare brown feet were visible above slippers which did not wholly cover them, her foot-gear struck Philip as suitable, and indeed entirely unexceptionable.

The girl turned and sulkily left the room.

"I object to her appearing in native slippers without any stockings on," was Van Homrigh's explanation.

They waited, and the girl returned after an interval, seating herself at the head of the table.

She walked with evident discomfort in the pair of high-heeled, fashionable, French shoes into which she had changed. Open-work silk stockings were distinctly in evidence, but Philip noticed with an inward chuckle that the stockings had been hastily put on, and one of them was inside out. Van Homrigh, not observing this "faux pas" however, was prepared to forget his disappointment at her failure to put her best foot foremost at the first appearance.

The meal went on.

Philip was astounded to see how far his companion had come under the influence of the girl, treating her with an obsequious and even exaggerated politeness that would have made any white woman ridiculous, but now and then being obliged to scold her like a spoilt child for some false step in the elements of table manners. The farce of the scene struck the newcomer acutely, but he simply registered the experience then as yet another example of the absurd manner of some white men towards brown women after a lengthy residence in Siam.

Later in the novel, Bua Phang throws the French shoes out of the window and vows never to wear them again.

Eric Reid, Spears of Deliverance, pp. 64-65

The Last Chukka

In Alec Waugh's story, the "burra-sahib" Arnold has reached a decision …

To his surprise he found Cheam alone. She was dressed, for he had never made any attempt to Westernize her, in a short blue silk jacket that fell shapelily over a gold and scarlet *sinn*; her feet were bare; her hair, that was bright with cocoanut oil, was drawn back tightly into the clutch of a high tortoiseshell and enamel comb. Her teeth, for from the betel habit he had discouraged her, were unfashionably clean. But from the corner of her mouth she was puffing slowly at a large white cheroot. As he came into the room she lifted her head in the calm, unemotional manner that had from the first characterized their meetings. There had never been at any time between them what Europe would have admitted as passionate relations.

She looked at him steadily and incuriously. But as their eyes met he was conscious on this evening of self-discovery, of a curious sense of kinship with her. They were in the same boat after all, exiles both of them; exiles from their youth and their ambitions. This life of theirs together had not been by any means the thing they had dreamed of for themselves. It was something quite other than they had planned. He had had his dream of Oxford, of English life and English shires and she, no doubt, of such a mating and such a life as had their roots in the dateless annals of her race. But for each of them fate had intervened; on each had been laid the duty of obligation to a family. He had come here that his brother might go to Oxford, and she in her turn had come to him because her parents could not afford to refuse the three hundred rupees that were her purchase.

They were both in the same boat. And that same curious sense of belonging to this woman and to this country of his exile, that earlier in the evening had made him forsake the round table and the laughter and the drinks, returned with redoubled force upon him. England had grown a foreign country to him. He had taken root here, by Babel's waters.

Softly across the night came the tinkle of a temple bell: the symbol of that Eastern doctrine which preaches subservience to one's fate: the acceptance unprotestingly of one's dharma.

"I shall be retiring, you know, Cheam," he said, "in a few weeks from now."

She bent her head slowly forward and he knew well enough what was passing behind that inscrutable masked face. "How much of paddy-field was he to offer her and how many ticals."

"Very likely," he said, "I shall be staying on in Pangrai. I am thinking of building myself a house across the river. It would be easier probably if you were to leave this bungalow and come and live there with me."

Again she bent her head. Her face showed neither pleasure nor surprise. Child of Buddha, she was subservient to her dharma; to her fate, as to his ardour, passive and irresponsive.

"In which case," he went on, "it would probably be simpler if we were to be married according to English law."

"It is as the Nai wishes," she replied.

Waugh, The Last Chukka

Staying On

"I've been here too long. Burma, perhaps, or Indo China, or I may go and have a look at Java. Not England, though; it's a foreign country to me now."

But that was not the reason. And Arbutt knew it. England was no place for a man with a Siamese wife and Eurasian children. That was why Carrington was staying East; to keep his children in their setting, where they could face their future on equal terms.

"Seen England for the last time," he said. […]

Lazily Arbutt stretched his arms above his head. The last elephant had wound its way into the compound. The noisy business of unloading had begun. In five minutes their beds would be set up. They would "lie off" for an hour or so. Then after tea, after they had shaved and tubbed, they would stroll down to the river and watch the bathing of the elephants. They would linger for a little exchanging gossip with the villagers, till the sun had set and the time had come for the first stengah. They would not talk a great deal as they sat there sipping at their glasses, but they would be glad and grateful for each other's company. Their limbs would be lax and weary after the long day's march. Their eyes would be soothed after the long day's glare. In their ears the chorus of cicadas would murmur wooingly. They would just sit there savouring the relish of accomplished labour, their senses tranquillised, at peace under the tropic night.

With a long slow sigh that was half gratitude and half regret James Arbutt drew the heavy sun-soaked air into his lungs.

Waugh, Waters of Babylon, p. 287

Two Teak-Wallah songs

A half-hour later I heard Malone's execrable voice rising from the bathroom. The rain, which was falling again heavily, had evidently inspired him, for this is what he sang:

> "I want to go home, I - ee want to go home,
> Mosquitoes are biting, it's pouring with rain,
> I don't want to go to the jungle er-gayne:
> Take me over the sea,
> Where I shan't see a single teak tree:
> Oh, my, I don't want to die,
> I - ee want to go ho-ome."

"Stop it!" I yelled.
"Don't like it? Then we'll have something else.

"We are all jungle wah-lahs,
No earthly use are we:
We cannot ride, we cannot shoot,
Because we are *tem-thi*:
And when we get to Bangkok,
Our managers will say,
Hoch, hoch, mein Gott,
What an awful, rotten lot,
Not worth a tical a day."

"Rotten," I boomed.
"Tem-thi" means something like "I've had enough".

Campbell, *Death in Tiger Valley, p. 189*

At the Club

The Chiengmai Gymkhana Club

William Harris recalls the foundation of the Club ...

In 1898 the Englishmen acquired twenty acres on the edge of town, erected a small pavilion, and inaugurated the Club. I joined the following year and continued my membership until we left Chiengmai.

The Club started in a very modest way: the fees were but Rupees 2 (66 Cents) per month; the only game, polo. As all men had to own ponies, we trained them to play the game at no extra expense. Later on three tennis courts, two squash courts, and a golf course, over the polo field, with hazards at the sides, were added. The fees were raised gradually, but were never high.

The administration of the Club was in the hands of a Committee of four men, of whom I was one for about twenty-five years.

The Club was, for me, a life-saver. My office work for twenty years (1900-1920) was very heavy; but five days a week, when we could get away, we went to the Club and played games – polo for me for many years – and sat out on the lawn in the dusk.

Nellie's presence at the Club was a steadying influence – an influence for good. The men

Evelyn van Millingen takes part in a shooting competition at the Chiang Mai Gymkhana Club. Oliver Backhouse.

liked and respected her; the talk after games was good – often worthwhile; for many of the men were well educated.

One rule of the Club I regretted: the number of Siamese honorary members was limited to five; none could be full members. There was fear – I felt, groundless – that, otherwise, the management might be taken out of the hands of the foreigners, to the detriment of the club life. This caused a certain amount of bitterness: our friend, Prince Dossiriwong, the Viceroy, who had been made a patron, spoke to me on the subject. He made a courtesy call, and, I believe, never went again.

William Harris, Recollections, pp. 12-13

Like an English Meadow

Alec Waugh visited Chiang Mai and the Club in 1926.

The white life of Chiengmai centres round the Gymkhana Club. It is a large field set a little way out of town which serves as polo ground and golf course and tennis court. By five o'clock, when the heat of the day has lessened, most of the white community is there, scattered about the field. There is seventy-five minutes of strenuous exercise. Then when the light fails there is a gathering round a large table on which have been set out drinks, glasses and a little lamp. There are rarely more and rarely less than a dozen people there. It is peaceful. In the swift-fallen dusk the large field, with its wide-branched trees rising from a hedge, looks heartbreakingly like an English meadow. Mosquitoes are buzzing round the table. The women have slipped their legs into sarongs, sewn up at one end in the shape of bags. The talk is subdued and intimate. It is the hour that makes amends for the heat and dust of morning and afternoon.

But you cannot picture it in terms of England. Chiengmai is so far, and the whites there are so few. Their life is hard and testing. It has many dangers, many difficulties. It is only by mutual tolerance, by interdependence, by loyalty and friendship that it can be made tolerable. In most small communities you will find gossiping and malice and petty spite. But in Chiengmai you will not. The white community has the solidarity of a small band united against a common foe.

Waugh, The Coloured Countries, pp. 141-142

Members of the Lampang Club in front of the Club House, 1930s. Oliver Backhouse.

A New Boy at the Club

Conversation at the Club was apt to be monopolised by one or two senior men, and juniors were expected to be seen rather than be heard. I soon got tired of this perpetual "new boy" business, and could not for the life of me see why priority of residence, especially in such a backwater as the north of Thailand, should intrinsically confer wisdom and wit on anyone. Unfortunately, during a sudden pause in general and disconnected conversation, I was overheard one evening informing my junior next-door neighbour at the round table that the Chiengmai Club reminded me of the fourth form at a smaller public school! This remark was largely overheard, and I was never forgiven! In the end we juniors used to go round to each other's messes after games at the Club, and play bridge rather than stay down and listen to the local "augurs." This was no doubt good for us, but bad for the Club's bar receipts.

Williams, Green Prison, pp. 149-150

Compulsory Games

In Eric Reid's novel, Spears of Deliverance, *the protagonist, Philip Harkness, learns about the importance of polo at the station. "Marlow" is probably a composite portrait of Arthur Queripel and David Macfie.*

For the male portion of European mankind in a place like Laowieng life became interesting only when a sufficient number of men had returned from the jungle to permit of two sides for polo being formed in the station.

These "teak wallahs" or "jungle wallopers" as they dubbed one another in mutual semi-disparagement, were wont to spend a couple of months or so in the jungle at a stretch, "girdling" trees, and generally supervising the extract of teak from the once abundant forests of Siam, now somewhat exhausted through a belated realisation of the necessities for state conservation.

As Morland pithily put it to Philip:

"After ten weeks or so of a solitary furrow in the Mae Chem, you generally come back to Laowieng in the hope that there will be polo going every day of the ten you spend in the station, while you're getting stores and so on for another spell in the jungle."

"And," surmised Philip," I suppose you manage to arrange that you are all 'in' at the same time pretty well."

"You bet! And after polo, we do a 'gin-crawl' from the Club to your house, where you finish up with more booze, and in this way most of us succeed in never going to bed sober while in station. Oh yes! It's a good life!"

"But," Harkness expostulated, "it doesn't seem to me so very unnatural that, after the solitude of the jungle, the relaxation to even the demi-semi-hemi-civilisation of the station makes one apt to ..."

"Let fly!" Morland found the phrase. "Quite so! Quite so! I don't deny it. But it's not until the Christmas meeting that we let fly at anything like a venture. And then it is a very long bow."

"Anyhow, there can't be much to spend your money on in the jungle, and I suppose in the working intervals one saves a lot."

Notwithstanding the paucity of Englishmen in Northern Siam

(Laowieng is the largest station with an English population of some thirty souls only) polo is indulged in fairly frequently throughout the year. Every man, hardly without exception, plays; and the healthy rivalry existing in the first place between the members of the teak companies, and in the second between the different stations creates a standard of play that is, comparatively speaking, high.

Every youngster who arrives in the North finds himself obliged primarily by the necessities of his work to learn to ride, and thereafter by the force of male public opinion to learn to play polo.

Marlow made no bones about it. He simply compelled all his men to play, and until he grew too heavy for the game himself, led his Company-team through an unbroken succession of victories over other teams. In addition he obliged his directors in London, in his own inimitably autocratic fashion, to grant allowances to his men for extra ponies chosen as suitable for polo purposes.

But then Marlow was the Uncrowned of Laowieng. A one-time All-England cricketer and a fine all-round sportsman, he was the oldest white resident in the North. So well had he developed the resources of his Company, obtaining such excellent results from his timber workings for so many years, that the Brunei Board had come to rely on his judgment in every particular.

Marlow it was who selected amongst the candidates for new posts in the Company or at least those youngsters destined to serve under himself up-country. Marlow seldom made a mistake, for his judgment of human nature was unerring – almost: but if it turned out that a man under him did differ from him on any of the essential points which he exacted that man had to go, whatever his other merits.

While fearing him, the whole station could not but admire Marlow. He domineered over Laowieng in the same irresistibly charming manner as that in which he compelled his juniors to fall into line with his own ideas of what constituted "a varie parfit, gentle" teak-wallah.

He dictated to the Gymkhana Club Committee as to how that institution should be run, and in much the same way he dictated to Laowieng society generally how it should conduct its affairs.

Polo at the Gymkhana Club, Chiang Mai. From Le May, *An Asian Arcady.*

To Siamese Laowieng he laid down what improvements in the shape of road-repairs and bridge-building he deemed advisable for his own comfort and the public weal: while by English Laowieng he was perforce accepted as the mentor on every subject, from the colour of puttees to the management of the one great annual social function in the North the "Christmas Meet."

Eric Reid, Spears of Deliverance, pp. 83-84

Stoker Scores a Goal

In Reid's story, the hapless new teak-wallah Stoker proves an unexpected success during his sojourn in the north. An "inter-interest" match is one between different companies or institutions.

As it proved, his stay up-country was the turning point in Stoker's career. For there he came into contact with an autocratic manager who, although imbued with all the ideas of his Bangkok colleagues that had served to render Stoker's life miserable, yet had the sense not to despise and ignore him because he did not know one end of a cricket bat from another, but rather, after his first shock of pained surprise, had the wit to set about cajoling and bullying, persuading and pommelling Stoker into some semblance of that ideal of good sportsmanship to which he and all his class aspired.

The result was that Stoker was compelled to purchase three polo ponies at fabulous price, to practise continuously at that and other games, and to risk life and limb in the endeavour to hit some sort of ball farther and straighter than anyone else present.

Rome was not built in a day and Stoker was not re-formed in a year. But in a year Stoker had done more things than straighten accounts. He had learnt the rudiments of cricket and football, had tramped through jungles and waded in creeks under a hot, hot sun, had learnt to keep his temper when he lost a game and not to wince when a fall or a concussion gave him grievous pain. Of all these good things he began to have a glimmering, but, best of all in the eyes of the jungle-wallahs, after falling off a pony not once or twice but several times, he had actually played in the Christmas meeting, having been given his place through a series of accidents to the proper members of the team. Lastly, he had by some unearthly fluke or other, hit a goal in the game which won the Inter-Interest Cup for his side.

Reid, Checquered Leaves from Siam, pp. 141-142

The Christmas Meet, 1922

The correspondent of The Bangkok Times *(here quite probably W. A. R. Wood) writes about the Christmas meeting of 1922. This was the Meeting that was attended briefly by Somerset Maugham, already a world-famous writer. He seems to have been given a rough time over dinner by the "junior mess", though our correspondent finds more to say about the sporting events. William Alfred Rae [W. A. R.] Wood (1878-1970) was born near Liverpool, the son of a prosperous merchant. He studied at Dulwich College and abroad before joining the Siam Consular Service in 1896. He became Consul at Chiang Mai in 1913, later becoming Consul-General. Wood retired in 1930 and moved back to England but he and his family decided to return to live in Chiang Mai the following year. His* History of Siam *was published in 1926 and was well regarded at the time.* Land of Smiles, *his anecdotal memoir, appeared in 1935 with a second, revised edition in 1968 as* Consul in Paradise. *In later life he was widely known as the "doyen of the foreign community" in Thailand. The* Bangkok Times *was an English-language newspaper that appeared daily from*

Evelyn van Millingen (standing, second left) and other teak-wallahs at the Lampang Club, 1926-1927. Oliver Backhouse.

1886 until the outbreak of the Pacific War. A convenient weekly edition containing the same editorial matter was intended for distribution to the provinces and abroad.

Chiengmai. Jan. 11th.

Our provincial serenity has been delightfully broken during the last few weeks. First we were honoured by a very pleasant official visit from the British Minister, Mr. Greg, who was entertained at dinner by the Viceroy and received the British Community at the Consulate in the course of an afternoon punctuated by boat races, sword dances, Burmese boy dances, and fireworks. The Nawarat Club held a tennis afternoon in his honour. His Excellency has left the pleasantest memories with all those who were privileged to meet him.

A Record Meet

Next the Christmas meet broke upon us with full force. It has been in point of numbers, I believe, a record meet, and has, I hope not fallen behind others in success. And first we are grateful to the ladies who have taken the trouble to come over. Mr. and Mrs. Lyle came up from Bangkok, Mr. and Mrs. MacNaught many days journey from the Salween and from Lakon Mr. and Mrs. Oakden and Mr. and Mrs. Norman. A large contingent came over from the Salween and greatly added to our pleasure. The Borneo Company and Bombay Burmah entertained over forty of us at dinner on Christmas night and one of the most delightful evenings eventuated. Thanks to the presence of ladies, dinner was followed by a dance and thanks to the new enthusiasm for dancing which has flowed out from home dancing was by no means confined to mixed couples.

After dinner on New Year Eve we all congregated at Mrs. Watson's, where dancing and other games of skill were kept up until the gramophone refused its office through sheer fatigue.

The New Year was seen in to the customary ceremony in which some forty-five people must have taken part. Mr. Somerset Maugham the distinguished dramatist was here for a few days, and tho' he has travelled many thousands of miles and seen many wild tribes. I fancy he can have had few more terrifying experiences than being entertained to dinner by one of the junior messes after the Borneo Company-Bombay Burmah polo match. However he came thro' unscathed and with the good wishes of all present.

Bumble Puppy day was the best of fun, and, owing to the excellent and hard work of the Sub-Committee responsible and the splendid paddock steward work of MacNaught, went with a swing and without a hitch. This day was a personal triumph for The Major.

Merry nights and strenuous days have left us a little tired perhaps, but happy with pleasant memories with new friendships and expectations of similar meets in the future. It is suggested this meet is becoming unwieldy and must be split into two. I hope this will be unnecessary. The whole point of this meet is the meeting of old friends and the making of new. If we are separated into our separate districts this falls to the ground. We lose the interest of inter-station and possibly inter-interest in events. It is hardly possible that representative teams could be brought together at any other time of the year, nor is any other time at all suitable for the various games involved.

It is certainly hard luck on jungle men who have little opportunity of playing games in the ordinary course of events to find the course so occupied by matches that they cannot get their games. I fancy, somehow, that there are many opportunities missed that might be taken. By a little management, really keen players can generally secure opportunities even though such opportunities may not occur at the exact moment desired. Judging by the difficulty of getting people up to scratch for matches, I am inclined to be a little sceptical about the number of ordinary games that would be played were there no or fewer matches.

Instead of walking four days over hoof – breaking tracks the Polo ponies came over in their own saloon carriage without accident of any kind. The cost, moreover, was not excessive.

Mr. MacNaught has had to go into hospital for an appendicitis operation and his many friends will be delighted to hear that he is doing especially well. […]

The weather has been perfect. Cold enough to brace without being too bitter, and we have avoided that day or two of rain which so frequently upsets tennis and polo during the meet.

The Bangkok Times, 15 January 1923, p. 8.

Bumble Puppy

The nature of "bumble puppy" has long been disputed, but this report of the 1918 events makes it clear it was a sequence of rather silly games for members of both sexes.

Bumble Puppy: The Bumble Puppy events took place on Saturday afternoon, with the following results:

Bending Race	1 Walton.
Polo Ball Race	1 Weston.
Bicycle Race	1 Norman.
Ladies Egg and	1 Miss Lloyd,
Spoon Race	2 Mrs. Wood.
Victoria Cross Race	1 Mrs. Gardner and Mr. Macleod.
	2 Miss Hatch and Mr. Watson.
Limerick Race	1 Mrs. Price and Mr. Weston.
	2 Mrs. Gardner and Mr. Williams.
Pig driving Race	1 Mrs. Lyle,
	2 Mrs. McDonnell.

In the Victoria Cross race ladies had to throw polo balls at the heads of dummies, which were covered with chatties; as soon as the chatty was broken their respective partners had to mount with the "wounded" dummies and ride off to the winning post. The throwing of the ladies was remarkably accurate and riders had not long to wait before taking their part.

The Limerick race required the men to ride up to their partners and hand over a slip of paper containing a key-word, to wait mounted while the ladies composed a limerick, and to ride back with the limerick; points were given for both the quality of the limerick and the order past the post. The winning limerick was

> There was a young girl of Bagdad
> Fell in love with a horrible cad:
> Her parents said "Jane,
> If you do that again
> We shall think you gone to the bad".

The Bangkok Times, 25 January 1919, p. 24

A Real Alchoholiday

Leigh Williams describes the less savoury aspects of the Meeting. Since he was very probably among the juniors at the dinner with Somerset Maugham in 1922, it is easy to guess what happened on that occasion.

I soon found this Christmas meeting was a wild orgy, an endless "binge," a real "alcoholiday." Most of the men were really abstemious in the jungle, and the reaction after months of loneliness, the excitement of meeting your fellow-men and talking and hearing your own language, went to the head and was expressed in a boundless hospitality that lasted all day and most of the night.

Nobody left the club much before nine o'clock, and formal and informal dinner-parties took place every night. The "burra-sahibs" or managers, most of whom came down to the club in smart little pony-traps with uniformed "sais" on the back seat, were rather inclined to keep to themselves except on big occasions. A party of drunken juniors would turn on the gramophone after dinner and dance with each other for hours. When they were no longer capable of dancing, there would be a "sing-song," most of the songs being unprintable and many of them uncomplimentary to those in authority. One of them parodied a well-known "aria" as follows:

It's the sime the 'ole world over –
Isn't it a bloody shime?
It's the rich wot tikes their pleshers
And the poor wot gits the blime.
See the blasted burra-sahibs
In their gigs' they proudly sit
While the wretched jungle-wallahs
Stumble home through slime and grit.

It was a fact that most of the juniors elected to walk home from the club in the evening, knowing from experience that they were quite incapable of sitting a pony!

Unfortunately for me, I elected to ride Rajah to a dinner-party given by another firm not far away. My arrival was unnoticed, but when the time came to go home a "rugger" scrum was going on in the middle of the lawn, and an ex-Welsh-international scrum-half was just putting the ball (an opera hat) into the scrum. As he caught sight of me trotting past, he yelled, "Here come the bloody Sassenach forwards!" and before I knew what had happened he had collared Rajah low! How the Welshman escaped injury was a miracle, but he hadn't a scratch on him. I was not so lucky. We were both flung to the ground, and as Rajah struggled to his feet one of his hoofs scraped down my shin-bone from knee to instep. A bruise on the shin-bone is painful, but to have the entire shin one long bruise is agony! Needless to say that in spite of my potations I got little sleep that night.

Williams, Green Prison, p. 98

An Unexpected Visitor

In Reginald Campbell's novel, the gigantic (and very angry) elephant Poo Lorn is frustrated by the obstacles erected to stop him attacking the railway line. His thirst for revenge is unsated. He turns toward Lampang where the Christmas Meeting is taking place at the Club complete with a polo match. The cup is to be awarded by a "very high personage" from Bangkok.

A huge marquee had been erected, inside of which were rows of benches. The coveted cup, of brightly polished silver, reposed on a table covered with scarlet cloth and bunting. The remaining table groaned under the choice assortment of sandwiches, cakes and wines that had been prepared for the delectation of the guests after the polo was over. From chairs arranged along the edge of the field the notabilities watched the game in progress. The very high personage wore the uniform of a Siamese general, and his breast glittered with a marvellous array of medals. Next to him were his personal staff, accompanied by their ladies.

Near these sat some of the teak-wallahs not actually engaged in the polo. They were lithe, red-bronzed men, with clean, hard features and alert expressions. A few missionaries and consuls completed the white element of those present, and their wives, conscious of the importance of the occasion, sported the latest Bangkok models in a worthy endeavour to look and be at their best. Parasols of various shades assisted greatly in the process.

Behind the chairs Siamese gendarmes, clothed in khaki and solemnity, kept the mobs of native onlookers from disturbing the peace of the elect. Laos, Burmese, Shans, Indians, Chinese, men and women of every type of face and form elbowed any another to gain a glimpse of (a) the very high personage, (b) the remaining occupants of the chairs, and (c) the polo itself.

The game was waxing fast and furious. The clean click of the stick on the bamboo ball, the thunder of galloping hooves, and the evening sun dreaming over the lush green grass, combined to please both eye and ear.

When Poo Lorn appears, chaos naturally ensues as the elephant tramples the marquee. Class distinctions are forgotten; the "very high personage" and the "fine ladies" mingle with the common people in their escape.

Rice-bowls, cups, champagne bottles, sandwiches and cakes amalgamated into one fearful mess, and the coveted cup was pounded to a shapeless wreck.

Campbell, Poo Lorn of the Elephants, pp. 197-198

Everyone Talked about the Club

Everyone who ever went to Chiengmai talked afterwards about the club. Not about the American Mission, the temple of the Emerald Rice Bowl on Doi Sutep, the leper colony or the old walled city, but about the club and the people who went there. It was quite understandable since it was quite different from any other club. Its almost English setting was beautiful and, had it not been for the rain, the heat and the tropical flowering shrubs, it might indeed have been a bit of England. In the cold season at Christmas time it was as near a bit of "home" as you were ever likely to get. From the moment you entered the gate it was impossible not to realize the years of patient planning that had created it. Its little etiquettes were such that it was like going to school again. There was one evening for "men only", heaven knows why. But in the end even the old hands rebelled against it. There was a small wooden room with covered veranda reserved for men only but none ever sat there except Hillyer who seemed determined to maintain a sort of squatter's right. Heaven help the new boy who hung his clothes on the wrong peg and displayed no interest in huntin', shootin', fishing'. But the old hands were really a kindly tolerant lot and fresh blood was soon accepted.

The solid, teak-built club-house buildings were clustered near the entrance and faced towards the race course which circled the polo ground. But polo was rarely played now and the races were only a memory. But the racecourse rails were always whitewashed and repaired. They seemed to lend an air of distinction. They hey-days of the club were over and the centre of the teak industry had moved to Lampang. The fairways of the eighteen-hole golf course with its pocket handkerchief greens, criss-crossed the polo ground which no bunker must desecrate. It was an interesting little course and the old hands told you proudly how its layout had been submitted to, approved by, and published by *The Field*. Very occasionally someone discovered enough energy to arrange a tournament but, as a rule, it was a friendly stroll round the course with drinks on the match. For the energetic there was squash or tennis.

And when it was all over, we cooled off on the lawn in front of the club house and watched the rays of the setting sun on the magnificent trees on the far side of the golf course. Some would settle down to chatty bridge, some to sterner stuff. Others stayed on the lawn and indulged in local gossip. Someone had been on leave, or was going on leave, and conversation would drift nostalgically to 'home'. But it was not always peaceful. In the hot season, and the rains, tempers could grow short and arguments develop which grew more heated as the bottle went its rounds. Quarrels there were at times, but they were short lived. Sometimes the older generation tend to scoff, forgetting that no generation is as good as your own. But there was rarely any bitterness. If ever a club was the hub of a community, then this was so in Chiengmai. It was fitting that the European cemetery should form part of its grounds.

Exell, Siamese Tapestry, pp. 166-167

Is That What Happens Every Night?

In Alec Waugh's story 'Waters of Babylon', Dorothy wonders what social activities await wives in Pangrai …

"What do they do?"

"Hang about the house. It's too hot to do much else. In the evening they go down to the Club."

"The Club?"

"It's a Sports Club, really. There's a polo ground and golf and tennis, and when it gets dark, we sit in front of the Club House and have drinks."

And as he spoke there rose clearly before him a picture of the Pangrai Club: the long polo ground, the wide-spreading trees, the great clumps of bamboo with their towering plumes; and the little table with the bottles spread out on it, round which they would sit talking when the light had failed, ten to a dozen of them attached to one another by those ties of mutual interdependence and reliance for which there was no counterpart in the self-contained, self-sufficient nature of city life. Very clearly he could see it all, but he could find no words with which to convey the hallowing content of those tranquil evenings. You had to go there to understand.

Otherwise it would be like looking from the outside at a stained-glass window: and he felt unhappy on account of his inability to explain the reality of that content; unhappy, too, on account of the strange puzzled look in the soft brown eyes that were looking up at him. She had sat there silently, taking no part in the conversation, but it seemed to him that in spite of his innumerable letters she was visualising now for the first time the life he was expecting her to share.

"And is that," she said slowly, "what happens every night?"

Waugh, Waters of Babylon, p. 283

The Chiengmai Library

On a front lot in one corner of the Prince Royal's College Campus stands the Chiengmai Library. The library plant belongs to the Library Association but its proximity to the residences and dormitories gives it added protection and reduces the expense of its maintenance.

The library began from a nucleus of some two hundred old paper covered novels, to these have been added several complete libraries donated by private individuals and in addition to these many up to date books have been purchased in England and America.

The English community have liberally contributed to the library not only money but expensive technical books, as well as large numbers of works of fiction and travel. Men resigning their positions in the Laos States or on being transferred to some other country, invariably donate their books to the Chiengmai library. Sometimes in case of death a man's entire library has been bought in and added to the shelves of the Chiengmai library.

The Chiengmai Library as it stands today is really a very creditable collection of books numbering over 4000 volumes of standard works covering almost every department of human knowledge, – Fiction, Literature, Travel, History, Biography, Natural Science, Religion, Medicine, Fine Arts and Useful Arts.

The books are well housed, well arranged, and the rules of the library are such that whether a book is taken to the jungle or the study the reader has ample time to use the book without the dread of embarrassing fines for petty technicalities. It might be said that all the men engaged in the lumber business use the library freely, and even though they are often out in the jungle four and five months at a stretch the books always find their way back to the library in good shape.

The missionaries derive much benefit from the library and take a pardonable pride in its growth and usefulness. We do not know whether the library idea in mission centers is unique or not. We can truthfully commend the enterprise as a splendid means of obtaining a maximum amount of literary benefit for a minimum of financial outlay.

Siam Outlook, July 1912, pp. 84-85

William Harris recalls the foundation of the Library:
There were very few books of a general nature in the Station and no circulating library. When I spoke to Willoughby Wood, manager of a British firm, on the subject in 1899, he replied: "We will support it, if you will run it." Having worked in the College Library in Princeton, I had learned something of library procedure, which now came in handy. Starting with hardly a shelf of books, we had received over 8,000 accessions when we retired. This was very largely due to the generosity of the British businessmen, most of them were great readers, who gave many of their books to the Library when going on leave or retirement. There were never more than thirty members at most in that up-country station so the growth of the Library was satisfactory.

By 1903, we were in need of a building; and, while on leave, I tried to raise funds for a small one. As I was also raising money for the School, I had to limit my appeals for the Library; however, I was given $600.00. This was supplemented by subscriptions in Chiengmai – mainly from the British – and we bought a small lot and built the Library.

I had one experience in raising the funds which amuses me to this day. I told people I was raising a thousand dollars in dollar subscriptions. Some people gave a dollar; and some much more. I called on a rich Scotch gentleman in Princeton who said he would be delighted to give me a dollar; pulling out a big wad of bills he found a dollar and presented me therewith!

Begging money is not all "beer and skittles." But it has its compensations.

As the teak trade was dwindling by the end of the first War and there would be fewer foreigners, thereafter, in the Station, books be given to our school; the school to be responsible for the up-keep; and all fees to be expended in the purchase of books of Prince Royal's College.

William Harris, Recollections, p. 12

Jungle

Green Mantle

The morning grew cold and a mist hung upon the earth. Followed by their baggage elephants and coolies, they would steal quietly along the silent jungle mazes, clothed in white wraiths of mystery. Soon the sun would pierce the mists and set the dew glistening like drips of gold on the quivering leaves. Arrived at the top of a hill, they would pause to admire the view. Beneath them rolls the landscape, but not a patch of land is visible. The ground lies hidden underneath a swelling green mantle of trees. Trees – they had never known there were so many trees in the world. Trees hide the earth from them, hide them, in turn, from the earth, trees make them feel as an aviator does, lost to mankind, with the sky above and the clouds below, only these are clouds of trees.

Campbell, Poo Lorn of the Elephants, p. 121

A Jungle Jamboree
By Allen Bassett

Rev. Allen Bassett was a teacher at the Prince Royal's College from 1920 to 1929.

Northwest Siam is a "district rich in timber, minerals and fertile plains, but cursed by fever, mosquitoes and blood-sucking flies," – shut in by hills on every side, and only open on the northeast where the Kok river leaves it in a series of rapids. The way in leads over hill and down dale. Climbing, tall oak and pine predominate, descending to palm and moss, bamboo and dense jungle – tiger infested, damp – impenetrable without ax and long jungle knife. The crowing of wild cocks never ceasing day nor night as they challenge for combat. Herds of semi-wild water buffalo – turned loose in the long jungle after the plowing season – proved to be the most dangerous of the jungle beasts; for on being the least startled they charge with lowered wicked three-foot horns, that can disembowel a man or beast with a single sweep. Before them the lordly tiger ducks his tail and flees. In this pathless tangle roam sturdy brown-skinned hunters, equipped, sometimes with an ancient flintlock, sometimes with crossbow and arrow; and the inevitable jungle knife which is used for everything from splitting a matchstick to felling a tree. Usually they travel in couples, a young buck straight and wiry, dressed only in loin cloth but tattooed from waist to knee with black dye, which gives him the appearance of wearing tight trousers. His wife is with him, lithe and supple as Diana herself with skirt from waist to knee. At night a few banana leaves spread over bamboo poles serves them for a place to rest. Berries, roots, and their kill serve for food.

Whenever a village was reached a crowd soon gathered to wonder how far beneath our clothes our white skin extended. One day investigation of some tiger growls that we had heard in the night led us to a place where a tiger and water buffalo had met in mortal combat. The ground and undergrowth together with some small trees were torn up over a considerable area but the tiger had gotten in the fatal blow first, so the men feasted upon what was left of the buffalo.

Barking deer encountered almost daily, running and barking in herds, very similar to dog packs; while the night is often made hideous by the yapping of the wild dogs, which run in packs on the trail of a deer which they never leave day nor night until the poor things drops from exhaustion. When the dogs are not heard there is still the scream of the flying fox to split one's ear drums. Overhead bands of monkeys follow the traveler from tree top to tree top, discussing his every action pro and con, and never leaving any abandoned object uninvestigated, but going into hysterics when the large maroon-bodied eagle with white head and tail, volplanes above them. An eye quick enough may detect a streak of black lightning which leaves wild pig tracks in the soft earth. The wild ox is always apparently ready for combat with all comers, and the streams dance with fish begging for a hook.

The Jungle Jamboree is well worth the price of admission collected in swarms of mosquitoes, leeches, blood sucking flies and sweat bees. Cicadas four inches in length almost burst one's ear drums, big jungle ants carry off everything bitable, fire ants raid a termite nest and leave not a single inhabitant to tell the tale. Monster grasshoppers, five and six inches long, looking exactly like fiery steeds from Fairy Land, and giant hornets like yellow tuckers under a microscope, furnish ever changing sights and sounds.

Siam Outlook, January 1928, pp. 231-232

All Life Seemed to be Stirring

By the end of a week's steady, continuous rain the change in Elephant Valley was almost unbelievable. From a harsh, yellow wilderness the valley slopes had turned to an ever-thickening tangle of green. The bare trees shot forth buds with incredible rapidity; creepers, vines, ficus climbed and coiled and twisted and strangled; from the ground dark evergreen leaves and fetid fungus sprouted. Even the air was changed; hot and dry before, it was now dank and steamy and malevolent. The jungle was coming into its own.

Down by the village the Mae Leen widened and deepened with each hour that passed; the sand bars became covered with a swirl of yellow water, and the river took on a new note, a note of quiet but relentless determination. The lazy water buffaloes, that for nine whole months had wallowed in idleness, were now brought out by the villagers to begin ploughing the little stretch of paddy-fields on the left bank of the Mae Leen below the valley's mouth. White egrets, following the wake of the ages-old ploughs for grubs and worms, flashed and swooped and cried. All life seemed to be stirring.

Campbell, The Keepers of Elephant Valley, p. 128

Infinite Charm

After leaving the "sala" we crossed a stream three or four times in quick succession and then began to climb. The hills were covered with woodland and undergrowth, but of a different nature from that which lines the hillsides between Nan and Muang Suat. There the mountain sides and ravines are covered with the densest and most luxuriant jungle growths; on the Chiengmuan hills Nature is not so profuse, but still with her infinite charm scarcely less pleasing to the eye. The jungle was what is termed in the North "pêh," and is in fact very like our English woods with their beech and firs at regular distances, not too close together, and bracken and fern beneath. For a further two hours we continued to climb, and gradually, as we rose above the mists, we were able to see the tops of the smaller hills, which surrounded us on all sides, steeped in the morning sun. The air was wonderfully clear and fragrant, and the mind seemed to be undergoing a sort of spiritual spring-cleaning with every step we took. At the summit, about 3000 feet above the sea-level, the view was unfortunately obscured by the encircling hills and woods, and we caught but the merest glimpse of the plain below. So we did not stop, but went on down the other side, and it took us three hours or more before we finally reached the level again, where the jungle became more dense and where the giant trees were choked and strangled by the creeping growths.

What horrible forms these parasites take, like great serpents twining their bodies round their prey. Striplings and giants were clutched alike in the creepers' coils. No matter how tall the tree, the parasite had reached the top; no matter how young and tender the shoot, the creeper sought to strangle it at birth.

Le May, An Asian Arcady, p. 183

Black Jungle

We were now nearing the sources of Mesong, and were almost continually in evergreen jungle. This is called by the natives "pa dum" – black forest – because it is in perpetual twilight owing to the density of vegetation. The branches of the huge resin or fromager trees and other, dark-leaved varieties meet overhead, the undergrowth is thick with thorny bushes, while giant creepers, many of them covered with spiky thorns, interlace above so that even at midday only a few shafts of sunlight ever penetrate the green gloom. In the north of Thailand this "black jungle" only occurs in patches, but in the central and southern provinces it covers many square miles at a time.

To enter this cool forest after climbing a bare, burnt hillside was at first a great relief. But one is never comfortable for long in the jungle. Every bush is a colony of mosquitoes, and from the dank carpet of rotting leaves underfoot leeches innumerable wave their foul questing heads in our direction. Groves of wild bananas add to the density of shade: the stench of decaying vegetation is overpowering, and we are glad to fight our way out to the sunshine again.

Williams, Green Prison, p. 117

King-Cobra

We'd gone about half a mile along the path when my companion stopped and looked around.

"Chappie seems to have hooked it," said he. He paused, then suddenly pointed triumphantly to a spot almost at our feet. My gaze followed the direction of his finger, and there, barely a yard inside the undergrowth that bordered the path, was an evil head and a long slatey-black body tapering away behind it. And I knew that we were in the presence of the most deadly of all jungle creatures: the great hamadryade, or king-cobra.

Now, a hamadryade differs from all other poisonous snakes in that it is the only one which openly attacks both animals and human beings; a banded krait or a viper or an adder will, or course, bite in self-defence if trodden on or otherwise disturbed, but normally they will slither out of the way on the approach of anything bigger than themselves; the hamadryade, however, rarely retreats and often attacks, and since its bite is certain death in the absence of serum, I realised that I and my companion were in none too pleasant a situation.

"Steady," I whispered to him; "keep your mouth shut and don't move an inch. I'm going to shoot."

I was longing to flash gun to shoulder with all the speed I could command, but I dared not; *it* could move like a flash of greased lightning, and so I was forced to raise my arms with maddening slowness. The cold eyes were staring all the time at my feet, and though they weren't meeting my own eyes they were enough to send a trickle of horror down my spine. I'd once endeavoured to out-stare a small crocodile that had been basking on a sand-bar of the Mae Lome, but there'd been something so utterly *soulless* in the brute's gaze that after a little while I'd had to turn my head away. I'd thought then that that croc's stare must have been about the most ghastly thing imaginable, but I now allowed that this hamadryade was winning handsomely; compared to these cold eyes the croc's had looked like a faithful dog's.

I knew that at any second we might be charged – I gathered afterwards from Algy that, luckily for him, the snake had been a good deal farther inside the forest when it had risen and hissed at him – but I didn't allow my movements to get flustered, and at last I felt the comforting pressure of the butt of the gun against my shoulder, whereupon I fired off both barrels at once. The shock of the discharge knocked me backwards a few paces, and when I'd recovered my balance Algy, looking as cool as a cucumber, was inspecting the remains. The horror's head had been blown clean off, but even then we made it over fourteen feet, and when we walked back to camp we did so in dead silence; a silence which told me that my companion, too, had fully realised the danger through which we had passed.

When we reached our tents he glanced significantly, first at my gun, and then at me.

"Good show," said he.

Two little words. Not much, perhaps, but of a sudden I saw the *real* Algy who only a few minutes gone by had stood, calm and fearless, at my side, and those simple words of praise moved me strangely.

Campbell, Jungle Night, pp. 166-168

The Lord of the Jungle

One incident on our upward journey served to remind us why the tiger is called the "Lord of the Jungle." We saw practically no animal life all day, except in the early morning hordes of chattering monkeys, who filled the air with their babel of noise. Suddenly, far down below me in the ravine, I heard a sound, not a roar, nor a bark, but, as far as I can describe it, like a compressed snarl. Its effect was instantaneous and startling. In a flash the troops of monkeys were still, and there was not a sound in the whole forest except the dew falling on the leaves. After a few minutes' interval the sound was repeated once more, and the deep, dead silence which followed the second command made one realise the power the tiger wields over other forms of jungle life. The old Lao guide who was with me confirmed this out of his own wide experience, and also told me a curious fact about the tiger, which others may corroborate or not; that, when it so wishes, it can imitate faithfully the call of a mother-deer to its young, and occasionally does so at dusk, lying crouched by the side of some forest pool. In this way it will not infrequently catch some young hind or doe that has strayed too far from its mother's side.

Le May, An Asian Arcady, pp. 151-152

A Man-Eating Tiger

On their return from annual meeting in Lakawn, a company of Chieng Mai missionaries camped in a rather lonely spot beside a stream. Nothing disturbed their rest, perhaps because a fire was kept up all night. Only a few nights later, a man was dragged from beside the fire at that very place, and carried off by an enormous tiger. From that time on, for months, that whole district was kept in terror by recurring instances of this tiger's boldness. Not less than twenty persons are said to have been killed, besides many cattle and pigs, by this ferocious beast. Hunts were organized, and traps set, but he always eluded his pursuers. Whether eventually he was killed, or simply left the district, no one knows, but after a time his appearances ceased. The writer has several times seen a tiger's footprints on his travels, but never has seen or heard the monster himself, although several very large tigers have been shot in the district through which he travels.

Freeman, An Oriental Land of the Free, p. 86

Another Tiger Tragedy
By Irene Taylor

The Nan tiger has become rather a joke to those living in civilized cities but to those living where one is liable to be snatched off his front porch any evening it is really not amusing. The farmer must not neglect the strictest vigilance while working in his field even in broad daylight or he may never return to his family in the evening. On January 27th one of our Christian men, Lung Ton, who has, off and on, worked as carpenter for the mission for twenty years, was chopping down trees for a new field about four miles from the city. At noon his fifteen-year-old son and a friend went to a stream to fish and when they returned to him in two hours found only his knife and hat where he had been working with tiger tracks around. They rushed to the city and a party of men went out but arrived too late to see where the tracks led to. The next morning they went back and by that time there was nothing left to be found except absolute proof that the man had been eaten by at least three tigers, a mother and two cubs. Why don't the people get together and clear the country of these beasts that are killing men, women and children every week? In the first place the Buddhist is forbidden to kill any living creature. In the second place these men-eating tigers are not real tigers, but angered spirits which have taken this form in order to get vengeance on their enemies. Killing one would only bring his full wrath to bear upon one self. It takes Christianity to save the heathen both physically and spiritually.

Siam Outlook, April 1929, p. 335

Good Hunting

Miss Minor, of India, tells of a pupil asking her, "How do you like living in the horrid zone?" Our Siam missionaries, too, know the disadvantages of that zone, which are more than its exhausting steaming heat. Mrs. Mason, from the new frontier station of Chieng Rung, writes of young tigers brought to her door for sale, and of an occasional lion killed nearby. Mrs. Palmer writes: "Our 73 Laos and three American boys do not yet seem able to make sufficient noise to frighten away the beasts of the jungle. Two weeks ago a tiger was shot within sight of our compound. He had been hanging about for two days and was a decided menace to the community." Another missionary tells casually of six scorpions in her bathroom in one day. Miss Starling wrote of approaching a village near Nan after dark and of missing the barking of the dogs which usually greeted the traveler. It was explained that there were no dogs in the village, the tigers had eaten them all. She tells, too, of a party of English sportsmen who killed five tigers in six nights. "Good hunting!" as Mowgli remarked.

Woman's Work, November 1919, p. 218

A Month in the Jungle

We travelled with an establishment of nine elephants and forty coolies. The hard work of camping was taken off our shoulders. At quarter to six in the morning we woke to a cup of tea and the sound of packing. While we dressed and breakfasted at our leisure the camp was struck. Our bedding and our food were stacked on elephants and coolies' shoulders. The supervision was in the hands of a head boy. By half-past seven our ponies were waiting for us and our procession was half an hour's march away. Elephants move slowly. Two miles an hour is the maximum. Fourteen miles is a long day's march. Not that you can picture jungle miles in terms of English miles. Along the majority of the roads you could not drag a bullock cart. For the most part you are piloting yourself with the aid of a heavy staff along steep and stony paths or slithering over slippery paddy fields. The streams through which you wade are high above your knees. The average village road is a narrow isthmus of caked mud running between bogs into which you are likely to slide every seven steps. You are caked in mud. You are soaked with sweat. The mornings are few during the autumn when you are not drenched with a heavy downpour of rain. You are very weary by the time you reach, after a seven-hour march, the compound on the stream by which you are to spend the night. You sit forward on a log, limp and motionless, while the coolies cut away a clearing in the bush and your boys run up your tent and your cook prepares your tiffin. You are too tired to talk over your meal, and the moment it is over you fling yourself upon your bed. In a couple of minutes you are asleep.

The country through which you travel is varied.

The word "jungle" evokes a picture of tangled undergrowth, of scarlet macaws, of monkeys screaming to each other from every bough, of large many-coloured butterflies, of snakes and bears and natives shooting at you from behind hills with blowpipes. It may be that in South America that is what it is. But in Siam it is a friendly landscape. There are cobras, it is true, but you rarely meet them. I only saw a couple of small snakes, neither of which was poisonous probably. You will hear the screech of monkeys, but they remain invisible. Though you will come upon the tracks of a bear, the bear is an animal that must be hunted. And though the foliage is in places overpoweringly luxuriant, the country is for the most part open. The flat land is planted with rice, and the undergrowth is inconsiderable in the actual forests.

Waugh, The Coloured Countries, pp. 143-145

"Entrance to 'Ngoke' where [the] river disappears into the mountain", in an area leased to the BBTC. Photograph by Tanaka, November 1918. Oliver Backhouse.

Mountains

The Charm of the Hills

2,300 feet above sea level.

In early 1914, the correspondent of The Bangkok Times *finds that work on the railway tunnel at Khun Tan has not marred the beauty of the surrounding hill country.*

Kuntan, Jan 29th.

A week ago we said goodbye to railway engines and construction trains, to travel on foot, or astride the sure footed and wiry ponies found in this part of the country. Those who know the roads of the north will agree that these tortuous and rough tracks up hill and down – often existing only in river beds – which in the main serve for roads in Monthon Bayap, are not the most inviting for a beginner to take lessons in riding on. But the assurance had been given that our animals were quiet and despite misgivings the journey was commenced. Our Chinese boy had been bewailing the sad fate that condemned him to wander in the Lao country at Chinese New Year. Where, he enquired with a touch of asperity, was he to *Wai Chao!* It needed some supervision to drag him from the comfortable quarters of compatriots at Pak Tar, where the Chinese were preparing to celebrate *kruit chin.* Once on the way, however, other and more pressing problems came up for his immediate consideration, and we did not hear much more about the great festival until Lampang was reached. A Lao boy, with a reputation for gallantry through the countryside and able to ride anything, took our man in hand, teaching him in a rough and ready manner how to sit a horse. The way took us along a winding riding path cut in the side of the hill for some miles, and the sun was well down before we reached the first camp, situated in an open place in the forest and beside a small stream. The carriers and servants had been in some time, and the former, squatting round in small groups before cheerful looking fires, were busy preparing their evening meals. Dinner in the forest can be as well arranged as in Bangkok, we found, and there was an added attraction of novelty and a healthy appetite, wholly uninduced by short drinks.

The carrier not only carries one's luggage, but like the coach drivers of old days home he conveys news from place to place. Within a short time of our arrival people had come in from huts in the forest to hear the latest happenings from other places. Fresh wood was thrown on the fires, and it was far into the night before the laughing and talking quieted down and the carriers lay down to sleep by their fires. Before daylight they were awake again, and long before the first rays of the morning sun had penetrated to the valley we were off.

Travelling at this time of the year, one sees the forests at their best. In a month or little more the trees except the evergreen patches will be leafless, jungle fires an everyday occurrence, and the heat intense. Then travelling is the reverse of pleasurable, carriers and water alike hard to find and no one sets out on a journey unless compelled to. Now the trees are in their full autumn glory. The path from Pang Buei to Koon Tan provides one long series of changing landscape views. For half an hour or more maybe the trail passes along a valley with rising hills on each side. Here it is deliciously cool. And on you start climbing and, reaching the top of the hill, find stretched out before you a seemingly endless forest, varying in height according to the contour of the land, and bounded in the far horizon by still higher hills. Leaving Meh Mok one climbs steadily for some time to the edge of a plateau extending for some miles. Looking backward furnishes a magnificent view. Ridge after ridge of hills stretch right across the country as far as the eye can see, the farthest range being a blurred mass of dull blue. In the valley beneath, substantially built teak sala appears absurdly small, and a band of silver in the shape of a mountain stream passes between banks of dazzling white sand. Ahead is Lampang. The plateau crossed, the road again begins to ascend, and at the highest point the first glimpse is obtained of the old city nestling in the plain below. The path passes in and out until one is about a mile from the town. Then the red bricks of the city wall stretch out to the right and left in a long straight line and immediately ahead is a large gap once occupied by the city gate.

The majority of dwellers in the rolling plains of the Maenam Valley have no idea of the glories of these northern lands. This article is being written on the verandah of a house which is 2,300 feet above sea level. It is built on a small ridge from which the land falls sheer for several hundred feet, and then gradually drops away to the valley of the Meh Tar over a thousand feet below. The high hills on the skyline form the last obstacle in the way of reaching Chiengmai. Westward Doi Bah has to be climbed and descended when one goes within reasonable distance of Lumpoon. On the east from a hill 3,800 feet high Doi Suthep can be easily discerned, and on a clear day Chiengmai stands forth. At the top of this mountain, access to which entails little trouble beyond that involved in climbing, one finds further to the east a taller neighbour in Doi Dap Chang, some 4,400 feet high.

So far, the railway works in progress hereabouts have not spoilt the landscape, and are not likely to. Work in the tunnel goes on night and day, but outwardly one notices little. Some of the small foothills are being cut into but from this height the view remains unspoilt.

In the morning a biting wind stimulates everyone to unwanted activity. Even at midday when cut off from the sun warm clothes are comforting. The forests are a never-ending source of pleasure. The red and brown of the dying leaves stand out vividly and in broad splashes of colour against the prevailing green. Owing to the position the glories of the dawn are denied to the workers here. Likewise the beauty of full sunset and the golden red afterglow one sometimes witnesses in the flatter south are missing. But as the sun is vanishing over the hill tops the air becomes wonderfully clear, and what the midday has concealed from view is now made plain. The rising smoke from a hundred small huts in the valley below tells of preparation for the evening meal, the sound of a mellow gong the signal for ceasing work, conveys its welcome message to the workers. The night has arrived and the stars in the now steel blue sky and the twinkling light from the houses in the valley far below seemingly come into being at the same time.

The Van Millingen family relaxes at their bungalow on Doi Suthep, 1933.
Oliver Backhouse.

On Tip Top

Bertha Blount McFarland came to Siam in 1908 and married George Bradley McFarland (1866-1942), a distinguished physician in Bangkok. Her memoir Our Garden was So Fair: The Story of a Mission in Thailand contains an account of their visit to Chiang Mai.

Doi Sutep is the 3,500-foot mountain at the foot of which lies the old northern capital, Chiengmai. We were carried up in chairs, being tenderfoots from the lowlands. Tough Chiengmai-landers boast of the short time it takes them to make the climb. About halfway to the top is the peak that bears the name Doi Sutep. A little temple nestles on the hillside. Nearby is the summer palace of Chao Dara, the Laos princess who became the wife of King Chulalongkorn. Her rose garden was one of the wonders of the Thailand world. At the temple and rose garden we stopped for a little breathing spell to give our carriers a rest, and to enjoy the roses. Then on we pressed, until the air grew rarer and we felt the change in atmosphere. On Tip Top we were in the temperate zone; the torrid zone lay down in Chiengmai. On the mountain top the sun loses its fiery character and one can go about bareheaded without fear. Even flora and fauna are different; pines grow easily. There we were on the top of the world and could look down in all directions and far off to the farther and higher mountain peaks.

McFarland: Our Garden was So Fair, pp. 89-90

My Mountain

Mary Lou O'Brien celebrates the beauties of Doi Suthep in this poem published in 1928.

My mountain has a wardrobe filled with frocks of varied hues,
And loves to change from gown, to gown, from dark greens into blues.
I think she tries to charm the sun, with all her garments fine,
And when she is successful you should see how he will shine.

She may be very moody, and I think she is quite vain,
In one frock or one color she will not for long remain.
She makes me rather dizzy, for I try to see them all -
Her garments for the summer, and her colors for the fall.

I can't decide which I like best, the purple, blue, or green
I seem, like her, to change my mind when each new frock I've seen.
She sometimes wears a mist of white, so gossamer and frail.
I think that she is playing bride in someone's wedding veil.
Of all her little vanities this is the worst by far,
At night she pins into her hair a shining, golden star,
Then she forgets the sun, this fickle one, and all too soon,
Begins to weave a spell about the old man in the moon.

I long to paint her portrait, but I know it would not do,
For she would want to change her gown before I quite got through.
Then, too, how could I find such blues, and sunshine-mottled green,
And color of a dew-drop with its cool and sparkling sheen?

My mountain is not young, I know, she's very cold, indeed,
And from such tricks of vanity her old age should be freed.
And yet the sun and moon are surely old enough to know
My fickle little mountain has a heart as cold as snow.

Siam Outlook, July 1928, p. 335

Visions of Beauty

Lucy Starling enjoys some respite from the heat of Chiang Mai on the mountain …

Here I am on the mountain, having the time of my life and getting fat.

I love to sit on my porch in the late afternoon, and watch the green rice plains below while the pink and blue on the mountains beyond fade into deep violet, and the stars come out one by one. Nor is it less beautiful in the morning. Then the trees in the plain look like regiments of soldiers, while the clouds above envelop them like the white smoke of a battlefield. Every hour of the day has a beauty of its own, every moment is a joy.

Tonight we killed an enormous scorpion while out walking. They sting with their tails and their sting is very dangerous, though I believe not fatal. When the men were bringing me up on Monday, they threw at a snake on our path, the first I have seen up here. If there were many, I wouldn't be quite so enthusiastic about this place.

This morning while taking a walk, I heard a great clattering and noise in the ravine, and creeping up, found the trees alive with monkeys. I sat down and kept very quiet, and watched them at play. One little fellow sitting

The wall at Chiang Mai, looking towards the west from Suan Prung Gate to the Khu Ruang Corner. Doi Pui in the background. Photograph by Tanaka. Oliver Backhouse.

between the forks of a high limb, watched me with as much interest as I did him. He would squat on his haunches, put his hands on his knees, and peer at me anxiously, as if to say "What is that anyhow?" I kept perfectly still, while he would go from one limb to the other, and view me from every angle. I saw quite a dozen in the trees, and there were more to which I could not approach near enough to observe. Before this I have not seen more than two or three monkeys, all the time I have been in Siam.

23 November 1910

I reluctantly leave here to-morrow afternoon. Annual meeting does not begin until Friday, but some of the guests will probably arrive tomorrow.

I sat on the steps this afternoon and looked over the yellow rice plains below, broken clumps of trees here and there, behind were the nets, a deep violet in the fading sunlight, about the sky was a blue gray, merging gradually into a deep pink. Here and there a cloud floated, like an enormous sea-shell, and as the colors gradually faded and the mountains were veiled in mist, a single star came out, to watch all night over the plain below.

This week God has revealed to me such visions of beauty as I have never seen before. The mountains wrapped in clouds of fleecy white at sun-rise, and violet robes at twilight, views of vast stretches of country, from various peaks, the grandeur of forest and waterfall, the ferns and flowers – how can I describe them? The words of the Psalmist continually rise to my lips, "The heavens declare the glory of God, and the firmament showeth His handiwork."

Miss Buck came up for over Sunday, and after a service for the natives, we took the watchman, and two girls, a lunch and books, and went to the woods for the rest of the day. After going downhill for nearly an hour, we came to, I believe, the most beautiful waterfall I have ever seen. Niagara, from its size, has more grandeur, but for delicate, fairy-like beauty and grace, I have never seen the equal of this. I went over this morning with my camera, and sat for three hours, trying to get a picture. But the sun was contrary, and the trees were thick and I couldn't get a good light on it. I finally took a "snap shot," but I do not hope much from it.

There is one peak, from which one gets a particularly imposing view of the opposite mountains. Across a ravine, it rifts like a huge amphitheater; it is entirely covered with trees, and against the unbroken mass of dark, dark green, gleam the white tree trunks, rising as straight and gracefully as palms, with no branches except at the very top. They look like the pipes of a giant organ. The amphitheater seems to close around one, as if to swallow one up in its vastness; you could easily imagine it peopled with giants, who use trees for clubs and boulders for ten pins.

One morning, in a venturesome mood, I climbed down the hill-side, into the ravine, to investigate the falls, the noise of whose waters reached me far above. I could not find a path, and had a desperate struggle getting through the bamboo thicket, the sunlight only peering through the vines and trees at rare intervals, and when I reached the bottom, I saw the water madly rushing down the rocks, like a huge, writhing serpent. On

"Going up the hill to the rest house". Oliver Backhouse.

the opposite side were black holes in the undergrowth, but whether rocks were there, or only trees, it was too dark to see. The roar of the water was deafening, and to tell the truth I shouldn't have been much surprised if a fiery dragon or a hydra-headed serpent had come out of one of those black holes. Well, I didn't stay there long to enjoy the scenery, but clambered up the hill again, into the sunlight, as fast as my legs would carry me.

Yesterday, as we wandered down the brook, we came to a very picturesque cave, high up in the rocks. The top was covered with a soft, fringy fern, making a ceiling of deep green. On the floor of the cave was a huge pile of rocks that had been smoothed and plastered on top, a priest's tomb. Directly above were some pictures in gilt, one of a reclining Buddha, another of Buddha standing, with a worshipper on either side. One could never want a more imposing or quieter resting place than this. As we crossed the stream to return home, we looked back for a last view, and as we did so, a group of priests in their yellow robes approached the tomb, and stood looking up at it, making a weird and most impressive picture. Siam only needs a poet to sing its beauties to make it world famous.

Dr. Campbell was up for a day last week, and gave me a final examination of my year's language work, so that is off my mind.

30 November 1910

Clouds Come in and Sit on Your Chair

Dr Cort is staying at Prince Bovoradej's house on Doi Suthep. The letter is hand-written and some of the words as transcribed here are "best guesses". The house still exists, though it is not open to the public. Trees now obscure the views over the city and the plain.

We are staying in the Viceroy's house 300 feet above sea level. It is a very comfortable place indeed. I am writing at his desk in the office – a room open on three sides and screened in – can be closed in by doors in case of storms. Back of this is a sort of dressing room & then bathrooms on one side of a little hall & toilet on other, then a comfortable bed room. Then to the north a big open dining & living room etc opened entirely on all four sides, with folding doors and a wide veranda around it.

Clouds sitting on Doi Suthep in the rainy season. The Editor.

It is well furnished and we are very luxurious. In addition there is a phone so I am connected with my work in a way and can keep in touch. So far this morning I have had four calls from the hospital in regard to cases.

From here you get a glorious view of the whole of Chiengmai plain and at this season of the year it is beautiful beyond words with its marvellous colorings – constantly changing and the miles and miles of river, plains, woods, & rice land, & the purple hills beyond.

It is the rainy season as you know and we are afraid it might be very damp and nasty. Sometimes clouds come in and sit on your chairs and loaf round on your table and even want to go to bed with you – they are like fogs only damper lots damper – and everything in the place drips, water trickles down the walls and you wring it out of your clothes. So far it has rained much of the time since we came up – this is the 2nd day & it rained all night last night. The clouds have been high.

1 September 1918

Six months later, the Corts are staying at Buak Ha, Arthur Queripel's house on Doi Suthep. This was dismantled during the Pacific War.

The house has two bedrooms with splash bath room attached on each side of a central dining room which extends out front into a comfortable porch. The house is furnished so all we had to bring was our food, clothing & blankets. We both are quite all right again & will walk down. This morning we went exploring, following the path past the spring where we get our water which is about 1/8 of a mile from the house. We found a fairly well beaten path heading around the shoulder of the slope and followed it for about half a mile or more & came to a beautiful deep ravine filled with giant trees, so cool & green where everywhere else things were bone dry. It has not rained here since October & practically none since September.

We found a delightful little run at the bottom, with ferns etc growing everywhere. After a cool drink we climbed up the steep side beyond. Then the path wound up along the shoulder of another slope. There had it been clear we should have had a glorious view down into the deep valley, with range after range of mountains piling away to the horizon beyond, but it is so smoky & dusty that we could just vaguely make out the forms in the valley & first mountain range beyond. Then along a practically level path shoulder after shoulder & along a hug-back with which we came to another ravine. We went down among the tall trees into delightful coolness, had a good drink from a leaf & then explored beyond for some distance. The wood we had passed through was fairly burnt & trees rather far apart, no undergrowth & the dry grass had been burnt over. But beyond this second run we went into a beautiful forest of tall trees with green undergrowth everywhere & great creepers hanging to the trees [...] As Mabel was getting tired we soon decided to come back. After recrossing this second run we followed down a hug back a little way looking for a site for a house. We plan to build a permanent house & while we shall probably build at "Tip top" where we spent some time two years ago, we are still on the look-out for a possibly better site. This led down to a grove of tall pines over a splendid promontory overlooking the valley.

11 March 1919

Mr. Queripel has a beautiful rose garden up here, great red beauties that look like American beauties – yellows, deep and a lighter shade, salmon pink, lovely pink and white – bush after bush about one hundred and all blooming their heads off.

26 June 1920

Tropical Flowers

The delicate spring flowers that are the charm of the American forest are hardly matched in the tropics. The so-called "ground orchids," that abound on the mountains in April, are nearest to them. The real orchids are mainly air plants and bloom in the clefts of tall forest trees. Just at the close of the dry season, whole forests of flowering trees blaze out in gorgeous red and yellow and pink. Many of these, as well as the more modest acacias, tamarinds and "fool beans," belong to the pea family which predominates among the flowers of Siam. Earlier in the season, thickets of certain compositæ make great masses of purple, of dull red, and of yellow, beside the path. However, flowers are sought by the Laos maidens, not for their color, but for their fragrance. The "jewel-tree" furnishes its delicate greenish flowers for their wreaths almost throughout the year. Tuberoses, golden acacias, jasmine and roses, are among the favorites. The young man is more apt to choose flowers of brilliant color, and places over his ear a sprig of "peacock-flower," or a brilliant-hued orchid.

Freeman, An Oriental Land of the Free, p. 82

Roses

The first cultivated roses must have been introduced a very long time ago, but in only a few kinds. In the seventeenth century they were apparently rare, as la Loubère tells us that he saw no roses, though he was told there were a few. The late Mrs. McGilvary of Chiengmai introduced, some fifty years ago, a number of varieties, such as Marechal Niel, Gold of Ophir and Gloire de Dijon. More recently other varieties have been introduced by Mr. A. L. Queripel and others.

Kerr, 'Notes on Introduced Plants in Siam', p. 210

A rose at Bhuping Palace, near the location of Arthur Queripel's former house Buak Ha. The Editor.

How Little they Dream of Siam, who only Bangkok Know

Le May visited Emil Eisenhofer (here identified as only "the Chief Engineer")
at the Khun Tan railway tunnel workings in 1913 ...

The Chief Engineer's house was built among the pines on the crest of a hill, about two thousand feet above the sea. Six hundred feet below, almost sheer down, was the cutting and the entrance to the tunnel, the yellow earth dazzling in the midday sun making a vivid contrast with the green foliage all around; and, as I watched, I could see the Lao coolies at work digging earth for embankments, like ants crawling on the face of a rock. On either side of the house the hills sloped gradually down from far above until, beyond the cutting, they almost met, yet did not interfere with the view of the broad plain beyond. They actually helped to focus the scene, for the eyes could not wander, and one seemed to be looking as through a telescope. On the plain could be seen the rice fields ripening to harvest, a sea of brilliant yellow-green, and beyond them again a long range of hills, stretching the length of the view, and standing sentinel over the country's treasure. A complete picture in itself; and above in the cool, clear air, one could gaze and think how little they dream of Siam, who only Bangkok know.

Le May, An Asian Arcady, p. 149

The Murder of a Teak-Wallah,
December 1910

On 8 December 1910, Evan Patrick Miller, the thirty-three year-old forest manager at Chiang Mai for the Bombay Burmah Trading Corporation, was shot and killed by "dacoits" (bandits) in the forest quite far from Chiang Mai. His colleague E. W. Hutchinson was severely wounded. The news was first reported in The Bangkok Times *on 12 December 1910, and reports were later carried by newspapers around the world. In January 1911,* Laos News *reported that "Mr. Miller was a man respected and loved, his wife is the intimate friend of our mission ladies both in Lakawn and Chiengmai. Our sorrow and sympathy go out to her in her bereavement". The story of the murder was later re-imagined by Eric Reid, who had been Acting Vice-Consul at Chiang Mai in 1910, for his 1920 novel* Spears of Deliverance. *Miller becomes "Morland" and Hutchinson "Philip Harkness", the protagonist of the novel, but otherwise Reid follows the account of events as printed in the newspaper quite closely. The missionary teacher Lucy Starling wrote about the murder and its aftermath in Chiang Mai in her letters home. Miller is buried in Chiang Mai's Foreign Cemetery (Grave D16). His widow, Daisy Laura Miller, gave birth to their second child at Chiang Mai in February 1911. She remarried in England in 1915. The dacoits were eventually killed or captured by the Gendarmerie.*

****

E. P. Miller and his grave at Chiang Mai's Foreign Cemetery. The Editor (photograph at right).

Dacoits Kill Bombay Burmah Man

A startling and tragic affair is reported from up country. On the 8th inst., Mr. E. P. Miller and Mr. E. Hutchinson, of the Bombay Burma Trading Corporation's Chiengmai staff were travelling with specie in the Mohat Forest, about 30 miles from Muang Tern, when they were attacked by dacoits.

Mr. Miller was shot dead and Mr. Hutchinson was wounded in the arm, the robbers getting off unhurt with the money.

A telegram was dispatched from Muang Tern to the Bangkok Office of the Corporation on the 9th and was received here on the following day, Saturday.

No further details have been received up to the present.

Mr. Miller, who had been in the service of the Corporation for twelve or thirteen years, was a married man with one child. Mr. Hutchinson had been in Siam for about half that time.

The Bangkok Times, 12 December 1910, p. 4

****

The late Mr. Miller. Authentic Details of the Murder

Yesterday's mail from Chiengmai brought us our first detailed account of the late dacoity upcountry. Messrs. Miller and Hutchinson were encamped on the bank of the Me Haht stream. Just before 8.30 on the evening of the 8th instant, they were sitting after dinner in the tent verandah, Mr. Miller by the entrance, Mr. Hutchinson farther in at the other side of the table which was placed between the two men. The latter heard three sharp reports, on the third of which Mr. Miller sank forward in his chair, struck by a bullet in the throat, which, subsequent medical examination has shown, must have caused death instantaneously or within a few seconds. Mr. Hutchinson jumping up, was struck by a bullet in the left arm above the elbow, and a rapid succession of shots followed, hitting various objects on the table including the lamp, but doing no more serious damage. Mr. Hutchinson after examining Mr. Miller promptly ran to the servants' quarters to summon help for Mr. Miller, in case there was any hope, but the latter was already beyond mortal assistance.

Of the assailants Mr. Hutchinson was in the darkness only able to make out a few blurred forms. These had in the two or three minutes which elapsed between his departure and his return to the tent made good their retreat, without however succeeding in removing any of the specie in Mr. Hutchison's or Mr. Miller's charge. Mr. Hutchinson took prompt measures to secure his camp against further attack, and to notify the nearest officials. He was able to cut the bullet out of his arm, and the wound is reported not serious. He had, it is evident, a marvellously lucky escape, considering the number of bullets which struck objects on the table and at a small distance off, and also in view of the fact that the arm in which he did receive the bullet, served to ward off the latter from the neighbourhood of the heart. Being lit up both by the light of the lamp on the table at which he was sitting and by that of the camp fire outside, Mr. Miller's form must have afforded a perfect target to the assailants, whose own figures would of course be correspondingly obscure.

Mr. Ryan of the Forest Department, who was in the neighbouring forest, immediately joined Mr. Hutchinson on hearing the news, arriving on the day following the outrage. He very kindly escorted the remains into Chiengmai, and the funeral service was held with all due solemnities on the 14th instant.

The Bangkok Times, 20 December 1910, p. 5; reprinted in
The Straits Times, 10 January, 1911

****

Dacoity

There was a sharp report!

Harkness looked towards the fire. For a moment he thought it must be the sound of a bamboo amongst the firewood, bursting with the sharp and curious explosion familiar to all jungle men.

Then a queer sound came from Morland, and as Philip turned, the head of the man at his side fell forward on his chest.

"I say!" Harkness jumped to his feet. "What – "

Morland's hand moved feebly upwards towards his throat. The night air was rent by a perfect fusillade, reports unmistakably of revolver shots.

Crash! The lamp on the table was hit and overturned.

In the darkness and confusion after it was extinguished Philip knocked his knee against the table. Strange to say, he was more conscious then of the pain from the bump thus caused than of the bullet wound received in his arm at the moment he rose to go to Morland's assistance.

"Oh, damn!" he cried, making a bewildered effort to lift the other's head and ascertain how badly he was wounded.

The shooting ceased.

Philip peered through the flame of the fire into the gloom beyond, and thought he could just make out a couple of figures flitting amongst the trees to the left of the tent.

He ran into the tent for his revolver and then stopped, suddenly recollecting that it was out of repair. As for Morland, he was a man who never carried weapons.

He thought he heard whispering quite near.

A hand or a branch clawed against the back of the tent. Harkness bethought himself of assistance. He lifted up his voice and shouted for his servant. There was no reply.

The whispering continued.

"Must get a light anyhow," he muttered, and he started off running towards the creek.

"Some water, too, for Morland!" he gasped as he stumbled on.

He was just in time to see the last of the panic-stricken camp servants disappearing up the other bank of the stream where they had been fishing.

"Good God! The brutes are bolting!"

He ran panting along the bank a little way, and then paused irresolute.

"This won't do," he told himself; "must get back to Morland."

Harkness must have fainted for a few minutes.

When he came round again he was lying on the ground, and his dead companion had fallen forward on his face again. He picked himself up. The excruciating pain in his left arm caused him fresh agony.

He pulled up his sleeve, and had a look. Above the elbow was a great clot of congealed blood. This he managed to wash away and the bleeding started again.

A whisky bottle lay where it had fallen undamaged when Philip had knocked against the table. He pulled the cork, and took a long straight draught of raw spirit.

He felt better and had another look at his arm.

"The bullet must be in there," he concluded, and he ran his other hand over the flesh and felt a hard protuberance on the underside.

His brain began to act clearly.

"My God!" he muttered. "Another couple of inches, and that would have been my heart!"

He remembered now! Just at the psychological instant when he had first risen to go to Morland's aid as the latter fell, his arm had been raised across his body covering his heart. The bullet was a small one, and it had evidently been deflected by the bone.

He paused with a sense of shame that he could think of his own trifling wound before ministering to the parlous state of his comrade. He did not know yet whether Morland was beyond all aid. But a look convinced him.

The face was setting in a ghastly hue, and on the skin's pallor great globules of perspiration stood out horribly. The body was already colder than normal.

Their first shot had killed Morland.

The brutes! Firing point blank from behind the shelter of the tent at the perfect target offered by the figures silhouetted against the fire and the lamp light.

As for the ensuing shots, of which Philip could now remember hearing at least half a dozen, some of them had hit the lamp, one had smashed a glass and another had come miraculously near cutting short the span of his own life.

Philip fell to piecing out the happenings of the last half hour, his mind working quickly and excitedly. He noticed that the tent was in some disarray.

He fetched the lamp and examined the interior. The chests of money, chained as usual in the jungle to the camp bed, had been dragged out to the full length of their fastenings. Apparently someone had been interrupted in the attempt to carry them off.

That much he noticed with a grim satisfaction, and then of a sudden a chill fear went over him. He went out and sat down to think as clearly and as decisively as he could.

Obviously they had been attacked by dacoits who had known of the money Morland possessed in his tent. Bold and desperate men they must be, for in all such robberies so far as Harkness had heard blood had never been shed for the sake of loot. Occasionally, if the marauders found themselves confronted by zealous guardians of a caravan's treasure, murder had been committed, but never had Europeans been attacked in this fashion before.

And then those gashes on Morland's face and neck.

Philip saw the reason now. It was when he had run down to the creek for assistance that the dacoits had rushed into the tent. There, apparently, they had found the chests of money too secure to carry off and, hearing the Englishman return with assistance as they thought, they had decamped, slashing (in the foul rage of their foiled disappointment) at the prone figure in their path as they fled from Philip's approach.

Something stirred.

Harkness jumped to his feet in a tremor of nerves.

"Damn you, you brutes!" he cried. "I suppose you are coming to finish me off next."

In sober truth a fresh attack might come at any moment. The situation might have appalled the bravest. Philip was alone, for it was certain their servants had bolted at the first shot fired. He was wounded and, save for a revolver out of repair, unarmed.

Worst of all, he was still seated in the full light of the lamp and the fire which had illuminated the dacoits' first target. How numerous they were he could not tell. He put the lamp out, and replenishing the fire, went to see if he could find any weapon in the servants' quarters. He was fortunate enough to come across an ancient fowling-piece and a Lao dah (short sword).

He stumbled over his dog lying some distance from the fire. Dead too, poor brute, he thought.

This left him quite alone!

With something like a sob he seated himself in the shadow. The native sword across his knees, and his ears and eyes straining to catch the slightest sound or movement, he prepared to pass the night watching. . . . Watching!

Followed a long vigil, a nightmare that Harkness never forgot in after life. His head dropping with exhaustion caused by loss of blood and his eyes closing always in weariness, he sat there with the dah across his knees sat and waited, every instant expectant that the crackling fusillade of Brownings would be renewed.

Once he got up, and searched in the medicine chest for a small lancet. Then, in the uncertain light of the fire's flicker he set to work on his arm.

By dint of slicing at the fleshy underpart he was able to extract the bullet. It was a small one and he placed it with whimsical care in the lid of the medicine chest. For future reference, he told himself, as he adjusted a rough bandage with some disinfectant over the wound.

Once a bamboo burst in the fire.

He started up. He had been almost asleep. Minutes dripped away into oblivion, and through his drowsy brain the hideous phantasmagoria bred of his terrible situation went careering madly. Along the corridors of memory there came and went the haunting dread of Death's legions. . . .

And once a cold, friendly muzzle was thrust into his hand. He looked down to find that it was his dog that had crept up beside him. Philip tried to remember, to account for its presence after having previously found it lying apparently dead.

It was piteously ill. It must have been given some poisoned meat which had just failed to kill it. It whimpered for sympathy. . .

But nothing could wake him for any length of time. Presently the dah dropped to the ground. His head went down on his knees as Night ran paling up the sky before the beams of Dawn.

Reid, Spears of Deliverance, pp. 110-115

****

A Death and a Christening

Lucy Starling writes home.

15 December 1910:

I suppose before this reaches you, you will have seen through the papers of the sad death of Mr. Miller. He was head man of the "Bombay Burmah Company," engaged in the teak business. He and Mr. Hutchinson were seated at the table last Thursday evening, when several shots were fired into their tent. At the first, Mr. Miller fell over dead, and Mr. H. went to his assistance, when another shot went through his left arm, just above the elbow, close to his heart. They had over a thousand dollars with them, and it is suspected an old employee, who had recently been discharged for embezzlement, knew this, and was responsible for the attack, with the purpose of robbery. We do not certainly know this, however. The officials of the province refused to do a thing to aid in the search, and it is supposed they knew something about it. Four pistols like the one that caused the death of Mr. M. have been found. Mrs. Miller was at our supper Friday night, and did not get the news until Saturday afternoon. The body did not arrive until Wednesday morning, as it had to be carried up river some distance, and then across country by the natives. Mr. H. is being brought in, and will probably get here today. Dr. Mason started out last night to meet the party. The circumstances are doubly sad, because Mrs. Miller is expecting a new baby early in Feb. But I have never seen anything like the way she is keeping up. She is making her plans to go home in March. I am sure that one great consolation to her will be the fact that she is going home to her little boy, whom she left in England a year ago, when he was only two and a half years old. I have often thought her love for him to be the only deep passion of her life. She is a refined lovely little woman, and we shall miss her very much.

25 January 1911:

I wrote you some time ago about the murder of Mr. Miller in the jungle. Well, one of the men who was caught has confessed, and says he was hired for about $700 to do it. He implicates three other men. In fact, it was seen that there were four men outside the tent. The motive was revenge, by a discharged employee.

16 March 1911:
Last Friday afternoon. Mrs. Miller had her baby christened, and Mrs. Kerr was at home afterwards, to give people a chance to tell her good-bye. Dr. McGilvary christened the baby, and it was a most painful ceremony. Mrs. Kerr was holding him, when the time came, she put him in Dr. M's. arms. But the old man is easily confused, and asked her to change the baby, which she did. This put the baby on his right arm, and when he went to reach for the water, he could not let go the baby. He tried to put his left arm under the baby, so his hand would support its head, but he could barely reach its head with the tips of his fingers. He began to tremble, and made a grab for the baptismal bowl three times, and spilled water all over the floor, but didn't get enough on his hands to baptize the baby. After each attempt, he would have to grab the baby, to keep it from falling out of his arms. The infant began to cry, and I don't wonder, and everybody was strung up to the highest pitch until it was over with. I felt very sorry for poor Mrs. Miller. She said, "Oh. I do hate to leave Chieng Mai," but it seems to me that there is very little in the lives of English women here to make it pleasant. We shall miss her very much, but there was "a balm in Gilead" for me in the fact that she took Winsie along. I don't think I would last a year, with that child around.

Crime in the North

Utopia in Miniature

According to Leigh Williams, violent crime was in fact rather rare in the north.
Unlike banditry in China, dacoity and river-piracy in Thailand are in the nature of an off-season's recreation rather than a full-time job. For this reason, except in the rare years of local crop failure, crimes of violence are not so serious or so widespread, but more difficult to bring to book. During the rainy season, everyone works in the rice-fields. In the hot weather, the Laos up-country go hunting or collecting jungle produce. Down-country, which means anywhere south of Raheng or Sawankalok, the more adventurous spirits vary these pursuits with a little gangsterism.

Williams, Green Prison, p. 45

With every day's march away from the large towns, the people are more primitive and more unspoilt. Many of these remote villages are a Utopia in miniature. Crime is unknown, and judging from the happy, open faces and gentle manners of the people one would hazard a guess that sin too is a stranger to these prosperous valleys. In later days when stationed in some down-country district where thieving and dacoity were rife, I often looked back wistfully to the simple peasants of Muang Wung.

Williams, Green Prison, p. 111

The Least Criminal Parts of the Kingdom

W. A. R. Wood writes confidentially to the British Minister at Bangkok ...
Consul-General Wood to Mr. Greg

Sir,

I have the honour to enclose herewith copy of a dispatch from Mr. Fitzmaurice concerning the prevalence of crime in Northern Siam.

This matter has been made the subject of reports by Mr. Fitzmaurice and myself on numerous former occasions, and has been brought to the notice of the Siamese Minister for Foreign Affairs at least three times. If any improvement has taken place, it is not yet noticeable.

It is, perhaps, almost unreasonable to call the attention of the Siamese Government to the prevalence of crime in this consular district, because, as a matter of fact, monthons Payab and Maharat are undoubtedly among the least criminal parts of the kingdom. In Petchaburi, Petchabun, Chantaburi, and some parts of the Mekong Provinces, crime of every kind is rampant to an extent which is hardly realized. No statistics are published, and only a few of the most sensational and notorious cases are ever referred to in the Siamese press.

In Maharat, crime is a good deal more prevalent than in Payab, presumably because the people there are, as a rule, poorer, and the rice crop in some parts often inadequate. But even in Payab, crime, especially cattle theft, is far too prevalent, in spite of an astounding statement recently made to me by Major V. Sylow, of the provincial gendarmerie, to the effect that the inhabitants of his district are among the least criminal in the world.

It appears to me that crime must be due to one of two causes, namely, either poverty of the people or bad administration. Now the people of northern Siam are not poor. Most of them never have any ready money, but they are able to feed and clothe themselves and their families comfortably, and that without doing any excessive amount of work. If, therefore, a large number of them prefer to spend their time stealing their neighbours' cattle or other property, the conclusion to be drawn is that this form of amusement is attended by far too little risk.

The explanation of the whole matter, here and in other parts of Siam, is, as I have often pointed out before, extremely simple. The detection and suppression of crime is a highly technical and complicated business, which cannot be efficiently carried out except by persons who have been specially trained for the purpose. In Siam a curious idea has always prevailed that anyone can do anything, and we find lawyers navigating ships or surveyors investigating cattle disease. As for the investigation of crime, it is thought that any ignorant deputy amphur or lieutenant of gendarmerie is good enough for that.

To give a single example – if any example be needed to illustrate so evident a fact – the strong-room of the Bombay Burma Trading Corporation (Limited), at Chiengmai, was recently looted of a sum of 27,000 ticals in notes and 2,000 rupees in silver. From what I have heard, the whole premises must have been full of what would have been, in the eyes of a trained detective, clues whereby the offenders could have been tracked down. For instance, a candle was found in the strong-room, and it is well known that a candle almost always shows finger prints. As there is, however, nobody in Chiengmai who has had any sort of training in detective work, naturally no advantage was taken of these clues. Several arrests have been made, but it is doubtful whether any convictions will result, and still more doubtful (which interests the corporation much more) whether any of the money will be recovered. Major Sylow has done, for an untrained man, wonderful work on this case; but this is a task for a detective, not for a Danish cavalry officer.

To sum up, I am convinced that crime in Siam will never diminish until competent officers are employed for its detection and suppression. As, however, the provision of a proper detective force would mean the engagement of several foreign officers for the purpose of training young Siamese in detective work, I presume that no real improvement is likely ever to be seen. Something might, it is true, be done in the way of setting aside a certain number of Siamese officers in each district solely for detective duties; but I doubt whether this would be sufficient without expert guidance.

I have, &c.

W. A. R. WOOD.

Elephants

A Magnificent Sight

Is there any spectacle, I wonder, that can surpass in magnificence the sight of one hundred elephants, all in the prime of condition, "ounging" timber down a swollen jungle stream? Crash! A great teak log collides with a rock head-on and swings round broadside to the current. The other end of the log is caught by a jutting-out portion of the bank opposite and the river is blocked from one side to the other. More logs are riding down upon the first. Boom! Boom! Hollow and sullen. A pile, a jam is forming. Four tuskers down here, quick, roars Orwell. What's that? The water's too deep? Nonsense. Get your elephants *in!*

Campbell, Teak-Wallah, pp. 44-45

Elephant Welfare

Elephants are not nearly so strong and robust as most people think. In proportion to their size and weight they are not able to carry or drag so heavy a load as a horse, mule, camel or man. This is partly due to the fact that they are ill shaped for dragging purposes. No howdah has yet been devised that fits an elephant back at all comfortably, and which does not tend to slither in all directions, and in dragging logs, for instance, an elephant's centre of gravity is in the wrong place relatively to the log, and it cannot therefore use its strength to the best advantage.

Elephants are rather delicate creatures. They are liable to all sorts of illnesses, and their condition has to be carefully watched when they are continuously employed on hard work. Moreover, they stand extreme heat very badly, and are often attacked by sunstroke or heat apoplexy. In their natural state they travel and feed mostly by night, and during the heat of the day they loiter about in some shady spot, smearing themselves with some nice cool mud, and powdering themselves with dust. Compel them to work in hot sunshine for any long period of time and they are certain to suffer.

Elephant owners in Northern Siam, especially the teak firms, give their elephants a complete holiday during the hot season of the year, about February to May, and have special camps for them in distant and shady glades of evergreen forest, where food is plentiful. Only by doing this can elephants be kept working year after year.

Wood, Land of Smiles, pp. 165-166

Elephant Stealing

In the early years of the century, the British Consul reported annually on the prevalence of elephant stealing in his Report on the trade and commerce of the Consular District of Chiengmai (as here, Eric Reid in 1909) – and every year the international press greeted the news with some hilarity.

This crime still continues to hamper the operations of the teak firms in Northern Siam. The official figures for Monthon Payab show that during the Siamese year 128 (April, 1909, to March, 1910) 46 elephants were stolen, of which total 35 were recovered. It would appear that although the numbers of elephants stolen during the past two years have not diminished, the crime has been considerably suppressed since 1907-08, during which period the number of elephants stolen was much in excess of and the percentage unrecovered was nearly twice as high as that of the present year.

Elephant stealing is most prevalent in the Salween district and one British firm there alone reports having suffered to the extent of 18 animals stolen, of which 5 were unrecovered, during the year, as compared with

Gathering elephants. Photograph by Knudtzon. Oliver Backhouse.

the Lakhon, Chiengmai and Raheng districts, where the returns of the principal teak firms show that 12 elephants were stolen and 10 recovered. In May, 1909, the enforcement of the Elephant Track Act was postponed for another year, but up to date no steps have been taken to bring the measure into operation. The officials on the Siam-Burma frontier render invaluable aid in recovering stolen elephants, but in the absence of definite regulations for registering and tracking elephants, and owing to the lack of an adequate staff, their efforts cannot meet with a full measure of success.

Consular report for 1909, p. 6

How Elephants were Stolen

Reginald Le May explains why the practice had not been quite as amusing as some journalists seemed to think. W. A. R. Wood had pointed out that it also involved considerable cruelty in that stolen elephants were "usually beaten and maltreated in a most brutal fashion".

Another subject, evidently not appreciated in the West, is that of elephant stealing. Most of us remember that time honoured joke in "Punch" about elephant-stealing in Siam, and the activity of the local pick-pockets. It has disappeared now, as elephant stealing has gone out of fashion, but I wonder whether it was ever realized how easy elephant stealing used to be, and how many animals were actually stolen annually.

Nowadays elephants are branded with an acid paste, the marks of which cannot be obliterated, and elephant-stealing has in consequence become a trade of the past, since the thief cannot dispose of the property; but under the old conditions, when elephants were merely branded with hot irons, the marks of which could be removed, the procedure was simple, and the thief did not even require a pocket in which to hide his stolen property. Let me give an example. Elephants, when used as "travellers" or transport animals, cannot be kept in a compound for any length of time, on account of the difficulty of finding sufficient food for them, but must be sent out into the forest under the care of their mahouts, to fend for themselves. Each evening the mahouts, who make a camp somewhere near, must go out into the forest and bring them into camp. What could be easier than for some expert thief and rider, who was watching his opportunity, to loose the hobbles of one of the elephants quietly browsing among the branches, to jump on to its back, remove its bell, and drive it twenty miles before its mahout came to look for it. Even then the mahout would probably think that it had lost its bell through some accident, or had wandered further than usual; and before he actually became convinced of the fact that it had been stolen, the animal would be fifty miles away, on the road to Burma. It would mean another day's journey for the mahout to come into the station and report the loss, and even then what could be done? The Burma authorities could be requested by telegraph to keep a watch for an elephant bearing such and such a mark, but by the time any search could be made, the animal would have lost its mark and been sold; in fact – to its owner irretrievably lost. It must not be forgotten that towns, even villages, are few and far between and that the jungle is very thick – also that telegraph lines and means of communication are not so universal as in Europe.

Le May, An Asian Arcady, pp. 159-160

Dr Heiser meets a Consular Elephant

Almost immediately upon my arrival in Chiengmai I met the British Consul, who invited me to dine with him. "I'd be delighted," I replied. "Where shall I come?"

"I'll send for you."

Twenty minutes before the dinner hour a tiny turbaned mahout, gaily dressed in crimson and white and gold, appeared before me. "The elephant waits," he announced.

"What's that?" I interjected. "I don't want any elephant." But the boy did not know enough English for any extended expostulation, and willy nilly I had to comply with what was apparently the customary method of attending dinner parties in Chiengmai. The little fellow conducted me to the door and with his hook prodded the elephant, which sank ponderously to its knees. I climbed the short ladder into the howdah and seated myself on a cushion. The mahout leaped nimbly to the elephant's head and we were ready. The great beast lumbered to its feet, the howdah lurching precariously. I was not at all prepared for what followed. As we set off I was shot forward and then suddenly back, until I thought my head would be jerked off. It did not seem possible that I could stay aloft.

Heiser, An American Doctor's Odyssey, p. 506

A Good Omen

A few weeks before my arrival a white elephant, the sacred symbol of the faith, the occasion years back of war with Burma, had been born on one of the teak company's workings. Such a thing had not happened within the memory of man. For miles round the villagers came to pay it homage. Every evening, when the calf was brought down to the river to be bathed, a hundred and fifty to two hundred people were gathered in the compound. They wore their richest and brightest clothes. They had brought flowers to cast before the infant's feet. And sugarcane to refresh the mother. There was a hush of religious awe. The brown eyes of the Lao maidens grew wide and solemn, luminous and dilated. Their lips parted in a sigh. Their little crinkled hands were joined together, lifted before their faces in simple and silent worship as a calf trotted turbulently towards the water.

The baby white elephant and its mother arrive in Chiang Mai. Photograph by Tanaka. Oliver Backhouse.

It was a curious and moving sight, and I could not help following the curving sequence of analogy as I watched the pink urchin bound and leap in the brown water. There it sported, like genius in a nursery, unaware that there was any difference between its playmates and itself, unconscious of its own importance, undreaming of its fate and future, the high rewards, the applause, the honour. All along the analogy held. Like genius it had won tardily to recognition.

Waugh, The Coloured Countries, pp. 146-147

W. A. R. Wood tells us what happened when the baby elephant was presented to the King and Queen.

The points of a white elephant are, in Siam, an extremely tricky technical matter, only to be understood by a few experts. An elephant which you or I might hardly deem worthy to be classified as "white" at all may well rank, in the eyes of an expert, well above another which to us appears infinitely superior in its degree of albinoism.

In the year 1926 a baby elephant of peculiar tint was brought forth by a female elephant belonging to the Borneo Company in one of the teak forests leased by that firm near Chiengmai. It was pronounced by experts to be a "white elephant", and as such, following immemorial custom, it was presented to the King of Siam. To comply with historical precedent, the official presentation had to be made in Bangkok by the hereditary Prince of Chiengmai. It so happened, however, that the King and Queen of Siam visited Chiengmai early in 1927, and a private presentation of the young elephant was made on the occasion of their visit by Mr. Macfie, Manager of the Borneo Company.

I was present when this presentation took place. For some time before the King and Queen arrived the young elephant was vigorously washed and polished, and by this means its peculiar reddish colour and light, almost bluish bristles were shown off to the best advantage. It was in a very frisky mood, and during the course of the preliminary proceedings knocked Mr. Macfie down and pushed me and two other men into a ditch. We were extremely nervous about its first meeting with the King and Queen, as it would never have done for the elephant to behave roughly toward them, and men were standing all round prepared forcibly to quell the rampageous infant if it showed the slightest signs of being naughty. As it turned out, the behaviour of the elephant was absolutely perfect; one would almost have supposed that some instinct told it that it was in the presence of Royalty. The King offered it a piece of sugar cane, whereupon it first raised its little trunk, as though in salutation, and then took the dainty in the quietest and politest fashion. After that, the Queen patted and fed the little elephant, and it never showed the slightest sign of roughness during the whole time Their Majesties were there.

It is popularly considered to be a good omen for a "white" elephant to be presented to a King of Siam during the first year of his reign, as was the case with the Borneo Company elephant, and great jollifications were held at Chiengmai and later at Bangkok, whither the new mascot, with its mother, was sent by special train.

One of the white elephants of the late King of Siam was a very savage creature. It several times smashed up rickshaws, carriages, and even motor-cars in the streets of Bangkok. Its end was a tragic one. It escaped, and when pursued, managed to jam itself between the pontoon and the river bank, where it was drowned.

Wood, Land of Smiles, pp. 182-183

An Elephant Ride

Mary Lou O'Brien enjoys an elephant ride …

Dear Friends,

When letter writing time comes I seem to have either no news at all or else so much that it spills out of one letter of polite size into a regular "special edition" sort of letter. This is one of the latter.

First of all let me thank you once again for the Christmas gifts, letters and cards which have found their way out to Siam, and to me. Our third Christmas in Siam was made even happier than it would have been otherwise, by the arrival of your thoughtful messages. Each Christmas seems just a wee bit nicer than the one before. One more, and then home, for furlough.

Oh dear! My typewriter fairly stutters and splutters in its haste to record all of the interesting things which it has to tell you. But what to pick first is a problem. If I had a neat and orderly mind (which I have not) I would take the very first thing first and then go on in chronological order.

Suppose, just to be different, that I begin with the latest experience, and then jump around a bit. I can't wait any longer to tell you that I'VE HAD AN ELEPHANT RIDE!!! And not just an ordinary elephant ride, either. No sir, the elephant which I rode wore a gold lacquer howdah and had the most red and gold trappings that you ever saw, and a mahout dressed in a red costume, like those worn in feudal times in Siam. So you see, I have a right to be excited about it.

The Chao Luang (Chief Prince, or feudal lord) of Lumpoon, eighteen miles from Chiengmai, was in the McCormick Hospital for many, many weeks last year while Dr. O'Brien was the only foreign physician at the hospital, and he pulled through after a very serious operation. In order to show his gratitude to the "Maw" and to the nurses who looked after him the Chao Luang invited us to come down to his palace two days ago for an "elephant ride" and tea. So down we drove to Lumpoon, four Siamese nurses who had looked after the royal patient, Miss Lemmon, Supervisor of Nursing, Dr. and Mrs. Cort and Dr. and Mrs. O'Brien.

We were not prepared for such pomp and display, at all, for a ride upon the back of any old working elephant would have satisfied us, so we were a bit dazed when we saw the gorgeous trappings, the mahout who looked as if he had just stepped out of a fairy-book, and four elephants. You really cannot blame me for being proud. Each one of us had a turn, and what a queer sensation it was, being up among the tree branches! Cameras clicked fast and furiously, for we all wanted to "go down" in history, photographically speaking. It was great fun, and not at all terrifying. And the Chao Luang was as delighted with our squeals of delight and excitement as we were with the novelty of the experience. It was a graceful way for our host to acknowledge his debt of gratitude to the mission hospital.

Life has been full of excitement these past two months.

28 January 1928

On the First Prize in the Red Cross "Our Day" Raffle, 1918.

The prize in the raffle at Chiang Mai was an elephant, the second and third prizes being a pony and a buffalo. The elephant in question was won by Nai Mar, a railway clerk at Khun Tan. He had previously worked as a syce for the Bombay Burmah Trading Corporation and as an assistant to the Japanese photographer Tanaka. He sold the elephant to David Macfie of the Borneo Company Limited for 2,500 ticals and bought a rice field instead. The Bangkok Times printed these exhortatory verses by W. A. R. Wood but regretted they could not print the photograph he had sent with them.

Of raffles, I ween, full many we've seen,
For motors and that sort of thing,
But the "Red Cross" to aid, as the above is displayed,
A prize more attractive we bring.
This photo is meant to (mis)represent
A northern Motor Dray
Which Britons up North present to hold forth
A helping hand to "Our Day".
For the "Tusker" portrayed a price has been paid,
Of ticals three thousand at least,
But when years have flown and taller he's grown,
His price will be vastly increased.
He's broken to harness, he feeds on bananas,
For petrol or oil you've no bill;
Let him forage at ease midst your neighbour's fruit trees,
And he'll carry you where you will.
A five tical touch won't embarrass you much
And if you the first prize don't gain,
A "Ma Ton Yai" and a marvellous "Kwai"
And other fine prizes remain,
An investment like this it were madness to miss.
Your natural instincts obey,
So do not be shy, in thousands draw nigh
And chance your luck for "Our Day".

The Bangkok Times, 21 November 1918, p. 21

The Peoples of the North

A Motley Population

As in the other towns of the north, the population of Nan is a motley one; Lao naturally form the majority, but Khamu, Shan, Burmese, and Toungsu (from Upper Burma), all have their settlements in the city. At the north end of the town are the barracks, where is quartered a moderately strong garrison. They are situated in well-wooded fields some distance from the actual market, so that the military is not evident to any great degree as one passes through the streets.

The only European element in the city is American – now that the French Consulate has been removed to Chiengmai – for the Presbyterian Mission has a station in Nan, as elsewhere, with a school and dispensary where the people can obtain an education and medicine respectively at the cheapest possible rates.

Le May, An Asian Arcady, p. 167

Wat Saen Fang, Chiang Mai. Photograph by Tanaka. Oliver Backhouse.

A Laos Village

The Rev. J. H. Freeman served "in the Laos field" from 1894 to 1922. The "land of the free" referred to in the title of his book published in 1910 is of course "Laos" or the north of Siam.

Almost every villager above the average in intelligence has some specialty that occupies his time when field or herd do not require attention. One is skillful in weaving baskets or matting, another makes better hats than his neighbors, a third is a blacksmith, a fourth excels in silver and brass work. This woman is a skillful trader and invests her capital in pepper, salt, or limes, when they are plenty; in the house opposite the women spend most of their time at their looms; others give time and strength to gardens of peppers, cotton, onions and tobacco. Weaving and the other processes that intervene between cotton boll or silkworm cocoon and the finished garment, have ever been looked on as peculiarly woman's work. Nowhere are to be found cotton goods of firmer texture, or with colors more cunningly blended, than on the looms of a Laos household. Beautiful silks are also woven, especially in Nan province. Though flax is raised, it is used only for cordage, and in making seines and nets.

Freeman, An Oriental Land of the Free, p. 54

In the Evening I Sat and Watched the Stars

Suddenly, without warning, we emerged from the forest and saw, rolling before us, a plain of golden rice faintly stirred by the breeze. At the end we could see a village with its clumps of tall palms, and beyond it, the hills shimmering in the haze. Down we went through the waving fields until at length we entered the village of Wiang Sa, some eighteen miles from Nan, and reined up at the rest-house, set in a compound of tall trees.

The village of Wiang Sa is a model for all Siam. At right angles to the road by which we entered lay the main street. It was about fifteen yards wide and lined on either side by a beautiful avenue of tamarind trees. Just outside the rest-house was a gate to prevent cattle from straying, and passing through this, we saw well-built wooden houses enclosed within their own fences. On the left was the "Nai Amphur's" office;

on the right, the gendarmerie station, painted white and with a neat garden, containing rows of crotons, clusters of rose-bushes, and well-trimmed lawns; further on, a store and a row of shops, all scrupulously clean and wearing a general air of prosperity. Near the rest-house was the village well, and in the evening, as in olden times, the maidens came in groups to draw the water for the house. As I watched them (which I could not help), I was struck by their comeliness, their well-developed figures, their splendid bearing and their bountiful hair. You might indeed search throughout Siam for finer specimens of womanhood. Their "sin", too, were of a different kind from those that I had hitherto seen, much brighter and with more tasteful blending of colour. They were in fact typical Nan "sin," which have the reputation of being the most beautiful in Siam. Some hundred yards away flowed the tributary of the Nan River on which the village was situated – picturesque enough, but very narrow. Buffaloes were peacefully wallowing in the water, just showing their noses and uttering long grunts of contentment. I could espy a stork on the further bank standing quite still, perhaps watching for fish; but I could not keep away from the village green, and so returned to wander up and down till dusk.

In the evening I sat and watched the stars, to the music of a flute and a Lao banjo, played by two of the syces, and to the "clock, clock" of the bells tied round the elephants' necks. The latter were hobbled and tied up in front of the rest-house compound, munching away at their evening meal of banana stems and coconut branches. I remember that evening well; a cool wind was blowing, and later the crescent moon rose, throwing the scene and the great bulk of the elephants into bold relief.

Le May, An Asian Arcady, pp. 165-166

The Lives of Farmers

Lucy Starling reports on the lives of people in the countryside …

A delightful summer you must have had, much more pleasant than the summer in Laos would have been, where we had to wipe the mould off our shoes and suitcases every few days, and hang all our clothes in the sun to dry whenever that orb condescended to shine. If you don't like a moist heat, postpone your visit to Laos until winter, and then you will agree that we have a nearly perfect climate. I know, and like Laos better every day.

The last few weeks I have been visiting in the out-villages. It is the best way to learn to talk, and the quickest way to get into the hearts of the people. I visited them in their homes, played with the babies and amused the older children; sat in the rice fields and talked with the people as they cut the grain, even turning reaper myself, and nearly cutting off a foot. I learned all I could about their tasks and diversions. The business life of the average Laos is divided between rice field and river sand-bars, – the two main sources of his food supply.

At the beginning of the rainy season, he sows his rice seed in beds and in due course the plants are set in the soft mud, by hand, one at a time, a most tedious process in the eyes of an American. From that time, if there is plenty of rain, his duty is mainly that of policeman, guarding his food supply for next year from crows, stray cows, horses, and his neighbor perchance. Then comes the harvest and, with a small sickle, he goes out to cut and gather into bundles, very much as reapers did in the days of Ruth. The bundles are stacked together and the grain beat out on the threshing-floor. A round bamboo tray is used for winnowing, and the grain is heaped into carts for distribution through the country. The first sound I hear, these mornings, is the tinkling bells of the rice carts as they start out to the fields.

It is a pleasant sound for the bells jingle "Plenty to eat, plenty to eat"; and the cry we have long been hearing was "I have nothing to eat!" The number of beggars has decreased remarkably since the beginning of harvest. Even the cows drawing the carts seem to rejoice and toss their heads in pride that they are carrying life and strength to the people. So the grain reaches the rice-bins and from there goes into the rice-pounder, an enormous wooden hammer worked by the foot.

Our great river is now very low and full of sand-bars, and the man who was busy in the field for many months has waded out into the river bed and built him a bamboo house on stilts, with a roof of leaves. All around his house down to the water's edge he has planted vegetables, many of them such as we have at home. Every afternoon, when the sun is low, he and his family go out to water the garden. Two square tin buckets are suspended from each end of a stick, which he slings over his shoulder; these he fills with water and pours the contents through a wide-meshed bamboo basket, a first-rate sprinkler. We Americans, who have been living out of "tins," bless the RETURN OF THE SAND-BAR GARDEN.

Woman's Work, May 1911, pp. 112-113

A Lao Homestead

Being far ahead of my party I crossed the stream and rested at a Lao homestead on the opposite bank. It was so typical of the country that it will be of interest to describe it. The homestead consisted of four or five bamboo structures, – it seems extravagant to call them houses – all built on piles with the main one in the centre, and the whole surrounded by a bamboo fence. The piles were stout, well-seasoned posts; the walls were of plaited rattan cane and the roof was built of dried leaves supported underneath by beams of bamboo poles. On the verandah of the main structure sat the good man and his wife, apparently with nothing in the world to do but sell their wares to hungry wayfarers; bananas, pumpkins, *miang*,* and other articles of food were set out to ease the traveller's hunger, while he might slake his thirst, at the cost of nothing but his own labour, from several jars, kept constantly filled with water from the stream. The man wore nothing but a loincloth, and the wife had apparently just finished her bath, for she was not wearing the *sin* and a close-fitting bodice, the usual dress of the Lao, but one single garment, which covered her bosom and reached down to her knees; it seemed to be a *sin* improvised for the time being. There was a cow in the byre, and a pony in the stall, while under the houses, in a continuous search for grain, a dozen fowls ran to and fro. Almost as numerous as the fowls were the children, for when I arrived I counted no less than eight fat brown bodies splashing in the stream, and laughing joyously as only children can laugh,

---

*   A species of tea-leaf, chewed by the peasants as the sailor chews his quid of tobacco.

with never a care or thought in the world. Seven girls and one boy, most of them seemingly of the same immature age, and all clothed in nature's garb. Certainly, except for the tiny babe, there was not a difference of three inches in height between any two, and the tallest could not have measured more than three feet nine. All but the smallest of the girls had already put up their hair, a curious sight to Western eyes, but the custom among the Lao. As soon as there is hair enough, up it goes into a coil, and I am sorry to say that, once it is up, it is very seldom taken down again.

Le May, An Asian Arcady, p. 77

Passers-By in Chiang Mai

The flood had attracted many of the townsfolk, and it was interesting to watch them as they went by – first a conservative old Chinaman, still jealously guarding his pig-tail, at least what there was of it; then a respectable Parsee dealer in gems, gravely discussing the affair with several of his fellows; next a Lao-Chinese boy of ten or twelve, with his head closely shaven except on the top, from which the hair hung down on all sides in tufts, like a coconut at a fair; then two Lao imps, who eyed us speculatively, but decided that it would be better to pass by. Close on their heels came a party of women, half Chinese and half Lao, in the midst of them the daughter of the richest Chinese storekeeper in Chiengmai, but lately married and displaying her new dignity. The *sin*, or skirts, were of shot silk, and had no doubt cost much money. Suddenly bearing down towards us with martial stride came a tall Sikh, clad in a suit of pale blue pyjamas, full bearded, and his black hair streaming down to his waist. We knew him well as the principal cloth-dealer in Chiengmai, but he reminded me at the moment of a giant picture of some Eastern Prophet. Lao, Chinamen, Indians of many castes and races, and women of all descriptions, passed in a seemingly endless stream before us, some with the day's work manfully done, some perhaps with it never begun.

Le May, An Asian Arcady, p. 81

Two Siam Villages
By Katharine Reichel

Katharine McLellan Reichel, the wife of the Mission architect Paul A. Reichel whom she had met while at Ohio State University, worked as a teacher at Chiang Mai between 1919 and 1924.

Not long ago, ten of us motored to the village of Maa Dawk Deng, the "river of the red flower," to hold communion. Word of our coming had been sent in advance and chairs and ponies were awaiting us at the point where we must leave the road and journey across paddy fields. The church had been gaily decorated with all kinds of ferns combined with flame-of-the-forest. The elders met us at the church and escorted us to the parish house which had been fixed up for our comfort. The village school formerly occupied the parish-house, but in these later days it has been abandoned.

The service was well attended. The chapel was filled, men sitting on one side and women on the other, as is the custom here. At the proper time, the collection was taken and, to our amusement, was counted and the contributions recorded then and there. There was no chance for a member to slip by without adding his bit to the fund! It occurred to me that some such public exposure might not be a bad idea to put into operation in some of our home churches.

We adjourned to the parish-house after the service to eat tiffin. The people brought in great dishes of rice and bowls of curry. There were also great fluffy rice cakes, eight or more inches in diameter. After eating, we went visiting in the homes of the village. The houses are well constructed and many comforts unusual to native homes were in evidence. This is the wealthiest village in the Chiengmai district. In some of the houses there were nice teak tables and chairs, pictures on the walls and foreign dishes. Some of the older people have been to school and their training was plainly shown in the homes. For some reason, however, they are not sending many of their children to school, although they can well afford to do so. Like many at home, wealth and comfort have made them stingy.

What a contrast one sees who visits the village of Ban Baw Sang! This is the home of the outcasts, the pariahs of this part of the country. When we drove up the long bamboo-fenced lane to the village, we were met by a host of ragged people, eyes all agog with wonder at the Ford. Many of the children were naked and the older people had barely enough clothing to make them at all respectable. As I looked around on the crowd, I saw only one head that showed any evidence of having been combed for several days. I do not need to dwell on the dirt.

This village has a history. Years ago the people enjoyed prosperity. The occupation of the villagers is paper-making and the industry was then in a healthy condition. Later, the price of raw materials began to rise, until it reached such a point that it was no longer possible for the people to "carry on". Then the Viceroy lent assistance by ordering the paper for government uses, paying a very fair price. Just as things were improving, the Chinese cornered the market on raw materials, thereby again boosting the price of the paper so much that the government could no longer afford to buy it. Such is the state of affairs at present.

Their existence is literally from hand to mouth. They get up early in the morning and go out to hunt food for breakfast. Perhaps they have gathered together enough for one meal by ten o'clock. The rest of the morning and afternoon is spent in searching for food to make the second meal of the day. The same routine must be followed the next day. Shiftless, you say? Perhaps so; but I wonder how many of us could do better if we were constant victims of malarial fever and were infested with thousands of hookworms eating the very vitality of young and old alike. Truly a very needy people and so few of us to help!

Woman's Work, November 1921, pp. 255-256

The Haw Train
By Mrs. Chas. H. Crooks, Lakawn

In a Haw train each one furnishes his own private conveyance and can either "stick" to the front or rear of the train according to his own heart's desire, but if he has any care for his own safety or any respect for the captain's opinion he will keep out of the middle of the train. And so it is in the queer land of the White Elephant that one can go with a train and still not be of it.

Getting into camp in the evening was always interesting – the head horse stopped and the others grouped around according to their places. The Haw boys would lift off a heavy load; out from under it would spring a tiny pony, make a dash for his neighbor with his teeth and deftly plant his heels in another's ribs. In the midst of this confusion ran the Haws screaming, grabbing, protesting, until all loads were finally off. All this over the tents would go up as if by magic, fires were built, and soon the kettle would be singing a merry song. Then began the unfolding of our house-hold cots, chairs, tables; and we ourselves while we did not unfold, at least expanded in the genial glow of the camp fires.

Later in the evening the full moon sailed majestically up in to the heavens and shone with all the brilliant radiance of the tropics. It transformed the rude jungle into a paradise, each tiny dew drop into a glistening diamond, and the heat and cares of the day into illusions. The breeze murmured and sang in the majestic teaks above our tiny white dwellings, and quietly we yielded to the power of Morpheus and soon were in his arms fast asleep. All the dangers of the jungle were round about us, and yet we slept in peace knowing that He who is all-wise and loving watched over us. We awoke to the musical din of pots and kettles, the old camp fires of the night before were stirred into a bright blaze, and soon all was life and activity once more. Long before the "eye of day" peeped over the mountain tops, we had folded our tent and noisily hurried away.

Laos News, February 1909, pp. 24-26

The Laos

Alec Waugh praises the people of the north …

The Laos are quiet, simple, decently-lived people. They cultivate their rice, carry their produce to the markets, tend their animals and chew their betel nut. And though, when you ask how far it is to such a place, you will be answered in such simple methods of reckoning as "Half a bullock's march" or "As far as you can hear a dog bark," it is hard to believe that you are a hundred miles from a road, from what is called civilisation. It is only at odd moments that you will realise how remote these people are from

A YOUNG LAO.

A YOUNG KHA-MU WITH TURBAN OFF.

A YOUNG KHA-MU WITH TURBAN ON.

A YOUNG KHA-MIT.

Young people from different ethnic groups. Photographs by W. A. Elder, from Le May, *An Asian Arcady*.

the practical organisation of the big cities.

It is at such moments that you realise how distant from civilisation the Lao still is, but for the most part you feel that you are in as ordered and developed a world as you would be in Europe within half an hour's stroll of telephones and cars. Their villages are tidy, their huts clean and airy, their single store is bright with printed cotton. Each village has its temple and its school. And the presence of the priests, with their cropped heads and their yellow robes, lend a dignity to life. The complicated Buddhist faith, over which metaphysicians will split hairs indefinitely, is a direct and simple thing to the simple Laos. They have retained the capacity to wonder.

Waugh, The Coloured Countries, pp. 145-146

Khamus

W. A. R. Wood writes about the hard-working Khamus ...

"New" Khamus must be about the simplest and most unsophisticated creatures on earth. They possess no written character, so are all quite uneducated, and have no religion beyond a system of propitiating various spirits; in fact, they know nothing about anything, and will agree to anything, believe anything, fear anything, and eat anything. They do not believe in the Biblical maxim about turning the other cheek – they prefer to turn their backs and run away as hard as they can after, or preferably before, the first blow.

Khamu immigrants never bring their women with them, and though there are thousands and thousands of Khamus in Northern Siam, very few people there, whether Siamese, Laos or foreigners have ever seen a Khamu woman. I have seen some of them, having once visited a Khamu village in the Nan Province. They looked very dirty and untidy, and had rather a masculine appearance; this is strange, because male Khamus are often distinctly effeminate looking. They wear their hair long, and have big, round, soft eyes and a shy and diffident expression. Many of them, when dressed in nice, clean blue suits, with pink turbans, may best be described as "pretty".

The Khamu language is very different from any of the Tai dialects. They are supposed to be allied to the Mon and Khmer races, but their language is not at all like modern Mon or Cambodian. It has no "tones," and possesses a strongly rolled R. The Laos and Shans have no spoken R, and the Siamese only a very mild one which frequently degenerates into an L, whereas the Khamus' R is rolled in a way to turn a Scotchman green with envy.

I have never met any people so devoid of racial pride as the Khamus. They are always saying things like: – "I can't do that. I am too stupid. I am only a Khamu," or "Do not expect too much of me. I am not a Lao, only a Khamu." They will cave in to a man half their size, and then explain that they could not probably resist him, "being only Khamus." It is only when they settle in Siam, marry Lao wives, and discard their national dress, that they succeed in throwing off their inferiority complex and forgetting that they are "only Khamus."

The reason why Khamus are in such demand as best labourers is that they work twice as hard as a native of the country for much less pay. On the other hand, they have their disadvantages, the chief one being a tendency to run away, either singly or in gangs, whenever they "feel unhappy". It does not, unfortunately, take very much to make them "feel unhappy." A few harsh words, a furious glance, or worse still, a threatening gesture, will produce a degree of unhappiness for which instant flight is the only remedy.

The Khamus are supposed to be racially allied to the Mons of Burma.

Their home is among the mountains of French Laos, but there are a number of Khamu settlements in the hilly districts East of Nan. A Khamu village is a good deal cleaner than a Meow or Yao one – perhaps I ought to say less filthy. The Khamus build their houses on posts, and do not usually lay on water like the other hill tribes.

Besides the indigenous Khamus, there are many thousands of Khamu immigrants in Northern Siam. They come from their homes in French Laos to seek work, mostly in the teak forests. Each gang of immigrants has a so-called Captain in charge, who arranges his men's labour contracts. They are paid by the year (often as little as Rs. 100, plus food) and as much as one year's pay is often taken by the captain as his commission for getting them the job. Why Khamus have always to submit to being bled and exploited by their captain I have never understood, but it is accepted as a necessary and inevitable state of affairs. The result is that every new Khamu has to get a big advance of pay in order to square his captain, and if he runs away or dies his employer has to bear the loss.

Wood, Land of Smiles, pp. 134-135

A Magic-Lantern Lecture

A man from another firm once told me that an American missionary, on an evangelising tour of this man's district, asked his permission to give a magic-lantern lecture to his Kamu coolies. The lecture was not a success from the missionary's point of view though the Kamus enjoyed it hugely. There was a good deal of tittering at the menial occupations of the white-faced disciples, but when Jesus Christ, an obvious "burrasahib," appeared carrying the heavy cross over His shoulders there was an uncontrolled and spontaneous burst of laughter which brought the house down.

Williams, Green Prison, pp. 49-50

The Coolie and His Money

The coolie is the most difficult person in the world to deal with in money matters – and the most conservative. Some time ago the Company imported a large quantity of King George rupees for the first time

BBTC saw-mill workers. Photograph by Tanaka. Oliver Backhouse.

(rupees were in the past largely used in the north of Siam), but out of the whole company of Khamu coolies, not one would accept the new coins. They were prepared to take King Edward rupees if absolutely necessary, but those they actually preferred were of Queen Victoria's reign. In this case the whole consignment had to be returned by road and rail to Bangkok and exchanged for those of an earlier reign. Even in the case of ticals the coolies are often very arbitrary and, while accepting some, will refuse others quite apart from their newness, for no apparent reason whatever. I remember another case in Lampang where the rumour suddenly flew over the countryside (as if by telegraph) that only those rupees stamped "Empress" were legally valid. Those marked "Queen" were of no value. Some bright mind had added up the letters and found that some coins had 7 and others only 5. It needed many proclamations on bridges and elsewhere to reassure the people that 5 was as good as 7.

Le May, An Asian Arcady, p. 187

British Shans in the North

One of the functions of the consuls in the north was to make regular tours of their district and to report on conditions there. In 1927, W. A. R. Wood was accompanied by Sydney Waterlow, the Minister in Bangkok, on the first occasion that a Minister had been on such a tour. They slept in tents supplied by the Borneo Company Limited. Here, Waterlow reports to Sir Austen Chamberlain, the Foreign Secretary ...

Bangkok, December 9, 1927

I have the honour to inform you that, with the cessation of the rains last month and the opening of the consular touring season, I recently took the opportunity to accompany Mr. W. A. R. Wood, His Majesty's consul-general at Chiang Mai, on a tour of part of the northern provinces of Siam. My objects in doing so were to get first-hand experience of the position of British subjects in that region, and to see for myself something of the work of the two northern consular posts (Chiengmai and Nakawn Lampang) in order to complete the survey of the conditions of the Siam consular service which I saw it necessary to draw up as a result of my visit to the Dutch East Indies. [...]

The country I traversed is prosperous and is being steadily developed by the clearing of jungle and the opening-up of new rice areas, by the reclamation of old ones which, after the depopulation following on the wars between Burma and Siam, had reverted to jungle. Mr. Wood tells me that, primitive though conditions still are, the change in the last few years is remarkable. Hamlets have become villages, villages have become towns, and "towns" which used to consist of a few hovels now have a row of shops stocking a miscellany of cheap European and Japanese goods. Narrow, overgrown paths have become broad mud-tracks (liquid during the rains) travelled by an unbroken stream of carriers and bullock-caravans that foul all the camping-places with their dung. And the standard of intelligence and efficiency among Siamese officials in remote places has markedly improved; it remains low enough, to be sure, but a few years ago the unsatisfactory state of things at Chiengrai would have been the rule instead of the exception. As it is, the British Shans in the north – gentle, law-abiding and likeable but very dirty people, – are obviously increasing apace, both in the course of nature and in the arrival of new settlers, who, except where Chinese competition ousts them, find it easy to gain a livelihood as small traders and cultivators in this peaceful and pleasant country.

The National Archives, F180/180/40

The Pu-Mia

In England, if a man goes about dressed as a woman he is arrested, and it seems to be assumed that a tendency in a man to assume female dress is a sign of some sort of moral perversion. In certain regulations annexed to the Indian Penal Code a similar assumption is made. In Siam, especially in the North, there are a certain number of men who habitually wear female clothing and grow their hair long. It does not seem to be thought that there is anything morally wrong about this, and so far that I have been able to make out, these *Pu-Mia,* (men-women), as they are called, really possess, as a rule, no moral eccentricities. Physically also, I am told, there is nothing peculiar about them. They prefer to dress as women, and that is all that there is to say about it.

There used to be a young fellow of good family living near us at Lampang who sometimes dressed as a man and sometimes as a woman, and it was popularly believed that during the earlier part of each month he actually was a male and during the latter half of the month became a female. I often exchanged greetings with him (or her) and found her (or him) very pleasant and polite: but I never got on sufficiently familiar terms to justify me in making personal enquiries as to his (or her) sex. So far as I could make out, he seemed to be a young man of very attractive appearance, though a trifle girlish looking. He did not wear his hair long, but when sporting feminine costume was very fond of decorating his head with flowers.

Wood, Land of Smiles, p. 111

Lepers

Apart from stolen elephants (and white ones), few stories from North Siam seem to have captured the imagination of the international press more than stories about lepers. This was almost entirely due to the tireless efforts of Dr James W. McKean, the founder of the Leper Asylum at Chiang Mai in 1908. Dr James W. McKean (1860-1949) was born in Iowa. He studied medicine there and in New York. His early years were marked by personal misfortune: he lost his parents in childhood and his first wife and a daughter after a few years of marriage. He also lost the sight of his right eye. In 1889, he left for Siam with his second wife, Laura Bell McKean, later becoming Superintendent of the American Mission Hospital at Chiang Mai. He founded the famous Leper Asylum in 1908 and tirelessly sought funding and support for the institution in Siam and abroad over the next few decades. He retired and returned to the United States in 1931, being succeeded as Superintendent of the Asylum by his son James Hugh McKean. Laura McKean edited a vernacular newspaper and Laos News *for some years; she also wrote, painted, and collected butterflies and moths.*

Chiengmai Leper Asylum, 1908-1929
By Dr. James W. McKean

Chiengmai Leper Asylum is closing its twenty-first year. A brief retrospect of the early days of the work for lepers in Chiengmai and the growth of the institution may be of interest.

Events and circumstances leading up to and rendering possible the beginning of this asylum had occurred from time to time during a period of fifteen years previous to the real initiation of the work.

Soon after beginning his medical service in Chiengmai in January 1890, the writer was deeply impressed with the dire need of the wandering leper. This came about largely because of the frequent visits of leper people to the medical compound to beg for alms and for medicines. Finding that

James W. McKean. The Editor.

their requests met with response they came in increasing numbers and in increasing frequency so that during a period of several years not a day passed in which leper beggars, in companies of from two to a dozen or more persons, did not come for alms.

On one occasion a leper woman came imploring aid to bury her leper husband who had died in a boat near the hospital landing. On two occasions leper men were found dead in public rest houses where, friendless and alone, they had passed the last hours of miserable and forsaken life.

It was discouraging to realize how very little it was possible to do to meet the great need of these folk, who, cast off by family and friends, were hungry and homeless.

Foreign residents of Chiengmai responded generously to a request for funds for a supply of blankets, food and clothing at the Christmas season. (This annual subscription was earnestly fostered by Mr. D. F. Macfie from before the days of the asylum until the present, a period of twenty-five years).

Drawn by our efforts to give a measure of relief, a company of more than fifty leper people made camp on an island in the river a mile below the city where food and medicines and other comforts were given out. The city authorities, however, drove these people away threatening them with death in case they should return.

It became increasingly evident that these sporadic efforts were wholly inadequate and that an organized work should be undertaken.

Perhaps the most important circumstance making possible the beginnings of the asylum was that the writer, during a period of some ten years and until the time of the Prince's death, was physician to Chao Inta Wichai Yanon, the Ruling Prince of the Northern Provinces. When the eldest son of Prince Inta Yanon came of age, his father gave him a Good Luck present. This present was none other than a very large and very choice elephant. Whether this elephant brought good luck to his young master is not known, but he seems to have brought ill luck to others. He proved to be a very vicious creature. He killed his keepers and became too dangerous for use. His front legs were hobbled with a heavy chain and he was placed upon an island in the river some four miles below the city. He soon became master of the island and ruled his domain with great rigor. He destroyed the gardens of the island villagers. He tore down their granaries and even their houses to secure the food he wished. Finally the villagers fled and left him the sole occupant of the island until the time of his death.

The Prince owner of the elephant became ruler upon the death of his father. He also was the writer's patient during many succeeding years. Generous in a marked degree, upon request he made a personal gift of the island-home of the elephant to the writer to be used by the Mission in establishing a leper asylum. After the death of the elephant the area grew up into a tangled jungle and in this condition was turned over to us. Later this gift was ratified by His Majesty's Government.

The beginnings of the asylum were auspicious only in the immensity of the task before us. With more than a hundred acres of land overgrown with briars and thorns, with six or seven leper people anxious to take up residence in the shade of the trees, with no funds in hand or in sight for the purchase of food and clothing, the outlook was not encouraging.

On making known to the public and to friends the needs of the leper, encouraging responses in gifts of money for maintenance were received in increasing numbers.

Nor were there wanting large hearted Siamese officials, men of real vision, who gave invaluable aid in meeting opposition. Chao Phya Surasi, the High Commissioner, and His Royal Highness, Prince Damrong, gave moral support and encouragement. To these two men in particular Siam is heavily indebted for fostering the beginnings of work for the many thousands of Siamese people who are suffering from leprosy.

During more than ten years the British Mission to Lepers generously gave financial aid to the Asylum. During later years the American Mission to Lepers has given most valuable aid and encouragement.

From the inception of the asylum until the present time one of the ideals to be attained that has been kept constantly in view is to render the institution as home-like as possible. Barring the prohibition of marriage, the asylum is in all respects a real community of three hundred and fifty persons whose activities move along the ordinary channels of community life.

The daily tasks pertaining to the household, the gardens, the roads, the laundry, the schools, the tailor shop, nursing, cooking, building etc. all find a place here. All of these tasks involve, of course, a greater or less degree of labor, labor being an integral part of a contented life.

In anticipation of a visit by Their Majesties, the King and Queen, the leper women made sixteen hundred Siamese flags which were used to bedeck the more than one hundred buildings at the time of the Royal visit.

Not only do the leper men keep in good order their own door yards, the roads and the gardens, but they also have a heavy yet agreable task in hulling the scores of bushels of rice that are issued to the whole community each Thursday morning. These occupations are of great value in relieving to a degree the monotony of asylum life.

Exercise is assuming, more and more, a prominent place in the routine treatment of leprosy. In the form of useful and increasing work it is of course a double value.

Those who regard a leper asylum as a dismal and utterly cheerless place would find no confirmation of that opinion in the Chiengmai Asylum. With the exception of the ward for the helpless patients, the so called "burnt out" cases, there are no revolting sights; and even among these, our most pitiable patients, there is a surprising degree of good cheer. Indeed one might travel far afield to find a village of similar size where there is a greater degree of community comfort and quiet.

The great majority of the patients have become Christians. Life has taken on a new meaning. They now know that they are not suffering for sins committed in a previous state of existence.

They know that they are children of the King and one day will go to dwell with Him, free from sin and disease. Such assurance as this is the prime cause of their contentment.

It was a fortunate circumstance that several of our nine original patients were already Christian before coming to us. Very soon after taking up their abode in our grass huts they asked for a chapel where they might meet for service. The chapel was built, a larger and better bamboo and grass hut than those in which they lived.

The buildings of 1929 are much superior to those of 1909. The chapel still maintains pre-eminence as the largest and best building in the Asylum. For this we are indebted to the late Mrs. Thaw, of Pittsburgh, Pa., who for more than a quarter of a century was an earnest friend and a liberal supporter of the world-wide work for lepers.

Siam Outlook, October 1929, pp. 366-369

Prince Damrong visits a model house for lepers, 1921. Dr McKean is standing second from right with Dr Barnes of the Rockefeller Foundation. The Wellcome Foundation.

The Leper Village, 1926

Ebbe Kornerup devoted a chapter to his impressions of the Leper Asylum in his travel book, Friendly Siam.

Outside Chieng Mai there is an ideal leper settlement, on the river, so that it is isolated from the outside world. The treatment is by the injection of *ethyl esters hydnocarpus,* an extract of chaulmoogra oil.

For hundreds of years Asiatic doctors have known that this oil is a medicine against various skin diseases, more especially leprosy. People apparently incurable used to go out into the woods to find the oil, which comes from the nuts of the taractogenos tree, settle down under a tree, sleep on its leaves, rub themselves with the oil from its nuts or smear their whole bodies. Perhaps they would chew the leaves as one chews betel, and many came home again fit and well after a year's sojourn; others remained and died in the forest.

This wonderful giant tree has its real home in a place high up in northern Burma near the Chinese frontier, but it may also be found in northern Siam. The press of the world has often spoken of it, ever since it was discovered that the oil could be used for leprosy.

The tree is rather rare and rises high in the virgin forest above all the other trees, with its dark, hard, shining leaves, which look rather like those of the coffee-plant. Its fruit grows in bunches.

The settlement is known as Leper Village.

Each house stands in its white-fenced garden with a wealth of flowers and creepers – roses, agaves, bamboos, and areca palms or erythrina: a true model village. Each family has its own house, or two live together and share the housekeeping; they do their own cooking and washing. When they are not looking after their gardens, they generally sit by the river and fish or bathe under the shady palm trees. Everything is given them free by the Government, so there is no want.

It is horrible to see their hands with the fingers eaten away, and their open sores. It is worse for the unfortunate women who do not come until they have lost a limb, and naively hope that it will grow again through the medicine's magic power. The Siamese is clean in his habits; he keeps his house beautifully and looks after his flowers. The Chinaman, on the other hand, stinks. When he falls ill he is hopelessly lazy and sits about listlessly all day long without stirring.

The cure works pretty well; the sores heal comparatively quickly when no complications set in to make the patient temporarily worse. One of the surest signs of leprosy is the decay of the muscle between the thumb and the first finger.

In order not to make too much of the operation, this is performed publicly in an open arbour. The box containing the miraculous medicine is brought in; the patient bares his arm or leg, the president of the settlement washes it clean with spirits of wine, then paints it with iodine, and the doctor makes the injection. All the horror is done away with; things are taken calmly in order to reassure the patient.

There are two villages: the men's, with a young man for president, and the women's, with an old one; he decides all disputes and arranges all business: so all goes peacefully in the colony.

There is an assembly hall, a temple, and a church. They burn their dead themselves in a primitive open oven, yellow-robed priests performing the solemn ceremony. Friends and acquaintances bring fruit and gifts; they live under the same conditions as other Siamese, nor do they wish they were out again.

But it is only a minority who can be taken in here; round about in Siam there are thousands of other lepers who have no help, no medicine. Siam is in dire need of leper hospitals and of a law requiring all patients to be taken in. You can see lepers any day in Bangkok with their stumps of fingers and their begging-bowls. No one thinks of money as a spreader of infection. But the slightest touch from a leper can infect, and as the incubation period is years long one cannot even tell where the disease was picked up.

The fame of this hospital is known far and wide. Six hundred miles away a man heard of it and wandered on his mutilated feet through forests where leopard and tiger roam, hungry and thirsty, until at last he reached the hospital. Now he sits cheerfully plaiting a mat, his feet well on the way to recovery and his courage high.

Another man, who has lost his fingers and toes, dragged himself along the ground even farther through the woods. His wife, who was also sick, went ahead and had a litter sent for him, but by that time they had already been months, wandering over high hills, through dense forests, sleeping on the ground by a fire, boiling their own rice in a saucepan, begging their way.

A blind boy was sitting beside a green stream, undressing for a bathe. His face was lined across and across with furrows like rivers on a map; his lips were swollen; they were full of holes and skinless on the inside. His sightless eyes were rimmed with red, the nails had fallen off his fingers, leaving them bloody; he smelled very strange. His nose was broken away at the nostrils and the upper lip had swelled.

He looked as if he were in a state of decomposition.

As he sat there, tugging at his *panung*, he suddenly yawned; evidently it exhausted him to take it off; he went on yawning; his tongue was thick and white, and very dirty; there were wine-red holes in the roof of his mouth, but his teeth gleamed white, nor was there anything wrong with his body; it was wonderful, built like an acrobat's.

This boy has come here led by a smaller boy who could scarcely find the way himself; they had had the most adventurous journey anybody could possibly have, and endured much on the way. One fine day they reached Chieng Mai, but got no farther, for he had been taken seriously ill there. They drove him out here and nursed him well. Of course he was sleepy – that was the effect of the medicine had on him; but he was well on the way to recovery, they said; his sight he would never regain, but he could sleep by the hour and enjoy bathing.

At last he got the *panung* off and slid into the green water, ducked, and rinsed his mouth. Then he smiled – a queer, distorted smile, and crawled out again; he looked like the crumbling antique statue of a Greek youth – the polished marble seamed and broken, but the classic form intact.

Kornerup, Friendly Siam, pp. 53-56

From *Siam – the need, the opportunity*, 1916.

Spirits, Ghosts and Charms

Pimpa's Ghost, October 1910

In October 1910, Pimpa, a boarder at the Girls' School at Chiang Mai, died during an operation for appendicitis. Edith Buck and Lucy Starling, missionary teachers at the school, both wrote accounts of her death and its aftermath. Starling's letter was written soon after the event and printed in her local newspaper in February 1911. Buck's article was written in January 1911 and appeared in Woman's Work *in August that year.*

Lucy Starling:
We had a sick girl for about a week, and on Saturday morning, the doctor decided she had appendicitis, and must be operated on at once. So she was removed to the hospital that afternoon, was operated on the next morning, and died on Monday afternoon. The doctor had waited too long, and she was literally rotten inside. The intestines were so soft, he did not dare search for the appendix. She was the only girl, and her mother, father and three brothers were all there, and were so distressed. But the mother, after the first outburst of grief, settled into a passive state, and at the funeral seemed no more concerned than any stranger. But these people are very heroic in death – in fact, seldom show deep emotion of any sort. Whether they are more heroic or less emotional than we, I do not know. These were very poor people, so Miss Buck and I paid the funeral expenses, which in this country, are very light. The girl's death struggles seemed to me dreadful, though Dr. Mason thought them very ordinary. But it took six of us to hold her. Her death disclosed some very painful circumstances, that I had better not mention, so on the whole I was very much shaken, and conclude not to go to the burial, and was invited to stay over at the doctor's for a game of tennis, after the funeral. Just as I was starting home, they asked me to stay to supper, and have some games

afterwards, so by bedtime, I had been able, to a degree, to get my mind off the last two days' happenings.

Last night after supper, Miss Buck went to the dormitory, to administer medicines, and found all the girls with their beds huddled together in a corner. As far as possible from where the sick girl had lain, with the old husband of the matron keeping them company. They were afraid (fifty girls and two teachers) and begging Miss Buck to stay with them, so she sat and talked with them a while. If I am not much mistaken, those girls will see a *pee*, or ghost, before they have forgotten about this girl's death, and I have been almost nervous enough to see one myself.

Edith M. Buck:
The third death that ever occurred in our school, was that of Pimpa last term. Hers was a bad case of appendicitis and she died in the hospital, her parents and brothers, Dr. Mason, Miss Starling and I all being with her at the time. The way the pupils and teachers of both the girls' and the boys' schools helped in the funeral and burial showed quite an advance in Christian fellowship here. According to native custom, relatives and people of the same village help each other in burning the dead. Toward a person dying away from home, no obligations are felt, no interest is taken, and it is difficult to get anyone to bury the body. But when Pimpa died, the girls who were able brought flowers and gave money, for her people are very poor – and some of the boys acted as pall bearers; two of their own accord stayed and helped fill the grave. This means much more than you who are accustomed to seeing all these things well looked after can realize. A mixed choir from the schools sang at the funeral service. Even among our Christian people there is still superstition, and we need not wonder at it. The night after Pimpa's death, I went over to the dormitory on an errand and found the mattresses, instead of being as usual side by side around the room, crowded on one side farthest from where Pimpa had slept, and a row of raised umbrellas formed a partition from the rest of the room. Each girl brings her own bedding and sleeps on the floor just as she does at home. I said, "What's the matter? are you afraid it will rain?" Some one remarked that they were "afraid" and one ventured that

it was "rats" they were afraid of. It was doubtless spirits. As I was about to leave they begged me to stay, they were "lonesome;" so I spent an hour. I told them they could trust Jesus to take care of them and Pimpa had gone where she would have no more pain. It was several nights, however, before they would sleep in the usual order.

I was pleased, last term, to notice marked improvement in regard to the petty thieving that we have always been troubled with. Satangs (the little copper coin of the country), pencils and handkerchiefs were often brought to me to find the owner – a thing that has rarely happened before, especially in regard to money

A Villageful of Demons

Dr Cort, like other missionaries, was much concerned about local belief in "demons" or evil spirits. One of the stories he liked to tell was about a village near Lampang that was harassed by demons and how he had overcome them. Here is the version in his unpublished memoir.

Another satisfying experience involved a village being harassed by demons. Most of the Thai are Buddhists, and Buddhists no more recognize the existence of evil spirits than Christians. But there is a strong underlayer of Animism in the more backward of the Thai, and it is a strange fact that Buddhism, by its insistence that man is bound to the Wheel, through its creed of accepting life as a prearranged state of existence, does tend to promote Animism amongst the masses. Just before I was transferred from Chiengmai a story came in from the backcountry of a man who had been attacked by a python. The snake swallowed one of his legs, but before he could proceed farther some neighbors came to the rescue of the victim. He refused their aid. He would not allow the snake to be killed. "This is my fate", he said calmly, "this is my fate." This strange combination of Buddhism and Animism is one of the few blights upon an otherwise intelligent people. A person in the grip of superstition and fear is difficult to help. A nation that has any superstition or fear in it just cannot take a place among the leading nations in the world.

Consider Ban Ling Kan, my village that was harassed by demons. Like all the Thai villages in the North, it consisted of a long, narrow street bordered by houses and lined by trees. I had gone there because we had heard that an epidemic had killed two hundred persons in it within a month and that most of the population was ill. As I entered the village I noticed that the first house was deserted, probably because death had struck there. It wasn't at all unusual for the surviving members of a family to abandon a house where death had come, where demons too malignant to be propitiated were lurking. No one else would dare to occupy a house under such a curse. Children would not play in it. The materials in it were taboo for firewood. It would stand there, empty and melancholy, until it rotted to the ground.

A person was lying on the porch of the next house, obviously very ill. Several members of the family came to greet me politely, – the Thai are invariably polite – but when I told them I was the Mission doctor come to help them they insisted there was no sickness in the village and most certainly none in the house. Their fear was in their eyes. I was confronted by a mass manifestation of that bizarre superstition having to do with offended family spirits. These spirits had moved in to punish the village, for what transgression no one knew. All the people did know was that the spirits were punishing them. The only way to placate them was not to give them greater offense by letting me do what I could for the sick.

I was boiling mad. I became angrier as I rode from house to house, each with its quota of sick and dying. Everywhere it was the same. Sick? Why, no one was sick. Someone must have fibbed to the doctor. But on the verandah of the last house a woman was tending a very sick boy. She looked up as I dismounted and begged me with great sobs to save her little son. Her daughter had died the previous day, she moaned, and now her son was dying. I raised her from her knee and learned that she had been a patient in our hospital a year ago. Of all the hundreds of people in Ban Ling Kan, she was the only one who was familiar with the work we were trying to do. But wasn't that enough, if I could save the boy? He was eight years old and he was in a bad way. His temperature was 106 and he was in convulsions and his pulse was almost uncountable.

The immediate diagnosis was malignant malaria and I gave him the usual injections of quinine and heart stimulants, following this with an enema and a fever bath. Within an hour his temperature had dropped, the convulsions had ceased and his pulse had improved. Presently he opened his eyes and spoke to his mother. I had been so busy all this while, working in the dimness of the gathering twilight as I had never worked before, that I had paid no attention to anything or anyone but the boy and his mother. Now I was startled to hear an assortment of sighs behind me. The compound was packed with people. Practically everyone who could walk was there. They had come to see what the foreign doctor was doing to the only patient amongst them whose family was willing to defy the demons.

As they realized that the boy was better, they besieged me with requests to treat their sick. In that one hectic hour or so I had breached the barriers which had separated us. I had, in the true meaning of the phrase, cast out the demons which had possessed them. For make no mistake about it: mental suggestion is a fearsome weapon, not only in the primitive mind, but in the cultured one as well. Every house was opened to me. In every house the disease was raging. In one house I found eight people stretched out on the floor and they were being cared for by a boy of ten who himself had a temperature of 103.

Cort, Yankee Thai, pp. 72-75

Trees at Night
By Mary Lou O'Brien

Trees at night look very strange:
Darkness brings a startling change
Just as if a spirit came,
Bewitching them – no two the same.

Some appear like ladies proud
Slim and upright; others bowed
Look like creatures grown quite old,
Trembling in the wind and cold.

Dancing girls with outstretched arms
Woo the night with fleeting charms;
Day transforms them into trees
Stirring lightly in the breeze.

Serpent trees that coil and twist,
Lover trees that keep a tryst;
Medusa trees with snaky boughs
Sense of fear and hate arouse.
Though I know they are but trees
A thousand shapes my fancy sees.
Magic power the darkness brings,
When such as I can see these things.

Siam Outlook, April 1931, p. 23

Ancestor Worship

In April 1911, Lucy Starling wrote to her parents on the subject of ancestor worship.

You must all know, from my letters home, that I have been very happy this year, though my chief task has necessarily been the acquiring of the language. This is a very dry subject, so I thought I'd tell you something of ancestor worship among the Laos. [...]

The Laos believe that at death the spirit of the departed takes up its abode at the place where its owner passed away. So rather than have the home infested by spirits, the sick are often taken out to the pig sty, or the roadside, and left to die. No matter how dearly beloved one has been in life, their spirits are greatly feared, and must be appeased by offerings of food, flowers, and even clothing. It is needless to say that those who profit by such a belief are the priests. Last term, we had a death in our school, and though the girl died in the hospital, for nights I would sleep in the part of the room where she had lain, but all our Christian (!) girls cuddled together in the opposite side of the room, with their umbrellas raised; evidently being ignorant of the belief in civilised America, that to raise an umbrella in the house is "bad luck."

Recently, a Laos of high rank, who lives just back of us, gave an all-day entertainment to his ancestors, and was kind enough to allow me to take some pictures – not of the ancestors but of their descendants. In the paved court-yard, a booth had been erected, under which the customary ceremonies took place. In the rear was a shelf, upon which was placed flowers and raw meat for the delectation of the departed. Underneath and at the sides, were hung some fifty scarves of every conceivable texture and color, for the dancing women. From the ceiling was suspended a long strip of white cloth, at which each woman took her turn. They swing around on this until thoroughly dizzy, after which they are supposed not to know anything that goes on, and sometimes dance until they fall from exhaustion. They often use liquor, to produce a rapture, though I saw no evidence of drinking at this place.

The band consisted of seven instruments, most of them being purely rhythmical. These people seem to have very few tunes and the one they played all day was the one I heard on my arrival in the country. It is very plaintive, a strain of five measures that ends on the fifth of the key, and of all of the sounds and sights, it alone seemed to belong to an unseen world. In its ceaseless repetition with never a note to bring it to a close, it seems like a wandering spirit seeking in vain for a resting place. The rhythm is as peculiar as the melody. The time is 4-4, and the accents come in this way: ONE and TWO and THREE and FOUR; or, on one, the ANDS on the 2nd and 3rd beats, and on 4.

After each dancer has swung around on the cloth until she is dizzy, she comes out in front and begins to dance. It is said the Oriental always does things backwards, and so with the Laos "Salome"; she starts out rather thinly clad, – though not considered immodest here – and adds her seven veils as her dance proceeds, selecting from the pile before her. She first winds one around her head, and sticks bunches of flowers around her ears. Then she steps into an extra skirt or two – or rather dances into them – and begins to wind the scarves about her shoulder and waist. By the time she is through, she looks like an animated rag-bag, or the victim of a rail-road accident, who has just left the surgeon.

While all this dressing has been going on, she has also tied strings around the wrists of the spectators, to protect them from the *pees*, or spirits; all the while keeping time to the music with her feet.

20 April 1911

Good Spirits

W. A. R. Wood and Reginald Le May took a more relaxed view of spirits than the missionaries …

Lao people do not only keep *evil* spirits. Almost all of them keep good spirits in their houses, or spirits, at any rate, which do not bite the hand that feeds them – for spirits, of course, have to be fed, just like any other domestic animals. Families moving to a new house often go to great trouble and expense to induce a suitable spirit or two to come and live there and look after them, and almost every house has a neat little shrine in which offerings for the spirits are placed.

Different spirits have different characters. Some of them are more or less lax in their moral principles, but most of them tend to be dreadfully narrow and puritanical. Once when my wife and I were staying at a small village, an old couple living nearby came to us in a very perturbed state of mind and complained that our cook had committed a horrible outrage in their house. We were greatly concerned, but on closer enquiry found that all our cook had actually done was to stroke the hand of their daughter. We said that we were sorry our cook had annoyed them, but suggested that, after all, the young lady's reputation would perhaps not be seriously damaged owing to her hand having been stroked. "But, my dear Sir and Madam," said the old father, "you do not understand. *We* really do not worry much about such things, if only your cook will make love to our daughter outside, and not in our house. We have a spirit living there which is extremely strict in its morals, and which is rendered furious if it sees even the slightest familiarity between unmarried persons. After what it has seen today it will, in its rage, bring down all sorts of evils and calamities upon us." So we had to pay several ticals to provide particularly spicy offerings for the propitiation of their spiritual Mrs. Grundy. The cook was made to contribute too, and was very annoyed about it, evidently thinking that he had not had his money's worth.

Wood, Land of Smiles, pp. 106-107

Spirits of the House

It should be said that not all the *Phi* are bad or malignant, and there is one kind, namely, *Phi Rüan*, or the "Spirits of the House," which may be compared to the penates or tutelary household gods of the Romans. These are of a kindly disposition, and a good story is told of how a new and unsuspecting missionary was trying to convert an old Lao woman to Christianity, and told her that, if she would allow his Master to come into the house, he would soon drive out all the *Phi*. This upset the old lady altogether and, rising in her wrath, she dared the missionary to bring his Master into her house, for her *Phi* was her guardian angel, and she could hardly conceive what disasters might happen if he were driven out.

Le May, An Asian Arcady, p. 139

The Sua Sen: A Were-Tiger at Chiengmai

W. A. R. Wood was evidently fascinated by stories of a "were-tiger" perhaps because the apparition may have been a British subject. Buak Ha was Arthur Queripel's house on Doi Suthep.

The inhabitants of Chiengmai are keeping a sharp look-out over their little boys and girls just now, for a Were-Tiger (*Sua Yen*) is reported to be wandering about the town, and several children have mysteriously vanished; at least, so people say, but the exact names and addresses of the victims are difficult to elicit.

The *Sua Yen* wanders about by day in the guise of a priest, some say an Indian priest, but it is impossible to examine him very closely, as he has a habit of disappearing suddenly in the middle of a conversation. At night he is – a tiger, with an insatiable appetite for little boys and girls.

There really is at Chiengmai an Indian, apparently insane, who dresses like a priest, and who runs away when spoken to, and there really is a tiger, which has been seen at Buak Ha on the Doi Sutep Mountain, and which has killed cattle at Ban Tong Fuang near Chiengmai. Perhaps a local romancer has combined those two visitors into a *Sua Yen*.

The Bangkok Times, 3 April 1928, p. 19

There are no were-wolves in Siam, but there are were-tigers, which are much worse. In the Peninsula were-tigers are comparatively common. I knew a young Malay at Patani whose father once put up a traveller in his house. Suspecting that there was something uncanny about the visitor, my friend's father told him on no account to let him out of his sight. At night the wayfarer crept out of the house; my friend crept after him and saw him hide behind a bush and let out a black and yellow striped tail! An alarm was given, whereupon the tail suddenly went back with a loud snap: but they took no more risks, and drove forth the *Rimau Jadi-jadian*, as a Malay call such folk.

In Northern Siam were-tigers are called *Sua Yen*. I have only ever met one of them, and he was an Indian of eccentric habits called Ram Das. His eccentricity first showed itself by his posing as a Buddhist priest. Later on he took to chaffing small children and giving them cakes and sweets. I do not believe that he meant harm of any sort, but unfortunately for him two children disappeared from their homes at about that time, and somehow or other a rumour got about that Ram Das had stolen the missing children away and eaten them. Next time he spoke to a child he was chased by an angry crowd, and narrowly escaped serious injury. I had him examined, and he was found to be insane, so I arranged for him to be sent over to the Mental Hospital at Rangoon. He was a most extraordinary looking person. When I saw him he had apparently not had a wash for years, and he certainly smelt very much like a tiger, only worse.

Wood, Land of Smiles, pp. 110-111

The Story of Ai Kham

While living in Lampang, I had at one time a round-faced, chubby Lao boy for a body servant, who not only gave full satisfaction, but was a far more pleasant and agreeable companion than his predecessor had been. Ai Kham was his name. After he had been with me for some time I contracted rather serious interior trouble, and was placed on a diet of milk and water. Now it appears that Ai Kham was not convinced of my appreciation of his services, and wanted to make me more fond of him. So he went to his father, who was cook to a friend of mine in Chiengmai and at the same time a doctor of witchcraft, and procured from him a supply of 'Ya Fêt, a potion concocted of the foulest ingredients imaginable. This he administered to me over a considerable period of time, with the result above recorded, and it was only by the merest chance that I discovered it.

Le May, An Asian Arcady, p. 138

Mr. R. le May, in his delightful book, an *Asian Arcady*, relates how a servant of his tried to dose him with some noxious substance in his drinking water, in order to render him more tractable. I knew the boy in question, and meeting him some time later, I told him that Mr. le May had published an account of his performance. He was rather flattered to hear that his alleged feat had been made known, as he said, "in every region of the earth," but he utterly denied that he had really put anything into his master's drinking water.

I was once warned that one of my servants had put a love potion into some fruit which he had given me. I at once said that I would eat the fruit, so as to show how little attention I paid to the matter, but when I was given details of the probable ingredients, I changed my mind; so I cannot say from personal experience what effect such charms may have.

Wood, Land of Smiles, p. 98

A Reputed Rejuvenator

Dr Arthur Kerr reviews a new wonder drug …

Some months ago Mr. H. B. Garrett wrote to me about a plant that was attracting much attention in Chiengmai, sending me a leaflet and a pamphlet on the subject. Later I heard from Dr. E. Cort about the same plant.

This plant is a well-known woody climber, *Butea superba*, called in N. Siam *kwao kua*. It apparently sometimes has tubers on its roots, which may be white, red or black. From these tubers, a drug, reputed to have miraculous properties, is made.

The first account of this drug seen was in the form of a single leaflet, printed on one side only, in Yuan (N. Siam) character, without date, author, printer or place of printing. This leaflet pointed out that the *kwao kua* had three kinds of tubers, black, red and white; of these, the black was the strongest and the white the weakest. In the directions given, the tuber had to be cut into thin slices and dried, then crushed into powder and mixed with honey. Of this mixture a pill the size of a peppercorn, half that size or a third that size had to be taken, according as the pills had been made from the white, red or black tubers. Only one pill was to be taken daily, and that at bed-time. Persons under forty years of age were forbidden to take the pills. A given charm (*kata*) had to be repeated twenty-seven times when the drug was compounded, and the five commandments had to be strictly observed while taking it. The leaflet goes on to say that, so taken for three to six months, these pills would cure all the ninety-six diseases, give long life and protect from danger.

It will be seen that this leaflet makes the extravagant claims often put forward for such drugs, and by itself would hardly merit further attention. Early this year, however, Luang Anusan Suntara, a well-known merchant in Chiengmai, had become so convinced of the virtues of this drug that he thought it his duty to give all mankind the opportunity of sharing in the benefits to be derived from it. Accordingly he published a pamphlet on the subject. This is in Siamese, and was issued in May, 1931. On the outside cover is a rough cut showing the *kwao kua* climbing up a tree, and the tubers on its roots. This is reproduced here. The reproduction, however, is not quite exact, as the artist has added details, such as venation of the leaves, not present in the original.

The main part of the pamphlet is a translation from the Burmese, by Nai Plien Kitisri, and that again is said to have been taken from an old palm-leaved manuscript found in the ruins of Pukam (Pagan). In the translation from the original various ways of making up the medicine

The Rejuvenator.

are described, and very extravagant claims are made for it; including its powers to rejuvenate, prolong life and cure all diseases, external and internal. Its ability to produce a soft, youthful skin, and to turn white hair black, are stressed. The most interesting part of the pamphlet is, however, Luang Anusan's own evidence, given in a foreword. Luang Anusan is, it may be said, a man well on in years. He tells us that, since taking the medicine, which he has done for more than ten months, he has been able to eat well, his bodily ailments have been lessened, and he feels vigorous. While formerly he had to use three or four blankets to keep him warm at night in the cold season, now he finds that one suffices. He also informs us that many witnesses have testified to him of women of seventy and eighty starting to menstruate again after taking these pills. I am told, however, by a reliable authority, that Luang Anusan himself has not yet developed a youthful appearance.

It will be interesting to follow the history of this medicine. If it soon drops into oblivion, as most of them do, we may take it that the claims made for it are baseless. On the other hand, it may turn out a serious rival to monkey-glands. Bangkok, August, 1931.

Journal of the Siam Society, Natural History Supplement,
vol. 8, 1932, pp. 336-337

Festivals and Rituals

New Year

Lucy Starling describes some New Year celebrations in Chiang Mai …

All this week, we have been enjoying the most delightful showers, a very grateful relief from the long dry season. It is too early for the rains to begin yet. and I can't say I enjoy that season, but I suppose the drought is broken. The first rain was last Saturday afternoon. The girls came down from the hill that morning in time to do their washing for Sunday. But Miss Buck stayed up until Sunday morning, so I had to watch the girls and it was very trying. New Year week is the one time in all the year, when the boys and girls are allowed to play together, and you may know the boys improve their opportunity. If I had charge of the school, I should not allow them to come on the premises, New Year or not. But Miss Buck allows it, and I was uneasy all day knowing they were in the place playing with the girls, and one of the boys even came up-stairs, but sent him down in a hurry. But we were invited out to Nawng Patit about a mile from here, that afternoon, and I was glad when the time came, and I got the girls out of town. Our matron has just built her[self] a new house, and we went out to attend the dedicatory exercises,

Wat Ku Tao, a Shan temple in
Chiang Mai with a "watermelon" chedi.
Photograph by Tanaka.
Oliver Backhouse.

"A beautiful temple at Nan." From Le May, *An Asian Arcady.*

and ate our supper there. As I may have mentioned before, one of the leading features of New Year time is throwing of water. Men and women parade the streets, in crowds, bearing big bowls of water and every passer-by is treated to a "sousing". The girls had told me that they were going to *hoat* me Saturday afternoon, so I went in an old dress, expecting to come home drenched. But when we were eating supper, a very heavy shower came up, and we had to wait some time before we could start home, and it was quite dark when we finally got there. So the girls' fun was spoiled, and we all got our "ducking" from the skies, instead.

Outside the temples on high poles, are floating hundreds of paper flags, of all colors, the flags being about a foot wide, and ten or fifteen yards long. They float gaily in the breeze, and every time the wind tosses them up, they are supposed to pull the person for whom they were raised, so far out of hell.

20 April 1911

The Spirit Ships
Mary Lou O'Brien describes the "fairy fleet" launched on the river at the autumn festival of Loy Kratong.

> I've watched the tiny boats float by,
> Upon a moon drenched stream.

A fairy fleet, a breath or sigh
Might make them but a dream.

I've seen the cargoes that they bear
To offer gods of fate;
Wee bowls of rice, some flowers to wear.
And coins, a precious freight!

I've seen the dancing points of light
Their small wax candles send,
(As if to mock the dark of night) –
With star-reflections, blend.

They say each craft bears far away,
To banish for a year,
All evil spirits which might stay
Too dangerously near.

If I could court good fortune so,
I'd launch a wee ship, too;
But I can only watch them go
And wonder what they'll do.

I've watched the tiny boats float by,
Upon a moon-drenched stream.
A fairy fleet; a breath or sigh
Might make them but a dream.

Note:- Each November, at the time of the full moon, many Lao householders launch small "toy" boats, bearing offerings to the spirits of the river. By so doing they believe that they send away their bad luck for a year, and assure themselves of good rice crops. This ceremony is called the "loi kratong."

Siam Outlook, October 1929, p. 390

A Laos Feast

Lucy Starling attends a Harvest festival service in the village of Ban Den.

"Harvest Home" among the Laos people comes at about the time of our New Year and is a season of feasting and merrymaking. Being coincident with our "week of prayer," the services held in different villages were made the occasion of feasts, several of which we attended.

One day we started at noon for Ban Den, and after a ride of about a mile left our horse by the roadside and walked through the narrow, winding paths of the village. After a few minutes, in which we had stirred up every pariah dog there, we came to a forest path cut through the bamboo, which towered above us like arches of a cathedral and pierced the green-leafed roof like the pipes of a huge organ. I for one would not exchange these wooded aisles for all the marbles and mosaics of Europe! And so we came to the pavilion that had been erected for the Christian service; its roof – bamboo poles overlaid with palm leaves; for pillars, the trunks of growing trees, entwined with green vines and the red and yellow blossoms of the tropics. From the roof hung festoons of tiny flowers in purple, white and yellow chains, while here and there through the leafage sifted the golden sunlight. There were no walls to shut out the forest beauty, and the people entered from all four sides through arches of palm leaves, and seated themselves on woven bamboo mats which covered the ground.

I have seldom seen a prettier sight than was before me that afternoon: the little girls – an abridged edition of their mothers who were seated behind them – with black hair combed straight back and rolled in a tight little knot (hairpins are unknown save as an American eccentricity), wearing white waists and striped skirts ; some with bright-colored scarves over the shoulder, all of them with flowers in their hair ; boys and men arrayed in white waists or duck coats, the loin cloth which falls in graceful folds to the knee. We had passed some naked urchins playing in a ditch, and they were covered with black mud from head to foot. I looked into the faces of these beautiful children and thought that no more powerful plea for foreign missions could be made than the contrast between the two groups.

And how the congregation did sing! Not the marches and two-steps we sometimes hear in American Sunday-schools, but "A mighty fortress is our God" and "The sands of time are sinking." As they sang, forest birds joined the chorus, and all Nature seemed to be praising God. I recalled the preacher at home who, at no little trouble and expense, secured a number of caged birds for his "Children's Service." Here, the birds join the children of Nature every Sabbath in their worship, and yet we pity the Lao with their so few benefits of civilization!

At the close of service, women appeared bearing lacquer trays, on which were bowls of food. I have often heard with pity of these people of the Orient "whose only food is rice," but pity is wasted when one sees the number of ways in which rice is served. You may have it ground and the beaten white of egg added; or, sweetened and pressed, it makes delicious rice cakes; cooked with cocoanut milk and cut into squares, it is a palatable mush; again, the whole grain is popped and mixed with cane sugar syrup, like pop-corn balls, and moulded into round and triangular shapes; mixed with peanuts or teal seed it becomes a toothsome confection. Besides these novel dishes, there is the endless variety of curries which all Oriental races eat with their rice. So I think it would be possible for even an American to eat this cereal the year round, without having it pall on the appetite.

The afternoon programme ended with songs and prayer, and then the people gathered around to bid us farewell. I have never met with a more gracious courtesy than among these simple Laos. Their bows would make a Frenchman green with envy.

I had not understood a word of the sermon, yet I went away from this little gathering with a spiritual uplift I have often failed to receive under eloquent preaching.

Woman's Work, May 1910, pp. 109-110

Processions

Mary Margaretta Wells taught at Prince Royal's College, where her husband, Kenneth Elmer Wells (1906-1980), succeeded William Harris as principal in 1939. She was also a writer and another editor of Siam Outlook. *She would later publish one of the first guidebooks to Chiang Mai.*

With a creaking of brakes our car jerked to a halt. The usually passable corner was a crowded thoroughfare of gesticulating people. It flashed through my mind that there had been an accident, but the smiling alert faces of the populace gave evidence of no alarming circumstances.

Then the mystical, enticing, indescribable sound of the cymbals and drums struck my ear, and I knew that I should witness another procession. I have a weakness for processions. The sound of the music so distinctly Oriental, so filled with the mysticism of the East, gets into the blood and holds one with an uncanny fascination. The vivid colors, unshaded yet harmonious, surpass in brilliance and fantasy the most abandoned Mardi Gras fete. The yellow robed priests seem a connecting link between the brightly clad people and the shining accessories of the religious pageant.

This particular procession was gorgeous and would make special merit. Preceding the first float, which carried gifts for the priests ranging from tins of sardines and notebooks to mosquito nets and umbrellas, came a band of small gong-beaters. These boys were all dressed alike in blue shirts and they wore new straw hats and dark glasses as a special mark of distinction. The floats were drawn by a double line of people, chiefly women and girls, pulling on the long ropes attached to these moving stages.

Following the first float came four little girls dressed in ancient costumes with long curved, gold tips on their fingers to elongate their finger nails and accentuate the graceful movements of their hands and wrists as they slowly performed a religious dance. There was a beauty, stateliness, and a certain sweetness about the dance that made it very fitting.

Drum and cymbal players preceded the next three floats. These were extremely interesting as they depicted portions from the *Ramayana*, the national epic. Marionettes mimed their little scenes to the huge delight of the children. Even in the passive, immobile faces of the priests were half concealed flickers of interest. Trooping along behind in motley formation came the inevitable assortment of children – the accompaniment of a procession in any land.

The sight of a procession such as this strongly reminds one of the old Miracle and Mystery Plays of England and Germany – miming while parading and giving performances in the churchyards.

All the world loves a procession.

Siam Outlook, April 1929, p. 324

Siamese Funeral Rites

Katharine Reichel reports on a funeral she attended in 1920 …

Picture to yourself a tropical afternoon at the beginning of the hot season; a long, dusty road; a procession of Buddhist priests in brilliant yellow robes; a motley crowd of people, official and common, following the funeral *cortege* of a Siamese Prince. Such a scene is stamped indelibly in the memories of some of your new missionaries who were seeing a cremation for the first time.

Early in the afternoon, four of us drove to the house of the late Prince, where we left a wreath and paid our respect to the family. The procession was almost ready to start. Just outside the gate stood a big dragon, made of paper-covered bamboo, mounted on a platform with wheels. The head of the dragon extended some fifteen feet into the air, while from head to tail it must have measured twelve feet. It filled the road. The body was covered with blue and white paper scales, and on each side there was a wing of purple paper, collapsible like a huge fan. A man inside the beast moved its head from side to side, now blinking the blue lidded eyes, now raising the wings and letting them fall. In the middle of the dragon rose a square tower, sparkling with gilt and spangles and ending in a pinnacle. Inside the tower were three caskets of graduated sizes. The lower two were false; the uppermost contained the remains of the Prince, now dead some five years. In the front, hung well up on the high tower, was the picture of the deceased draped in black.

Just behind the dragon several friends of the Prince had taken their positions. One bore the Prince's gold sword, another carried on a pillow of royal purple, his helmet and accoutrements. Behind them came the priests, followed by the crowd and the band playing the weirdest and most haunting of funeral dirges. When all was ready, many willing hands, whose owners wished to make merit, pulled on the long ropes tied in the funeral car and the slow walk began. We followed for a few roads, then, taking a short cut, we hurriedly drove to the cremation grounds just outside the old city wall. Under a bamboo pavilion we watched the officials arrive and awaited the procession.

The long line came to a halt some fifty yards from where we sat.

A funeral in Lampang. From Kornerup, *Friendly Siam*.

The picture was taken down; all the decorations which were to be used for some future cremation were removed, straw in large bunches was placed where it would aid the conflagration. After some time, a hush fell on the crowd. From the right, a large group of priests, led by an aged man who had to be assisted, moved up and sat around the base. Some kind of solemn rite was observed, but we could hear nothing of it. Some of the priests carried red Chinese umbrellas; others had white ones, while the head priest was sheltered from the sun by a huge umbrella of flaming orange silk.

I wish there were words to describe the beautiful coloring of that scene. When the priests had resumed their places, each having been presented with a new yellow robe, the crowd surged forward. The women led, walking once around the car, carrying little torches to be thrown on the fire at the proper time. The King had sent the sacred fuse from Bangkok which was to start the conflagration. One old Princess, however, became excited and threw in her torch before the fuse was lighted. In less time than it takes to tell it, the whole was a mass of fire and soon crumbled to a heap of glowing embers. While the gruesome thing burned, a man in a tree nearby threw limes filled with money among a crowd of small boys who scrambled wildly for the prizes. There seemed to be no general air of sadness, but rather one of festivity.

Woman's Work, November 1920, pp. 228-229

Celebrations

The Peace Celebrations, September 1919

The end of the Great War was celebrated at Chiang Mai some months after the signing of the Treaty of Versailles. In this undated letter, Cornelia Harris describes the ceremonies and the prominent role played in them by the boys of the Prince Royal's College. The boys had been "smartened up" by the adoption of a school uniform designed by Harold Morrison of the Borneo Company. They had been drilled by Major Sylow, the Danish Commander of the Gendarmerie.

Sunday the 21st was the first of the three days set apart by the Siamese Government for Peace Celebrations and the Mission arranged a special service in the church for the morning. Mrs. Campbell had decorated the interior of the church very prettily with Siamese flags grouped around the walls, and signal flags hanging from the crossbeams overhead. All the Europeans who were in Chieng Mai were present – also all the Siamese officials from the Viceroy downwards. Unfortunately he had misunderstood the time, and only arrived shortly before the Benediction. It showed some courage on his part, I thought, to put in an appearance at that late hour – I couldn't have done it – but he made his apologies like a man, in front of the whole congregation.

I left my home early as I knew that the school had arranged for the Army band to play them down to the church, and I waited to see how they looked. Outside the church, I found Major Sylow who has also an interest in the school, for lately he has been drilling the boys every morning and has smartened them up wonderfully. Shortly before church time we heard the band and from where we stood, we could see the whole length of the column as they came round by Mrs. McGilvary's over a slight rise in the road at the end of the bridge, and on to the church. It was an extremely pretty sight – to see the boys swinging along, harmony of blue and white, punctuated at regular intervals down this column, with the red, white and blue of the flags of the various Allied nationalities who are represented in Chieng Mai. About ten paces behind the band came the Siamese flag (6 x 4, as were all the other flags) carried by one of the bigger boys. Ten paces behind him, again, marched the first company of about twenty boys. Then at the same distance came the school flag and judging by his face, the boy who carried it wouldn't have changed places with the King himself. He was followed by the boys who were to sing in the choir, a company of about fifty. After him and always at the regulation distance came more flags and more squads of boys, American, British, French, Japanese, and Chinese. I heard afterwards that the Chinese were awfully pleased at having been represented. I wish you had been there to see it all. The whole thing was so pretty and so smartly done. A brighter and smarter looking lot of boys, you won't find anywhere in Siam, and though I shouldn't – the school uniform is distinctly becoming. I thought of "Alice in Wonderland."

"Their faces washed, their hair brushed
Their shoes were cleaned and neat,
And this was rather sad because
They hadn't any feet."

Only in this instance "they hadn't any shoes", bare feet being the fashion in this country. Major Sylow was as much taken as I was, and the way the boys marched did him credit.

We went into church when the procession halted, and watched the rest of the proceeding there. Each standard bearer took his flag up to the dais in turn, the whole congregation standing, knelt down and planted it in its place.

Later, she writes to her daughter ("my dearest Kiddie") about the dinner at the Viceroy's who at the time was Prince Bovoradej …

I was much surprised when the Viceroy told me he wanted me to sit at his table and on his right hand. Mr. Wood the British consul was the only other foreigner there. It was very kind of the Viceroy and showed he appreciated what we had done for him. Your father was at Chow Dara's table. It was a very informal supper. The Prince and other men served the ladies, had several toasts. First to the King proposed by the Viceroy. Then the British Emperor and Great Britain, French President and France, President Wilson and America. Then the Viceroy who was replying toasted all the Allies. The toast to America and the Mission in this country was really wonderful. It was put on too thick but it showed that our work was appreciated.

After supper there was a play given by the Royal Pages' school. It was entirely too long. We left before it was over and it was then after one o'clock. They do not know how to condense things enough. So now we have celebrated Peace. We hope and pray that Peace has come to stay in the world.

We are getting very anxious about the rice crop. We have had very little rain. I have never seen such a rainy season. If more rain does not fall in the next ten days I am much afraid there will be a famine.

26 September 1919

A Coronation Garden Party at the British Consulate, 1911

Lucy Starling joins a group of missionaries at a garden party in the grounds of the British Consulate.

This is a great day in Chieng Mai, in the English colony. The English consul is to celebrate the coronation with a garden party. There are to be boat-races, fireworks, and other games in the afternoon, and a Burmese theater in the evening. Miss Buck, Marie Collins, and I will take dinner with the Kerrs, – they live near the Consulate, – and go back in the evening to the theater. The boat course has been laid out in the river for some distance, with flags of all nations, and the men are busy practising for the races. I think they will wear themselves out before time for the show. A big float has been made, decorated with flags, and full of sailors, and is now in the water, going up and down stream, exciting the wonder of hundreds of natives. We have been hearing the music all morning, too. I could very easily dispense with that part of the entertainment, as the native music soon grows monotonous. Just now, it looks as if rain might spoil the show, I hope it won't.

24 May 1911

King George's Birthday, 1914

The Bangkok Times reports on the celebrations of King George V's official birthday at the British Consulate in 1914.

On Monday June 22nd the birthday of H.M. King George V was appropriately celebrated at the British Consulate. Mr. and Mrs. Wood were "at home" in honour of the King's Birthday. The Consulate was fittingly decorated with flags and mottoes wishing the King and Queen long life and prosperity. The programme consisted of native boxing, a relay race by the soldiers, a tug of war between the soldiers and Shans, climbing the greasy pole and a race carrying a greased coconut. Music was furnished by the military band for the barracks. Besides the foreign community among those present the following were noticed; H.E. Chao Phya Surasi, Lord Lieutenant of Monthon Bayap, H.E. the Chao Luang, Maj Gen. Phya Phiphit, Phya Warawichai, Commissioner of Chiengmai, Phra Inta Sat, Chief Judge of Monthon Bayap, etc.

Fun and games at the British Consulate, on the occasion of George V's Silver Jubilee in May 1935. The Consul's House had been built in 1915. Oliver Backhouse.

King George's Birthday, 1920

Mabel Cort is less than impressed by the entertainments (and the catering) in 1920 …

We had walking a greased pole over water, relay races, tugs of war, sack races, with the contestants tied up in the bags, heads and all and a hundred yard dashes. The Shans won the tug of war twice and the child-like people in their joy at victory turned handsprings, tore off their turbans and threw them in the air. The military band furnished the music and some of it was pretty weird. We were served cake, sandwiches, candy and tea as usual.

4 June 1920

The Birthday that was Grim

I celebrated my thirtieth birthday by getting myself cut off in the sources of a very gloomy creek called Mae Meeung, by going down with a bout of fever there, and by having my red dog taken by a panther.

On this birthday morning of mine I encountered a particularly heavy rain-storm; for some reason the rain also seemed particularly cold, and in a few minutes I was drenched through and shivering. I broke off inspection and returned to my gloomy camp, but by the time I had changed I knew I was in for a go of fever. Glancing out of the tent through the rain, I saw that the bed of the Mae Meeung was in high flood, and I knew, therefore, that for the time being we were completely cut off from the outside world. My transport couldn't cross over to the next creek owing to the steepness of the hills, it couldn't go down either bank of the Mae Meeung for the same reason, and were it to try the bed, the men would be swept off their feet by the rush of water. With this comforting knowledge I turned in.

At four o'clock my boy brought tea. The rain was still falling in a steady cataract, the sound of it on the canvas above my head resembling the muffled explosions of countless tiny bombs; mingled with the noise was the whining of mosquitoes and the thrumming of the spate in the Mae Meeung; on the ground-sheet the usual runs of ants were exploring for food.

I opened a tin of biscuits to go with the tea, not because I was hungry, but because I wanted something to do. When the dogs heard the crackling of the paper inside the tin they cocked their ears, and I tossed them some biscuits, being only too glad of their company. After tea I relapsed into a sort of vague coma, thinking, if I thought at all, about the singing of my quinine-sodden head and the pricking of the fever chills.

Just before dark, and it became dark before sunset in this gloomy gorge, my boy arrived with the lamp. It was then I noticed that the red dog was missing, and, assuming that in spite of the rain he had gone out for a nose round, I told the boy to call him in.

This produced no result, and a great disquietude assailed me. *Why* should the red be staying out so long in the rainy jungle just before dark when he might be in a comparatively safe and dry tent? I summoned the coolies, and soon I heard the "ugh, ugh, ugh" with which a Lao or Kamoo calls to an animal.

Campbell with Sclave at the Club in Lampang. From Teak-Wallah.

My boy reappeared, looking sombre: "Master," said he, "one of the coolies says he heard a cry in the jungle some time back. He thought nothing of it then, but now . . ."

So that *was* it. The red had gone out for a moment, only to be bagged by the sneaking panther that had probably been crouching for hours in the fringing jungle, watching the camp and waiting for its chance. I had been fond of the red, but were Sclave to be taken . . . Regardless of my fever, I jumped out of bed, threw something over my shoulders, assembled the parts of my gun, loaded both barrels, rushed out of the tent into the rain, and stared at the grim and dripping jungle wall that seemed to mock me.

Campbell, Teak-Wallah, pp. 225, 226-228

The King and Queen visit the North, January 1927

In January 1927, King Prajadhipok and Queen Rambai Barni visited the north of Siam, the first reigning Chakri monarchs to do so. In retrospect, the visit can be said to mark the apogee of the Anglo-American community at Chiang Mai. The royal couple visited the main institutions of the Mission and spent time relaxing at the Gymkhana Club and on Doi Suthep. The leading, non-official male members of the community (Dr McKean, Dr Cort, Rev. Harris, Mr Macfie and Mr Queripel) received royal honours.

Arrival at Paknampo

Leigh Williams is presented to the royal couple at Paknampo.

My most interesting contact with the Siamese ruling classes also occurred in Paknampo, when I was actually presented to His Majesty King Prajadhipok. The King and Queen were starting on a tour of the Northern provinces, and the royal train was due to stop at Paknampo station for the General and the Lord-Lieutenant to present their staffs, as well as the prominent local merchants, to His Majesty. I received an invitation from the Lord-Lieutenant to be present, and noted with dismay that the time of the royal train's arrival was two in the afternoon. This was about the hottest time of the day: I should have to wear tails and a white tie, and very much doubted whether my stiff collar and boiled shirt would not melt on me before my turn of introduction arrived! Knowing I should have to stand in the open or under a very thin awning, I had to add a white but incongruous "topee" to my attire.

The central royal saloon was a beautiful coach, painted white in distinction to the buff of the rest of the train. At a central window, beneath which the royal arms were emblazoned in gold, stood a slight figure whose inscrutable yet benevolent features reminded one of an image of Buddha,

His Majesty King Prajadhipok. The resemblance was strengthened by the fact that a party of priests seated on the ground opposite the royal coach broke into a religious chant. As the train came to a standstill a party of soldiers clattered out of the next coach and formed a guard with fixed bayonets on either side of the royal window. Then the presentations began.

After the officials had been introduced, an apparently private individual, carrying a golden bowl such as are used in giving offerings at a temple and from which protruded a rolled piece of parchment, knelt down in front of the King, who took the parchment, and handed it to an official in the coach. It was evidently a petition, and proved that direct access to the sovereign was by no means frowned upon in this absolute monarchy.

After I had made my bow, I was beckoned by a figure just descended from the train who wore the uniform of a general. It was H.R.H. Prince Purachatra of Kampengpet, whom I had met at home. He shook hands and chatted affably for a few minutes. I felt my stock with the local dignitaries rising quite considerably!

The presentations were over, His Majesty took the salute of the guard of honour, and the train steamed out. My last sight of it was the observation car at the rear, where one of Prince Purachatra's staff was busily filming the route with a cine-camera.

Williams, Green Prison, pp. 190-191

A Gorgeous Welcome

Mary Lou O'Brien writes of the mounting excitement in anticipation of the royal visit to Chiang Mai and of the recognition shown to the Mission's institutions.

For the past ten days Chiengmai has been in a state of feverish excitement for the King and Queen of Siam, and their royal attendants, have been visiting here. It was the first time since feudal days that a reigning monarch had come so far north and Chiengmai welcomed them in a manner that was simply "gorgeous". I wish that I had time to tell you about the welcome procession when eighty-four elephants resplendent with their lacquer and gold-leaf howdahs, cloth of gold covers, flower garlands, bells, etc. escorted and carried Their Majesties from the railway station to their temporary palace, or about some of the "homage processions" when subjects by the hundreds marched by with flowers, and when all of the odd, shy little mountain tribe people came out in all of their interesting costumes to pay their "respects" to the King, and to get a good look at the really pretty little Queen of the Kingdom. And how I should love to tell you about some of the wonderful Siamese dancing, it goes on for hours at a time, you know. And how we entertained the royal visitors at our Gymkhana Club for polo and tea, but time is flying, and I am going to tell you instead about the King's and Queen's visits to missionary schools and to our own McCormick Hospital where my husband spends his waking hours!

It was a great morning for McCormick, January 28th, and when I came over dressed in my almost best dress to see if I could be of any aid the place was buzzing with excitement. The hospital was all shining and clean, the patients were all ready and excited and there seemed to be nothing for an amateur to do so I whiled away the hour of waiting by practicing my curtsy in front of the instrument cabinet which has a glass case. I became quite good at it I thought, and I was all prepared to be presented to Their Majesties along with Dr. and Mrs. Cort. Miss Agnes Barland, Superintendent of Nurses, Hugh McKean, Business Manager, and my husband!

There was a great shrieking of the siren whistle on the pilot car which always precedes the royal motor, and in almost no time the royal cars were sweeping up the drive and the visitors were alighting. Something happened to my well-trained knees when I saw the King and Queen enter very quietly and shake hands with Dr. Cort! I had not expected this and when after shaking hands with Mrs. Cort they came to me and repeated the ceremony I was so overcome that my curtsey, my darling little curtsy, was a total loss.

We took the royal party all through the hospital, even into the kitchen, and they seemed really interested. I was perfectly delighted to discover that one of the ladies in waiting, whom I was escorting about, had gone to Western College, in the same town as Miami, where I went, Oxford, Ohio.

Mabel and Dr Cort are standing to the right of H.M. the King and the Queen. To the right of the couple is Prince Purachatra. From the *McCormick Hospital Report*, 1926-1927.

The King told Dr. Cort that he was surprised to find so fine a hospital outside of Bangkok.

As a result of the royal visit mission work in the northern province has received a gift of five-thousand ticals from the King, and Dara Wittaya Academy for Girls has received eight-hundred and fifty ticals (a tical is equivalent to about forty-five cents American gold) from the Queen. I think that is a very beautiful tribute from Buddhist rulers! The King has told Dr. McKean that he wishes to build a cottage for the Leper Asylum, too.

1 February 1927

A Fine Sight
Cornelia Harris writes to her daughter in America …
My dearest Kid
I am very sorry that I have not been able to write to you for two weeks. I have never been so rushed in my life – and now that I have some time, there is so much to tell that I hardly know where to begin.

First of all the King and Queen came in the afternoon of the 22nd. All officials, the Consuls, heads of the companies and the senior members of the Mission were asked to go to the Station to meet him (or rather them). All the other foreigners went to a pavilion just beyond the bridge in front of the Judge's house. The train was due at 2.45. We all had to be there at 2. The train was late, not arriving until 3.10. Waiting around was interesting as all the officials were in full dress. The ladies were in beautiful *sinns* and this place looked very gay. They had a red carpet from the train to the King's room at the station. It was most amusing to see men brushing any specks off if any one happened to step on it. When the train came in sight the army men were lined up on the western side of the shed. On the Eastern side were the officials and foreigners. The Tesa and Government met the party way at the end of the long train and then the King followed by his whole retinue came. In front of the foreign crowd he stopped and the two consuls and their wives were presented. No one else. The King was in uniform and the Queen was in a very simple dress of a *sinn* and blouse to match. The uniforms of the retinue were very gorgeous. The party were driven to the rest house where the elephant procession was in readiness for them. The people not in the procession took a new road which has

been cut from the freight station to Wat Pa Koi. In front of that wat a pavilion was ready for us.

We watched the procession from there and it was a fine sight. I can't begin to tell you how wonderful it was. There were over 80 elephants with all the wonderful trappings. I shall try and get photos of it for you. On the first half of the elephants,

A postcard with the Royal Elephant on which the King rode through Chiang Mai in January 1927. The Editor.

men dressed as they dressed in olden times when they went to battle. They held long spears. In the middle of the procession came Chao Luang riding the neck of an elephant and after him came other Lao Princes. Then came the King's elephant with an open howdah. A Lao Prince rode the neck of that elephant and another sat behind holding the royal umbrella over the King. Next came the Queen's elephant. This had a howdah with a cover over it – all gilded and with cloth of gold curtains. After that came Prince Damrong, Prince Kampaeng Pet, […] and the ladies in waiting and maids of honor. Then the Lao Princesses. It was a very fine sight and all through it I kept wishing you were here to see it. They say there will never be such a procession again.

We came home and changed and went down to the Club.

On the morning of the 23rd we were all asked to go in to watch the ceremonies. We had seats on each side of the royal pavilion built in front of the government building which had been turned into a kind of Palace. The pavilion is lovely, all red and gold. […] In the center is a raised dais on which are the two thrones. In front of the thrones are steps leading down to a lower floor where chairs (the school's by the way) face each other with an aisle between. On the day of the big ceremony the ladies sat on the right of the aisle and the men on the left. The officials wore full dress with all their decorations. The two Consuls were in their uniforms. And all foreign men were in evening dress (tails).

When the King and Queen came out the procession began to pass. First was the Boy Scouts band leading over a thousand scouts in companies. We had two companies. As the Scout master leading each company came just in front he and the boy holding the banner with the company number made a bow and then fell in behind his company. After the scouts came the rest of our school in school uniforms holding flags. Then came the different schools both girls and boys. The scouts and school children turned and formed in line on the opposite side of the street from the pavilion. […]. Then a long procession of women who turned and came and sat on the grass just by the pavilion. Then came different hill tribes – Haws, Maws, […] Kamoos, each with a float representing something peculiar to their tribe. The Chinese had a wonderful long dragon. The Burmese had a peacock, etc. Then came the B.B.C. float – an elephant dragging a log – one pushing a log, a little house with a little figure of a man [...]. The two elephants were perfect. Next came the Borneo Co. float which was very good indeed. There was a large elephant which could shake its head and turn his trunk. There were several quite big teak trees. There were Kamoos felling one and men standing around. Dr. Cort had a miniature hospital with dolls dressed as nurses and one dressed as a baby with a nurse feeding it with a bottle. Dr. McKean had a miniature of the Leper Island. The Haws had their pack mules.

After these had all filed past the Lao Chaos (men) headed by the Chao Luang of Chieng Mai, then were the Chao Luangs of Nan, Lumpang, and Lumpun. Next came the Lao Chaos (women) led by Chao Tipanan. Then two men in old Lao costumes and had the long gold fingernails. There were almost fifteen of them. In olden times the King and Queen would have danced out to meet the tributary princes. In this case they had four little Princesses and daughters of Chao Khuns who danced out to meet the Princesses instead. One of these was Prince Kampaeng Pet's little daughter who lives with Chao Dara. Another was the smaller of Chao Khun Pet's daughters. They were very pretty.

After this the four Chao Luangs took up offerings. They went on their hands and knees. As the Chao Luang of Chieng Mai can't read, the Chao Luang of Nan read an address. Then came the ceremony of tying the cord around the wrists and ankles of both the King and Queen. This is to keep the vital forces from leaving their Majesties.

The King presented a sword of state for the city to the Chao Luang and then presented decorations to the three Chao Luangs, Chao Dara, Ma Chao Luang, the Tesa and Chao Khun Pet. The band then played the National and that ended that ceremony.

In the afternoon we went to see the King present colors to the Boy Scouts.

The next 3 afternoons the King and Queen and the party went to the Club to play golf. No one was presented. They are all crazy over golf and it is a very good thing as the King is not strong and could hardly stand his hard life without exercise.

On Thursday evening we went in to see the dancing. The girls dancing with tapers around the elephant – with lighted tapers on its tusks. Also the dance of thirty of our boys and thirty government school boys dancing with the lighted lotus lanterns. That was beautiful and very wonderful.

Friday they came here but I will tell you of that in my next letter. The greatest excitement now is that your father, Dr. McKean, Dr. Cort, Mr. Queripel and Mr. Macfie are to dine with the King and Queen tomorrow night and be decorated. Dr. McKean and Mr. Macfie are to get one of the Orders of the White Elephant and the rest – one of the Orders of the Crown. It is the first time that missionaries have been decorated in Siam. […] Your father of course is very pleased that what he has done has received recognition. […]

The King has sent Tcs 5000. to Uncle Roderick (Secretary of the Mission) to be divided among the medical and educational institutions of the Mission. I shall also try and send you a copy of that letter and Uncle Roderick's reply.

You can see how tired I am by this miserable letter so I must close. I shall write the next letter soon to tell you the rest of the news.

I can't get over wishing that you were here. Katherine certainly is in luck and she is a dear. With love for Cousin Nellie and heaps for you.

Your devoted
Mother

1 February 1927

The Changing North

Are the Laos Lazy?

The Laos are often called lazy, unjustly, I think. No man who is not compelled to do so, works regularly if he does not expect to receive the fruit of his labor. When the conditions I have described were prevalent, what possible motive was there for industry or thrift? Conditions have changed, but the habits of a lifetime are difficult to change. The older men are still indolent, but a spirit of industry and thrift has grown greatly among the younger men in the past fifteen years. Now well-built frame houses with tile roofs are to be found in almost every village, better vegetables and fruits are in the markets, a better quality of foreign goods is demanded; the whole country is more prosperous. These advances have been brought about largely by the change in governmental conditions.

Freeman, An Oriental Land of the Free, p. 102

Progress in the North

According to a correspondent of The Bangkok Times *in 1914, people in the North were making great progress in many areas ...*

Chiengmai, March 12th
Your readers, or some of them, may possibly be interested in the following observations by a friend who travels around the country a good deal, concerning progress or the lack of progress in the North: –

In travelling through the country one is favourably impressed with the signs of progress. Roads are gradually improving; shade trees are being planted along the highways. Bullock carts are fast superseding the old-time cattle trams, bicycles speed back and forth between the different large government circles of the provinces, and in practically all the cities and environs carriages may be used with comfort.

The people eat better, dress better and receive higher wages than ever before. The minds of the people are becoming more enlightened; schools are springing up rapidly through the country.

The Bangkok Times, 24 March 1914, pp. 14-15

Acceleration of Mails

As the Northern Line edged closer to Chiang Mai, the city and the north began to lose their status as the "back of beyond". Here, The Bangkok Times *reports on improved communications in 1914.*

Slowly but surely Monthon Bayap is being drawn into closer touch with the capital. Opinions are inclined to differ as to the advisability of this, and one has to consider individual points of view in arriving at a decision. But on the whole the north welcomes any means whereby the distance may be shortened. Up to quite recently to get to Lampang the majority of people made Phrae the starting point of the journey by road. The progress of the railway, however, has made the journey very much easier, and Phrae will in course of time only be used by those going to Nan and further north and north east. Recently by carefully planning things beforehand, the journey from Lampang to Bangkok was made in three days. Most people do not care to travel like that, especially in March, even to put up a record, but it has served to bring home to people how the line is bringing the outer marches into closer union.

On the 15th June the next section of the northern line will be opened, i.e. from Pak Tar to Pak Ping. Pak Tar has no claim to remembrance other than that the junction of the Meh Yome and Meh Tar at this point rendered it necessary to bridge the river. This has not been a particularly easy work, and although construction has been busily proceeding on the other side of the Meh Yome at the same time as the bridge was being built, the river has proved an obstacle in the way of any further extension of the regular passenger service. Construction trains have been running on the other side for some time and at the present time the actual rail-head is at a point not far from the northern end of the tunnel which marks the beginning of the serious attack of the line on the foot hills leading to Pang Buei. When the line is opened for regular traffic to Pak Ping, we understand the Post and Telegraph Department will utilize the extension for accelerating the postal service between Bangkok and Lampang, Lampoon and Chiengmai. It has been remarked that the Department did not do this when the regular service ran, as now, to Pak Tar, but it must be remembered that the Department could only rely on the mails being carried to this side of the Meh Yome. Transport across the river in the high-water season is not the easiest of propositions, and once across the mails would have had to be transported by construction trains. Wisely, we believe, the Department resolved not to alter the existing arrangements until certain of a regular service.

The same problem has confronted the Department regarding the mails in the Peninsula. A number of people have written urging the authorities to take advantage of the construction trains running between various points to accelerate the present services. But those who know the vagaries of a construction train stopping here and being derailed there, do not question the soundness of the official reasoning, as regards both lines. The result of the line being opened to Pak Ping will mean at least an acceleration of two days for mails between Lampang, Lampoon, Chiengmai, and Bangkok. At present the mail is due in Lampang on a Sunday, and the mail for Bangkok closes on the same day. It is only by a rare stroke of luck that one is able to receive the mail and answer it the same day. It may be added that there is no real wish on the part of folk there to do this; the main desire seems to be to receive the incoming mails quicker. We have so far had no serious request for an accelerated dispatch. We incline to the view that generally the mails in the north mean much less than they do in the south, except as regard receipt. It has long been a matter of complaint in Lampang at any rate that the mail is not sorted as promptly as in Chiengmai. Say for instance the mail reaches Lampang about four on a Sunday afternoon, it is not sorted till the following day, whereas in Chiengmai they view things differently. The arrival of the mail means it must be sorted forth with, and if it is after regular office hours callers can always obtain their letters. The gain in time to the different Government Departments and especially the Ministry of Interior will likewise make for better administration.

The Bangkok Times, 8 April 1914, p. 19

A construction train crossing a viaduct around 1913. From Le May, *An Asian Arcady.*

Dr Cort's First Ford

Laura McKean's Miltonic poem on Dr Cort's first Ford (1920) was typed up by Mabel Cort who sent it to her family. It has been orthographically corrected here. The Corts had acquired the car in September 1919. Mabel Cort tells her family that it had "features that are not on Dr. Campbell's car", although it was expensive to run: "We shall not do much joy riding because these days at the present rate of gasoline here it costs us 15 satangs or about five cents a mile." At the anniversary party, there were various "stunts", including sketches and especially written poems. A highlight was the vanilla and chocolate ice cream made by the Barnes' Chinese cook. Presents were received from the Chao Luang and Princess Dara Rasami who received some of the ice cream "which she greatly enjoyed".

> Of Cort's first automobile and the fame
> Of that hard-earned car, whose speeding wheels
> Take pills unto the sick to ease their pains,
> I sing, O Muse and on suppliant knee,

Invoke thy aid to my adventurous song,
That with no ox-cart pace intends to move.

Through Chiengmai's palm-lined street and far beyond,
The Doctor can be traced by Lizzie's track,
Or, if within a mile you chance to be,
You'll hear the rattle of her loosened parts.

Now if within the templed city of Lampoon.
With glistening spires delight thee more,
Tell Cort to furnish Liz with gas and oil,
Then rain or shine, deep dust or quaggy mire,
That city's gates will soon appear in sight.

Perchance Cort's called some sable-vested night
When dark the moon and stars forget to shine
One lamp, her own or mayhaps a neighbor's
Is all Liz needs to light her tortuous way.
Where once the elephant and cattle train
Pursued their placid way with tinkling bells,
Now Lizzie's honk and rattling chains
Scatter with vulgar haste these ancient owners
Of the King's highway and pagoded lanes.

Where Sutep's templed peak and pine-clad hills
Once looked upon a city calm and still
And life slow moving seemed as though asleep,
A speck swift dashing here and there, they see,
And wondering from their heights, resentment hiss
What means this strange invasion of our land?

An answering wave from far Atlantic seas
And e'en beyond from Detroit's buzzing shores,
Repeat the magic name of Henry Ford,

And peak and hills and Maping's surging flood,
As o'er Elysian flowers, rolls its dirty stream,
Murmur, the past is lost, the future his.

E'er long all scared precincts he invade,
We must submit and welcome, tho deplore.
So, here's to Henry Ford's ubiquitous Liz.
Long may she rattle on to carry pills.

And here's to Lizzie's owners, kind and true
Long may they live to wear out many Fords.

2 October 1920

A Motor-Bus

With modern roads came buses, though bus rides were something of an adventure ...

There is now a good metalled road covering the fourteen miles between Den Chai and the town of Phre, under the charge of the Royal Railway Department, but at the time of which I write this road was more a grassy track than anything else, extremely bumpy in the dry season, and a quagmire in the rains, the period of my visit. We found a motor-bus plying for trade, and hired it for the ride, but it was a very old one and came near to proving our undoing, since at the foot of a hill it stuck in a morass, the left wheel spun away, and the suddenness of the shock shot us all out of the car. Fortunately we escaped with only a few bruises, and thought no more about it, for if one travels by motor-car in the interior of Siam, one must be prepared for these mishaps. The only unpleasantness was that we had to walk the remaining four miles in the heat of the afternoon.

Le May, An Asian Arcady, p. 70

I was also lucky in finding an acquaintance at Lampang. Unfortunately she and her husband were just off on leave, but able and willing to arrange that elephants should work in the forest for me to see and sketch if

I could make my own way there. The 'buses made this easy, and though something of a gamble, one worth risking, being so much less expensive than to hire a private car. The advent of the motor-bus has had the demoralising effect of magic on the native, who looks on it as a means to get-rich-quick. Encouraged by the salesman he invests his savings in one of the marvellous carriages that go so quickly, carry so many paying passengers, and mean so little work to the driver. Never having hitherto seen any machine more complicated than a Singer's sewing-machine, which I saw in places incredibly remote – he learns to drive and to change a tyre, and do the roughest sort of repairs. Then he proceeds to drive his 'bus to death, sometimes, but wonderfully seldom, to its death by accident, afterwards sorrowfully awakening to the fact that he has killed the goose that laid the golden eggs and must return to labour or starve.

Whitehead, Siam and Cambodia, p. 241

The Chinese Bus

The next morning, while it was still dark, Miss Niblock and I got on our Chinese bus for Chieng Rai. It had to be completely reloaded in order to make room for the two of us and even so we were tightly packed. You must always make the driver arrange everything to your satisfaction before you start on your journey, for *en route* he will do nothing. Bus and truck travel hereabouts is an art. You must know which drivers are reliable, which trucks are least likely to come apart on the way (a difficult decision since they all look fit for the junk yard), how best to bargain for the fare, and how to have the truck reloaded so that one survives the journey without suffering permanent dislocation of the joints. If you don't watch out, the driver will, at the last moment, sneak gasoline tins into the space where you had planned to place your feet. It is also a good idea to take along a blanket and pillow, as well as drinking water, cup, and food, though you can always buy fruit on the way. As for rest rooms, you might as well forget about such Western luxuries and be on the lookout for suitable bushes when the need arises.

Rickover, Pepper, Rice, and Elephants, p. 202

Old and New

In 1927, Laura McKean reflects on the changes she had seen over the years, and their meaning.

There is an elusive, inarticulate something termed, "The Call of the East" which old residents of the Orient are supposed to hear when they are in the West and which irresistibly draws them eastward. Distance seems to lend an enchantment that metamorphoses the dark blue experiences of torrid heat, mosquitoes and malaria into a rosy memory of palm and bamboo, the tamarind, and the mango, of the gorgeous poinciana and the yellow glow of the tree of "Summer Breezes". So back we each come to his particular spot in that mystical East.

The particular spot in mind just now is that old city called new (Chiengmai, New City) when it was built on the ruins of its predecessor (the original city was founded in 1296) and is the last capital that has ruled this delightful valley nestled neath the shadow of Mount Sutep. Peace days were established before its encircling walls and lotus covered moats were destroyed by hostile neighbors. And now like a moth breaking through its chrysalis to a greater perfection, the city is spreading beyond its crumbling walls along the river's bank and to the neighboring rice fields, turning them into streets of commerce or suburban homes.

Here in this old city called New the centuries jostle each other in friendly conflict. French and English and American cars throttle their engines by the side of the King's Highway till the cumbersome elephant sidles timidly by.

At the McGilvary Seminary representatives of the National Church were discussing ways and means of caring for the needy orphans of the city while with all the pomp of royalty a baby white elephant, escorted by a train of elephants, was being conducted through the street to the Governor's country place. Admiring crowds in Gala dress lined the streets. On the backs of some of the elephants were pipers who filled the air with the weird music which custom or tradition has designated as suitable rhythm for the stately stride of the elephant. Beneath the spreading branches of forest trees this royal baby was sprinkled with holy water and garlanded with flowers. And all because according to the ancient tradition, a white elephant is a harbinger of prosperity and good luck.

The birth of this elephant at about the time our new King ascended the throne has created the general feeling of reverence and loyalty toward him and a general expectancy of prosperity during his reign. The psychological effect on the people in general is good and so in a way augurs "good luck" for the young King.

Transition times are always interesting as old customs give way to new. This does not occur without a struggle, however. Now and then an old custom long discarded will come to life unexpectedly, to the amusement and irritation of the younger generation.

Recently a gentleman of the old school gave a garden party in which men and women guests were received in separate pavilions. There was a general raising of the female eyebrows in disapprobation, while a few voiced their displeasure by "Why the very idea, it is a long time since this custom was in vogue".

In a recent Siamese magazine was an article discussing the growing sentiment against absolutism throughout Asia and favoring the rights of people to share in the affairs of government.

Organizations unheard of a generation ago are growing in popularity as the Red Cross Society, co-operative association, nurses' training schools and temperance societies (not confined by any means to the Christians but joined by all creeds). These are just a few that might be mentioned.

The East is changing. Kipling's dictum needs revision, for those Ten Commandments hurled eastward from Sinai's peak are encircling the world and are coming back to their own East from the West. One of the problems of the East will be to keep the beautiful in her customs and traditions, and even in her superstitions, while selecting the true and the essential in modern civilization.

Chiengmai.

Siam Outlook, April 1927, pp. 129-131

The Virile North

"Chang", writing to the editor of The Bangkok Times *in March 1920, describes four veterans of life in the north – a forest manager, a missionary teacher, a diplomat and a forest conservator.*

Dear Sir,

Happening to drop in at the Chiengmai Gymkhana Club the other evening. I wandered over to watch a strenuous tennis four in progress. Whilst watching this four I was suddenly struck with the fact that the four players engaged had each put in a long number of years in this country, and on reckoning up, I found to my astonishment that their years of residence in Siam aggregated not less than 140 years. The players were Mr. D. F. Macfie (37 years) the Rev. Wm. Harris (37 years) Mr. W. A. R. Wood (33 years) and Mr. H. E. Garrett (33 years). As a tennis four, I imagine their years of residence here creates the record for this country, and what is more, the average pair of griffins arriving today would stand a very poor chance against any two of these veterans.

The Bangkok Times, 19 March 1929, p. 19

Big Ben Chimes in Chiang Mai

By 1929, the radio had reached Chiang Mai and the world seemed ever closer. Reception was said to be better than in Bangkok.

Chiengmai which has always declared that what it does today Bangkok follows to-morrow, now keeps its clocks, or some of them, according to Big Ben in London. The striking of the hours is clearly received by at least one set in the northern capital, and the programmes broadcasted in London which end up "Good night everybody." These come through in Chiengmai in the early morning and listeners have no difficulty in tuning in and receiving these items.

The Bangkok Times, 19 April 1929, p. 35

Gradually Going Forward

Speaking in a general manner, with the opening up of the country by communications, the north of Siam is going gradually forward, and the next ten years will no doubt witness greater strides still. The east side is much more backward than the rest, and, unless the teak forests are opened up again round Nan, there is not much scope for development there, but in the far north, just south of Chieng Rai, there are enormous tracts of land just waiting for a population to cultivate them. There have been rumours for some time past that large bands of Japanese are coming to Siam to take up land in this district for rice-cultivation under the new treaty which has just been signed between the two countries, but it is doubtful whether this will eventuate.

Le May, An Asian Arcady, p. 101

Not the City it was Half a Century Ago

In 1924, Siam Outlook *described the nature of the change since the foundation of the Mission station some fifty-six years before:*

Neither is Chiengmai as a city what it was half a century ago. Ninety long weary days did it take the pioneers to come up the river by boat from Bangkok to Chiengmai. Now you may have your afternoon tea in the capital and on the following evening sit down to dinner in the second city of the kingdom. In those days they picked the way through the winding lanes of the city or walked from village to village in the country. Now bridges of concrete or steel and macadamized roads reaching out into the country in all directions provide smooth roadways over which we swiftly arrive at our destination in motor cars. In the early days many long months did they await news from the outside world. And now before another year will have passed the buzz of the airplane overhead will announce the mail to have arrived from Bangkok.

More importantly, Siam Outlook *concluded:*

Thus Chiengmai has changed. More and more have the ideas of the outside world pressed in and changed the old ideas. And not only have there been these physical changes but spiritual changes have taken place as well.

Siam Outlook, January 1924, pp. 18-19

The old Khua Kula teak bridge at Chiang Mai, irreparably damaged by logs, July 1932, and replaced by a steel construction. Oliver Backhouse.

Then and Now

It is difficult, indeed almost impossible, for those of us who have come to Siam but recently to even begin to realize what the Siam of the pioneer missionary days must have been like. We who travel over wonderfully fine roads, ride in automobiles, (albeit they be Fords) read by electric light, have daily supply of ice, travel to the north on the express which makes the bi-weekly trip in twenty six hours' time (a trip which is the early days consumed six weeks' time and had to be made by boat), take for granted the friendly attitude of the Siamese toward us and our work, read daily papers, English and Siamese, and go about Bangkok in trams can only travel at the courage of those pathfinders, and at this safe distance of time wish, half-heartedly, that we had experienced some of the hardships of those days.

Even in Nan, the most remote station of all, a missionary Ford has opened the way for road improvement, and within four years' time a motor road from Prae to Nan will be ready. Thus does the romance of olden times give way to the spirit of modernity. The most beautiful road in Siam connects Lampang with once-remote Chiengrai, a distance of about one hundred and twenty-five miles, and buses fly back and forth each day of the week.

Siam Outlook, October 1928, p. 304

The Tropical Congress - Travellers Return from Chiengmai

In December 1930, delegates from the Eighth Congress of the Far Eastern Association of Tropical Medicine visited Chiang Mai in what was almost certainly the first group excursion of its kind to the north. The Bangkok Times reported on the programme in some detail.

The express from Chiengmai bringing back the members of the F.E.A.T.M. and their families ran gently into the Hua Lampong terminus this morning at 9.45 a.m., five minutes ahead of time. The travellers expressed themselves delighted with the excursion, and they were loaded with curios, Chiengmai roses and *sins*, etc. But the treasures of the north have not been unduly depleted, although the pockets of the tourists are lighter than when they left Bangkok.

Writing from Chiengmai yesterday morning at one a.m. a correspondent says: -

Early on Tuesday the visiting delegates, their wives and friends called in a body to pay their respect to His Highness Prince Dossiriwongs, the Tesa. A visit was then made to the new Health Centre, a building but recently completed, beautiful in appearance and modern in equipment.

Shortly after 10 o'clock the visitors arrived at the Leper Asylum. This institution is located on an island in the Meping River. It is reached by a drive of some five miles from the city along a winding and interesting road.

The Van Millingens motoring near Lampang. Oliver Backhouse.

The visitors were received in the newly completed Community House, where a brief address of welcome was made by Dr. McKean, who introduced the Superintendent, Mr. J. Hugh McKean, and the other members of staff.

A string band of leper boys provided music. A drive through the Asylum grounds enabled the visitors to see most of the more than one hundred buildings. Much interest was shown in the samples of Chaulmoogra fruit grown in the Asylum gardens. The visit closed with a visit to a newly completed Administration Building, where refreshments were served.

Dr. Deggeler, Secretary General of the Far Eastern Association of Tropical Medicine, gave a brief address expressing the thanks of the visitors.

Dr. McKean replied briefly by expressing the appreciation of the management in the visit of so many noted men and women from other lands.

An interesting afternoon was afforded the guests by a tea at the McCormick Hospital. Opportunity was given for inspection of the many departments of the hospital, and the manner in which the many activities are carried on. Many words of approval and appreciation were heard from the visitors.

The evening hours gave opportunity for a visit to the winter fair in operation at the Agricultural School. Interesting displays of samples of handicraft, and curios peculiar to the North helped to give additional understanding of the people of the North to the visitors from the foreign lands.

On Wednesday morning through the kindness of the Borneo Company Limited, there was staged a very interesting illustration of the method of working into the river teak logs that have been stranded on sandbars.

Three large well trained hounding elephants exhibited their skills, their strength and their remarkable understanding of their task, by dragging, pushing, rolling or otherwise moving the great logs from the bank into the stream.

The location was conveniently near to the iron bridge in the city so that the spectators who lined the bridge in the city had a most excellent opportunity to see the whole of the very interesting spectacle, a sight quite unfamiliar to most of the guests. Words of appreciation were tendered to Mr. Hoare of the Borneo Co., who had the work in charge.

After nine o'clock the guests drove to Lampoon, the charming little walled city some eighteen miles south of Chiengmai. Upon arriving in Lampoon the visitors were received and conducted by guides over the grounds of Wat Luang (Haribunjaya). There they viewed the temple, the big pagoda, library, the large gong and the museum containing many objects of interest.

A very interesting display of weaving, carving, etc. was arranged for the visitors on the outskirts of the city on the grounds of Topless Pagoda. Each one had an opportunity of seeing the weavers at work on the national looms. The finished articles were on sale in the many booths encircling the Pagoda grounds.

A temporary sala was provided with chairs and "smokes", a very welcome arrangement for those who had so strenuously viewed and bargained for the various articles on displays. The party returned to Chiengmai at noon.

At three o'clock guests were driven to the Municipal Offices, and the historic Wat Prasing with its beautiful temple and library. From there a steady stream of cars, marked by dense clouds of dust, proceeded north through the White Elephant Gate to visit the two statues of the white elephants, the Lion Grounds and Wat Chet Yod the temple of Seven Spires.

To many this last temple was the most interesting as it appeared in its original, somewhat scarred and defaced by time, but still revealing everywhere the skilled workmanship of ages long gone by.

The March of Progress

But these primitive, arcadian conditions in Siam are going to change, and with them the lives of the people. The railway is forging rapidly ahead, and with it will go many of the accompaniments of our modern Western civilization. Roads are springing up on all sides, and hundreds of Ford and Chevrolet cars and trucks are pouring into the country to serve the up-country districts. The cinema hall, put up in a day with tin roof and bamboo sides, is early in the field, and cheap American cigarettes soon begin to oust the native-made tobacco. Townlets arise, seemingly from nowhere as in the pantomime, conjured up out of the brain of the ubiquitous Chinaman, who is prepared to buy and sell anything that will bring grist to his mill. What of my arcadian peasant, after a few years' mingling with all the rogues and vagrants of the place, irresistibly drawn by the thought of sheep to be fleeced? I have heard it said already that when the emigrants now return yearly from their work in the Ayudhya plains, they have to be guarded to their homes by the gendarmerie, or they would lose their little all at the hands of the pack of wolves that stand hungrily round the station of Korat with protruding tongues, waiting for the sheep to arrive.

We cannot stop the march of progress if we would. The world is growing smaller and smaller every year, and scarcely any action of importance can take place nowadays in one country without its echoes reverberating throughout the others in a short space of time. But although you can within a few years develop a country materially by introducing all the most modern inventions, you cannot automatically, by pressing a button, develop the moral and spiritual nature of the people of that country, to enable them to appraise these material changes at their proper value. You and I know how much more real pleasure is to be obtained from a walk through beautiful surroundings, costing nothing but the effort, than from the most lavish theatrical or cinematograph display. But how are they to know it? Still the future must be faced with confidence and the present looked upon as a transitional period from which the people will in time emerge *with a higher standard of living and* better equipped to maintain themselves against all comers.

Le May, Siamese Tales, pp. 191-192

The bridge at Tha Chompu between Lampang and Chiang Mai, built 1919-1920. The Editor.

Afterthoughts

Chiengmai
By Laura McKean

Chiengmai, with your stately palms,
Etched on summer sky so calm,
I dream of you.
Crumbling walls along the moat,
Where blooming lotus gaily float,
I dream of you.
Rice field green with growing crops.
Dotted with swaying bamboo tops.
I dream of you,
Brown maid decked with orchids rare
Swarthy swain piping an amorous air,
I dream of you.
"Dawk Keo" sweetening the summer breeze
"Pitchaleo" in the tamarind trees,
I dream of you.
Old friends whose years of kindly thought
Have bonds of previous friendship wrought,
I dream of you.

Siam Outlook, April 1931, p. 83

The Importance of Good Manners

The universal friendliness of the Siamese people has been the subject of remark not only by foreign residents but by casual visitors. Consul Wood entitled one of his books, *The Land of Smiles*, and the Dane, Kornerup, *Friendly Siam*. It used to be said that a foreigner could travel about with empty pockets and not go hungry. Courtesy was the universal rule; any display of temper was considered bad manners. The Siamese followed the injunction of the cowboy in *The Virginian*, "when you say that, smile!" Severe reprimands were accepted respectfully, if given without a frown.

Gaucheries were, as a rule, committed by foreigners, *not* Siamese. The code of etiquette was the growth of centuries and was strictly observed; it was founded on innate courtesy, respect and consideration of others. Where such "breaks" were made from excusable ignorance, the Siamese were quick to forgive; but when through indifference, they were not quick to forget. I shall never cease to be thankful that my wife, who spoke the language faultlessly and always observed Siamese etiquette, coached me in both; wherefore I was able to avoid many pitfalls.

How, then, may the foreigner – whether businessman or missionary – successfully meet, and win the regard of the native? The fundamental rule is friendliness; for "the greatest of all is love;" the next is modesty – native manners are not ours, but they are *good* manners; and finally, the determination to learn the language to the best of one's ability, language, to that extent will the native forget he is a foreigner, and will "open up" to him.

William Harris, Recollections, p. 43

Night in Chiengmai
By Mary Lou O'Brien

There's a whisper of a breeze in the slim palm trees,
There's a crescent of a moon riding high;
There's a fragrance in the air, blossoms wafted everywhere,
And a billion stars or so bedeck the sky.

While the sound of hollow drums lightly beaten faintly comes
To my ears from Buddhist temples far away,
I hear banjo gently strummed and a Lao tune softly hummed,
And I feel the peace that comes with close of day.
There's a bobbing orange light which is mocking at the night,
There's the tiny silver tinkle of a bell,
And a bullock cart goes by on its way home from Chiengmai
With the driver tired but sure that all is well.

From the barracks down the river comes the sad-sweet first long quiver.
Of a bugle sounding taps for soldiers there;
And our mountain seems to speak from her darkened lofty peak;
Sleep in peace for God is always everywhere.

Siam Outlook, April 1927, p. 167

Epilogue

Dear Reader, we have come to the end. And you, who are sitting by your winter fireside, with the curtain drawn and the cold north wind shut out, and have just put down the book, where has your spirit been the while? With your body, still in its western home, or with me, wandering through this enchanting, eastern land? Can you close your eyes and see the evergreen jungle, with its deep ravines, its gigantic, mysterious tree-ferns, its parasitic growths coiling themselves round the smooth tree trunks, its myriad insect life, its running, rocky streams and fairy-like waterfalls? Can you hear the tiger's snarl, or the hoopoe's call? Can you see the "tawny," smiling Lao, whose cheerful countenance and independent mind cover a multitude of minor human failings, pitching a tent or saddling a horse, or playing on his banjo those plaintive airs he loves so well, or climbing on to his elephant's neck by the route of the latter's bended knee? Can you see the Lao girls, with their pretty faces framed in coils of coal-black hair, and their supple bodies draped in *sin* of variegated hues? Can you see the waving fields of golden rice, burning in the tropical sunlight and fringed with lines of tall and stately palms, through which the houses of the villagers peep? Can you see the flowing lines and graceful spire of the Lao pagoda, and the *naga*-tipped, heavy, tiled roof of the temple-hall, the whole in its still, leafy garden setting? Can you see the fat, ugly old buffalo, the real basic coin of the Far East, wallowing in the mud, or lumbering across the field with its snout nearly touching the ground, and the smallest of naked children sitting astride its ponderous back, guiding it where he will? Or the majestic elephant, the very acme of dignity, come glistening black from his bath in the stream, or dusting his back, in airy fashion, with a coconut-leaf held in his trunk? What more can you conjure up? What other picture can we throw on the screen? The long stretches of high green-clad hills; the mighty rivers, flowing, some from the hills of Siam, some from the lakes of far-off Thibet, but all finding their way at length to Far Eastern Seas; the long, romantic caravans of mules and ponies bringing down the products of China from the heart of Yunnan; the teak forests, and the masses of seasoning logs jammed at low water on the river rapids.

Yes, and many more such sights which serve to make this country of the Lao, if not the Promised Land, yet one which grows dearer to the heart the more one knows it, and the stranger feels that, if he must be exiled from his own native shores, he could not find a land of greater charm and sympathy in which to spend his days. And now. Dear Reader, farewell – we have occupied the stage long enough – 'tis time the curtains fell; so both my elephants and I will make our bow, and leave you to your dreams.

Le May, An Asian Arcady, pp. 263-264

The British Consular Elephants, 1913. From Le May, *An Asian Arcady*.

Appendix – Facts and Figures

The entry in the famous eleventh edition of Encyclopædia Britannica sums up the situation of Chiang Mai as foreigners saw it shortly after the turn of the twentieth century. In 1930, the Siamese Ministry of Commerce and Communications provided an up-to-date account of the city in the handbook Siam: General and Medical Features. *This was produced for the delegates at the Eighth Congress of the Far Eastern Association of Tropical Medicine, held in Bangkok in December 1930.*

Chiang Mai in the 1910 Britannica

Chieng Mai, the capital of the Lao state of the same name and of the provincial division of Siam called Bayap, situated in 99° 0' E., 18° 46' N. The town, enclosed by massive but decaying walls, lies on the right bank of the river Me Ping, one of the branches of the Me Nam, in a plain 800 ft. above sea-level, surrounded by high, wooded mountains. It has streets intersecting at right angles, and an enceinte within which is the palace of the Chao, or hereditary chief. The east and west banks of the river are connected by a fine teak bridge. The American Presbyterian Mission, established here in 1867, has a large number of converts and has done much good educational work. Chieng Mai, which the Burmese have corrupted into Zimmé, by which name it is known to many Europeans, has long been an important trade centre, resorted to by Chinese merchants from the north and east, and by Burmese, Shans and Siamese from the west and south. It is, moreover, the centre of the teak trade of Siam, in which many Burmese and several Chinese and European firms are engaged. The total value of the import and export trade of the Bayap division amounts to about £2,500,000 a year.

The Siamese high commissioner of Bayap division has his headquarters in Chieng Mai, and though the hereditary chief continues as the nominal ruler, as is also the case in the other Lao states of Nan, Pre, Lampun, Napawn [sic] Lampang and Tern, which make up the division, the government is entirely in the hands of that official and his staff. The government forest department, founded in 1896, has done good work in the division, and the conservator of forests has his headquarters in Chieng Mai. The headquarters of an army division are also situated here. A British consul resides at Chieng Mai, where, in addition to the ordinary law courts, there is an international court having jurisdiction in all cases in which British subjects are parties.

The population, about 20,000, consists mainly of Laos, with many Shans, a few Burmese, Chinese and Siamese and some fifty Europeans. Hill tribes (Ka) inhabit the neighbouring mountains in large numbers.

Chieng Mai was formerly the capital of a united Lao kingdom, which, at one time independent, afterwards subject to Burma and then to Siam, and later broken up into a number of states, has finally become a provincial division of Siam. In 1902 a rising of discontented Shans took place in Bayap which at one time seemed serious, several towns being attacked and Chieng Mai itself threatened. The disturbance was quelled and the malcontents eventually hunted out, but not without losses which included the commissioner of Pre and a European officer of gendarmerie.

From Encyclopædia Britannica, 11ᵗʰ edition, Cambridge and New York, vol. 6, 1910

Chiang Mai in 1930

Chiangmai, the second largest city of Siam, with its suburb has a population of about 350,000, the majority of which is Thai or Lao (the word Lao is sometimes used to designate the Thai population of Northern and Eastern Siam. This word is derived from the word Lava, the name of the original population of these regions). Chiengmai is a city of beautiful and interesting temples built on a broad and fertile plain watered by the clear stream of the Me Ping, one of the northern branches of the Menam Chao Phya. Chiengmai was founded in the 11ᵗʰ century by Meng Rai, the Thai chief. Subsequently it became the centre of a large kingdom, and very often the point upon which the struggles between Burma and Siam converged. The town is surrounded by massive walls and ramparts, and is the headquarters of the Lord-Lieutenant of the North-Western Provinces. It has well laid out streets and shady avenues.

Chiengmai is the most important centre of the teak industry. Being the capital of the North, it is naturally looked upon as the head station by several companies. The importance of the teak trade may be gauged from the extent of its export which in 1928 amounted to over nine million Ticals.

Like practically all other towns in Siam, one of the chief products of Chiengmai is rice. There still exists in this part of the country, an old system of irrigation by water wheels. In addition to rice, the other products grown are cotton, sugar-cane, indigo, beans, and all kinds of vegetables. The climate of Chiengmai is suitable for many species of cold climate plants. Chiengmai's rose is well known for its extraordinary size and colour.

A great number of Chiengmai's population engage in handicrafts, of which weaving, pottery and silverware and lacquerware manufacturing are the leading ones. Visitors to Chiengmai seldom resist the temptation of purchasing some of these products, for souvenirs. The workshops where these products are actually made can almost always be visited.

The American Presbyterian Mission has a large headquarters here also. The Mission manages a school, a hospital, a nurses' training school and a leper asylum. The works of the missionaries in Chiengmai have proved most beneficial to the population.

As already stated, Chiengmai has numerous temples and objects of interest for the visitor. Among the many temples, Wat Phra Singh and Wat Chedi Luang are the two outstanding ones. Wat Chedi Luang is important in that it was at one time the most important temple of Chiengmai and ranks as one of the grandest in the whole of Siam, while Wat Phra Singh which was constructed in the 14th century is still maintained in an excellent condition. This temple contains a collection of fine buildings. The burial place of the ruling Chaos of Chiengmai at Wat Suan Dok is also of considerable interest.

From Chiengmai there are highways leading out to several places of interest. The road to Doi Suthep, the mountain overlooking the city is 6

The Hua Rin Corner, a bastion at the north-west of the ancient walls of Chiang Mai.
Doi Suthep visible in the background, probably before 1920. Oliver Backhouse.

kilometres in length. Huey Keo with its waterfalls may be reached within
ten minutes, while the village of Meh Rim, 16 kilometres away, as well as
that of Chom Thong, 30 kilometres, are also accessible by car.

The average height of the peaks in the neighbourhood of Chiengmai
is 1,600 metres above mean sea level. The ground level in the city is 300
metres. Doi Intanon, 2,576 metres, the highest mountain within the
boundaries of Siam, is about 50 kilometres south-west of Chiengmai while
Doi Suthep is 1,676 metres in height. Doi Chiengdao on the north and
Doi Pa Cho on the north-east are 2,185 and 2,012 metres respectively.

All in all Chiengmai deserves at least four full days of the visitor's
time. Its numerous attractions will supply the visitors with so many
varied interests that the time allotted for sight-seeing and shopping will
be fully occupied. The express trains from Bangkok arrive at Chiengmai
on Thursdays and Mondays and leave the city on Tuesdays and Fridays.
By this schedule, a stay of three or four days can be arranged without any
difficulty. There is a good rest-house near the railway station.

Siam: General and Medical Features, Bangkok 1930, pp. 168-169

Timeline

1867   American Presbyterian Mission station founded at Chiang Mai

1883   Anglo-Siamese Treaty

1889   Borneo Company Limited (BCL) opens Chiang Mai operation

1898   Gymkhana Club founded

1899   William Harris becomes Principal of Chiang Mai Boys' School

Chiengmai Library Association founded

1902   Shan Rebellion in North Siam

1903   Queen Victoria statue set up at British Consulate

1904   *Laos News* founded

1908   Dr McKean founds Leper Asylum

1909   Anglo-Siamese Treaty; abolition of "extra-territoriality"

Lucy Starling arrives in Chiang Mai (December)

1910   Prince Nawarat succeeds as Chao Luang of Chiang Mai

Leigh Williams arrives in Lampang

E. P. Miller, a Teak-Wallah, murdered by dacoits (December)

1911   Lucy Starling's letters start

to appear in the *Hopkinsville Kentuckian*

1913   Reginald Le May arrives in Chiang Mai

Dr E. C. and Mabel Cort transferred to Chiang Mai

W. A. R. Wood becomes Consul at Chiang Mai

Official opening of Leper Asylum

1914   Great War breaks out

1915   Consul's House built at British Consulate

1916   Northern Line reaches Lampang

Prince Bovoradej becomes High Commissioner (Viceroy) in Monthon Payap

Laos News becomes *North Siam News*

1917   Siam declares war on Germany and Austria-Hungary

1918   Armistice ends Great War

1919   W. A. R. Wood becomes Consul-General

Reginald Campbell arrives in Siam

Celebration at Chiang Mai to mark end of Great War (September)

1920   Eric Reid publishes the novel *Spears of Deliverance*

Glossary

*The words are mostly derived from
Siamese or from Anglo-Indian usage.
Many cited definitions are extracted from
Leigh Williams' Jungle Prison (the revised
edition of Green Prison, 1955), pp. 193
ff. Williams lists words as Siamese (Thai),
Hindi or Malay but does not refer to
Khammuang, the northern language.*

Bale A fruit-bearing shrub.

Ban, Bang (Siamese) Village (Williams).

Banyan A species of fig tree.

Barking deer A muntjac deer, latterly established in Britain.

Betel A species of vine (Thai: *maak*), the leaves of which were chewed as a quid.

Boy A servant or valet: used in the Far East irrespective of the man's age (Williams).

Bumple Puppy A sequence of silly games at the Christmas Meeting.

Burra (Hindi) big, very big, e.g. "burra-sahib", i.e. "boss, manager" (Williams).

Chang (Thai) Elephant.

Chao (Siamese) Chief, Lord. Chao Luang: "very big chief"; head of a Lao state (Williams). A royal personage.

Chatty (Hindi, Tamil) an earthenware water jar

Chiengmai or Chieng Mai Former spelling of Chiang Mai.

Chiengrai or Chieng Rai Former spelling of Chiang Rai, a city to the north of Chiang Mai.

Chin-chock Small house gecko. Perhaps better transcribed "jing-jok".

Chukka or chukker (Hindi, Urdu) Period of play in polo.

Cicada Insect best known for its extremely loud song.

Cocoanut An obsolete spelling of "coconut".

Compound Enclosure, fenced or walled, containing buildings or a plot of land; precinct; domain (Williams).

Cone-yam Nightwatchman (Thai: khon yam).

Coolie (Hindi) an unskilled manual labourer; now outdated and considered offensive.

Dacoit (Hindi) bandit, armed robber; cf. dacoity.

Dah (Siamese) Long knife, native two-handed sword (Williams).

Dawk keo (Thai) A flower with a fragrant smell.

Deva A celestial being in Hindu cosmology.

Dhobie (Hindi) a washerman.

Doi (Khammuang) Mountain.

Doi Suthep or Sutep The mountain (or rather, range) at Chiang Mai.

Durian An edible fruit with a pungent smell.

Durwan (Persian) a doorkeeper.

Farang (Siamese) Foreigner, European (Williams). Westerner.

Fromager A kapok or "silk-cotton" tree.

Gharry (Hindi, Urdu) A wheeled cart or carriage.

Girdling A way of stopping the sap rising in teak trees and thus preparing them for felling.

Godown (Malay) warehouse, wharf (Williams).

Hamadryade A king cobra.

Haw Also: Chin Haw, people originally from Yunnan in southern China.

Hoopoe A bird with a distinctive crown of feathers.

Hwe (Thai) stream.

Jheel (Hindi) pool or marsh.

Ka Indigenous (i.e. non-Thai) peoples.

Khao or khow (Thai) rice, cf. "khow lahm", a northern delicacy.

Khamu or Kamoo An ethnic group, largely settled in Laos; associated with the forestry industry.

Khun (Thai) Mr or Mrs.

Khun Tan or Khun Tal Location of the railway tunnel linking Lampang and Lamphun.

Krait A venomous snake.

Lakon or Lakawn or Nakon Lampang. A northern city to the south-east of Chiang Mai.

Lamphun or Lampoon A northern city, to the south of Chiang Mai.

Laos, Lao The northern region, its people and language, distinct from Siam; an area covering modern north and north-eastern Thailand, Laos, parts of Myanmar and even parts of southern China.

Laowieng Eric Reid's fictional name for Chiang Mai.

Mahout (Hindi) elephant rider (Williams).

Matayome Secondary school classes or grades.

Maung (Burmese) "younger brother", but sometimes part of a given name. Abbreviation: "Mg.".

Maw or Mor (Thai) Doctor.

Menam (Siamese) "mother of waters", i.e. river (Williams).

Meping or Mae Ping The river that flows through Chiang Mai.

Meyome or Mae Yom The river that flows through Phrae.

Mia (Thai) wife, woman. Cf. *mia yai* (main wife), *mia noi* (minor wife).

Monthon Circle, region. Cf. Monthon Payap, North-Western Circle.

Mot (Siamese) ant (Williams).

Muang (Siamese) country, province (Williams).

Musth (Hindi) periodic state of excitement in bull-elephants (Williams).

Naga (Siamese) sacred serpent, often flanking steps in temples (Williams).

Nai (Siamese) master, Mister, Mr.; prefixed (Williams).

Nam (Siamese) water (Williams).

Nan A northern city, to the north-east of Chiang Mai.

Ohm (Thai) Large water pot.

Ounge (Burmese) push logs to ensure they move downstream in a river.

Pa (Thai) forest

Padi, paddy (Malay) rice plants, rice field.

Pangrai Alec Waugh's fictional name for Chiang Mai.

Panung A skirt.

Pasin See sin.

Pathays Chinese Muslim inhabitants of Burma.

Pee (Siamese) spirit, ghost (Williams).

Poo (Siamese) male. Poo, followed by name, used of male elephants (Williams).

Poo or Pu-mia A man/woman or non-binary person.

Prae or Pre or Phrae A northern city, to the south-east of Chiang Mai

Prarachaya The Princess Dara Rasimi, whose full style was H.R.H. The Princess Consort or Chao Dara Rasami Phrarachaya.

Raft Teak logs bound together for floating on a river; sometimes of gigantic size.

Raheng A northern city to the south of Chiang Mai; modern name: Tak.

Ricsha or rickshaw (Hindi) A wheeled cart pulled by a person.

Rise That which occurs when a river fills with water, e.g. when replenished by rain.

Rua sadao (Thai) River boats; "great squat barges of teak" (Eric Reid).

Sahib (Hindi) Master, sir, suffixed to name.

Sais, syce (Hindi) groom, horse attendant (Williams).

Sala (Siamese) rest-house, usually attached to a temple (Williams). In fact, a pavilion-like structure open on all sides.

Sambhur A large forest deer.

Satang (Siamese) cent, small coin, a hundredth of a tical (q.v.) (Williams).

Sawankaloke or Sawankhalok A rafting station ("R.S.") on the Mae Ping south of Chiang Mai

Shan An ethnic group, largely settled in the Shan States of Burma but represented in northern Siam through emigration. Regarded as "British Asiatic subjects".

Sin (Siamese) skirt (Williams).

Stengah (Malay) a whisky and soda (preferably with ice).

Sticklac Substance derived from a secretion of the lac insect; used to make shellac, as e.g. in gramophone records.

Syce See sais.

Tabloid Medicinal tablet for oral use.

Teak (Hindi) Latin, *tectona grandis*, a valuable hardwood found in India and S. E. Asia (Williams).

Tesa The highest Siamese official in a Monthon. Cf. Viceroy.

Tical (Hindi) Siamese coin of currency, value about two shillings. The Siamese name for it is baht (Williams). Possibly of Burmese origin and apparently pronounced "ticARL". Abbreviation: "tcl."

Tiffin Lunch.

Tokay Large gecko capable of inflicting a nasty bite. Perhaps better transcribed "tuk-kae".

Topee or topi (Hindi) A helmet-shaped hat made of pith or cork; considered essential for foreigners in the tropics to avoid sunstroke.

Wallah (Hindi) man, fellow (Williams)

Wat (Siamese) temple (Williams).

Wheel Bicycle, as used by Lucy Starling.

Abbreviations

BCL Borneo Company Limited, a British trading and forestry company

BBTC Bombay Burmah Trading Corporation, a British forestry company

Sources

Most texts and any unattributed images are believed to be out of copyright according to Thai and international law. The author and publishers would be grateful for any corrections with regard to copyright that should be incorporated in future reprints or editions of this book.

Newspapers and Periodicals:

The Bangkok Times (daily and weekly editions).

The Hopkinsville Kentuckian (Lucy Starling letters, printed 1911-1914).

Laos News (1904-1916; title change: *North Siam News*, 1917-1919; superseded by: *Siam Outlook*, 1921). Chiang Mai: American Mission Press.

Woman's Work for Woman. Philadelphia: Woman's Foreign Missionary Society of the Presbyterian Church.

Manuscript Collections:

Cort, Edwin Charles and Mabel: Letters, Church of Christ in Thailand Archives at Payap University Library, RG 007/90.

Harris, William and Cornelia: Letters, Church of Christ in Thailand Archives at Payap University Library, RG 004/91,92.

O'Brien, Mary Lou: Letters, Presbyterian Historical Society Archives, Philadelphia, Henry R. O'Brien papers, 1376G.

Single Published and Unpublished Works:

Campbell, Reginald Wilfrid: *Fear in the Forest.* London: Hodder & Stoughton 1932.

Campbell, Reginald Wilfrid: *Jungle Night.* London: Hodder & Stoughton 1933.

Campbell, Reginald Wilfrid: *Poo Lorn of the Elephants.* London: Hodder & Stoughton [1930].

Campbell, Reginald Wilfrid: *Teak-Wallah. A Record of Personal Experiences.* London: Hodder & Stoughton 1935.

Campbell, Reginald Wilfrid: *The Keepers of Elephant Valley.* London: Heinemann 1939.

Campbell, Reginald Wilfrid: Uneasy Virtue. London: Chapman & Hall 1926.

Cort, Edwin Charles: *Yankee Thai.* Presbyterian Historical Society, Philadelphia, MS C795y (digital copy via website).

Exell, Frank Kingsley: *Siamese Tapestry.* London: Hale 1963.

Far Eastern Association of Tropical Medicine. Eighth Congress: Siam – General and Medical Features. Bangkok 1930.

Freeman, John Haskell: *An Oriental Land of the Free*. Philadelphia: The Westminster Press 1910.

Harris, William: Recollections for My Grandchildren. Typescript dated: 1950. Church of Christ Archives at Payap University Library 922 H317R.

Heiser, Victor George: *An American Doctor's Odyssey. Adventures in Forty-Five countries*. New York: W. W. Norton & Co. 1936.

Kerr, Arthur: 'Meteorological Observations Made in Chiengmai. 1910-1914', in: *Journal of the Siam Society*, vol. 17, 1923, pp. 21-34.

Kerr, Arthur: 'Notes on Introduced Plants in Siam', in: *Journal of the Siam Society*, Natural History Supplement, vol. 8, 1932, pp. 205-206.

Kornerup, Ebbe Erland: [Siam] *Friendly Siam*, translated by M. Guiterman. London, New York: G. P. Putnam's Son [1928].

Le May, Reginald Stuart: *An Asian Arcady. The Land and Peoples of Northern Siam*. Cambridge: Heffers 1926.

Le May, Reginald Stuart (translator): *Siamese Tales Old and New. The Four Riddles and other Stories*. With some Reflections on the Tales. London: Noel Douglas 1930.

McCarthy, James: *Surveying and Exploring in Siam*. London: John Murray 1900.

McFarland, Bertha Blount: *Our Garden was So Fair. The Story of a Mission in Thailand*. Philadelphia: Blakiston 1943.

Reid, Donald Eric: *Chequered Leaves from Siam*. Bangkok: Bangkok Times Press 1913.

Reid, Donald Eric: Report for the Year 1909 on the Trade and Commerce of the Consular District of Chiengmai. Edited at the Foreign Office and the Board of Trade. (No. 4550. Annual Series. Diplomatic and Consular Reports. Cd. 4962-162). London: His Majesty's Stationery Office 1910.

Reid, Donald Eric: *Spears of Deliverance: A Tale of White Men and Brown Women in Siam*. London: Stanley Paul & Co. 1920.

Report of Deputation sent by the Board of Foreign Missions of the Presbyterian Church in the U.S.A. in the Summer of 1915 to visit the Missions in Siam and the Philippine Islands, and on the Way home to stop at some of the Stations in Japan, Korea and China; presented by Mr. Robert E. Speer, Mr. Dwight H. Day and Dr. David Bovaird. New York 1916.

Seidenfaden, Erik: *Guide to Bangkok with Notes on Siam*. 3rd edition. Bangkok: Royal State Railways, Passenger and Information Bureau 1932.

Starling, Lucy Mercer: *Dawn over Temple Roofs*. New York: World Horizons 1960.

Waugh, Alec: *The Coloured Countries*. London: Chapman & Hall 1930. US edition: Hot Countries. New York: Farrar & Rinehart 1930.

Waugh, Alec: *The Last Chukka. Stories from East and West*. London: Chapman & Hall 1928.

Waugh, Alec: 'Waters of Babylon', in: *The Windsor Magazine*, February 1928, pp. 277-287.

Wells, Margaretta B.: *Guide to Chiengmai*. Bangkok: The Christian Bookstore 1962 (reprinted: 1967).

Wheatcroft, Rachel: *Siam and Cambodia in Pen and Pastel*. London: Constable & Co. 1928.

Williams, Walter Leigh: *Green Prison*. London: Herbert Jenkins 1941. Revised 2nd edition: *Jungle Prison*. London: Andrew Melrose 1954.

Wood, William Alfred Rae: *Land of Smiles*. Bangkok: Krungdebarnagar Press 1935.

Index

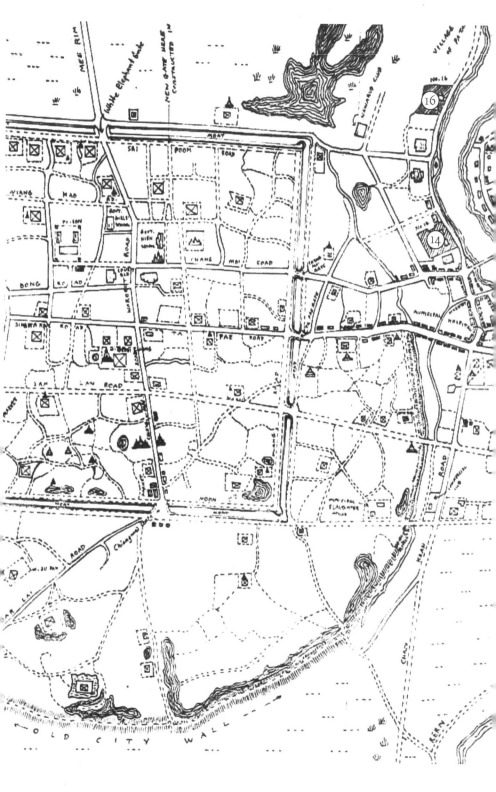